I0670586

LEGAL WRITING STYLE

SECOND EDITION

By

HENRY WEIHOFEN
Professor of Law, University of New Mexico

ST. PAUL, MINN.
WEST PUBLISHING CO.
1980

COPYRIGHT © 1961 By WEST PUBLISHING CO.
COPYRIGHT © 1980 By WEST PUBLISHING CO.
All rights reserved
Printed in the United States of America

Library of Congress Cataloging in Publication Data

Weihofen, Henry, 1904–
    Legal writing style.

    Includes index.
    1. Legal composition. I. Title.
KF250.W4   1980   808'.066'34   79–23662

ISBN 0–8299–2066–8

Weihofen—Leg.Writing Style 2d Ed. MTB

FOREWORD

Professor Henry Weihofen has completed his excellent work on style in legal writing. The title is a precise one but I am not fully satisfied with it for the book is more than a mere work on good writing style. Its contents are bottomed on sound pedagogical and legal foundations because the author is both an experienced advocate and a skillful teacher of law. Professor Weihofen is a member of the Bars of Illinois and New Mexico, and for some years has been a Professor of Law of the School of Law of the University of New Mexico, teaching both criminal law and legal writing. He has lectured on legal subjects at many universities and has written extensively on criminal law and on law and psychiatry. One of his books, written with Dr. Manfred Guttmacher, Psychiatry and the Law, is recognized as a standard work in the field of forensic medicine and is widely quoted as an authority. In 1955 Professor Weihofen was the recipient of the Isaac Ray Award of the American Psychiatric Association, an honor conferred upon a psychiatrist or a lawyer who has made a distinguished contribution in the field of relationship between psychiatry and jurisprudence. He has served also as a Special Assistant to the Attorney General of the United States and has had extensive experience in administrative and constitutional law.

I agree with him that there is nothing more useful for the attorney or judge than the ability to express legal concepts clearly and briefly. I am convinced that the most difficult problem confronting him who deals with clients and judges is one of communication. This thought is succinctly expressed by Professor Weihofen when he writes, "For the lawyer more than for most men, it is true that he who knows but cannot express what he knows might as well be ignorant". He properly describes language as "the greatest of man's inventions". While the primary subject of this book is legal writing much of it is equally applicable to the spoken word. Buffon, the French epigrammatist, said: "Style is the man himself". Weihofen improves on Buffon for he writes that style is "non-detachable, unfilterable". We will all agree that without style, writing is but dust whether the subject matter be law or romance.

In his early chapters Professor Weihofen outlines the rudiments of successful legal writing. He lays emphasis upon the need for precision, conciseness, simplicity and clarity, and illustrates his points effectively. He points out that it may be unnecessary in every case to strip legal writing or speech in every instance to the admirable minimum achieved by Chief Judge Murdock of the United States Tax Court. A taxpayer had testified, "As God is my judge, I do not owe this tax." Judge Murdock replied, "He's not. I am. You do." But the author makes it clear that every unnecessary word in a legal document should be omitted and that circumlocution must be avoided. On tautology Professor Weihofen is superb. His examples are acute. I cannot resist the temptation to make a sentence of three of them. Three are enough for they are painful: "The resultant effect" was that "he died of a mortal blow" "invisible to the eye".

The author points out that the creation of a simple style is not a simple matter and that the complicated subjects with which lawyers habitually deal require hard mental labor for proper briefing and adequate argument. Very few of us, and this includes practicing attorneys, professors of law and judges, have the gift which the gods so rarely bestow, the genius to be able to explain complicated legal and governmental ideas in simple terms. There is no reason, however, why an educated man, be he lawyer or layman, cannot express himself plainly and briefly in writing or in speech. This is the message implicitly but clearly conveyed by this book.

On the subject of clarity Professor Weihofen adds an interesting gloss. He points out that there are some situations where too great a degree of definiteness is not desirable. He cites a cogent example. Article IV, Section 3, of the Constitution of the United States provides that "New States may be admitted by the

FOREWORD

Congress into this Union * * * ". I think it will be conceded, as Professor Weihofen suggests, that at the time the Constitution was framed a precise definition of the terms of admission of new States in the Federal Union would have been injurious to the acceptance of that document.

The author approaches his subject matter with a humor rarely found in books dealing with writing style. For example, and this is but a small matter among some very large ones, the book contains a priceless list of clichés, a hundred or more, which the writer of this foreword meets in speech or in print like braces of weary woodcock almost every working day. To paraphrase, and but slightly alter, one of them, the list of clichés alone would make the book "Worth more than the paper it's written on".

The final chapters of this book deal with matters well beyond the first principles of good legal writing. These latter pages have been composed with genuine discernment of what a court needs —indeed must have—from counsel if it is properly to decide issues of law whether at the trial or appellate levels.

This is no mere book of rhetoric, no legal grammar. Though its contents are directed primarily to law students, what is written is of value to experienced lawyers and judges. It should be made available to every law student. Every practicing lawyer should have a copy. It should be in every judicial library.

> JOHN BIGGS, JR.
> Chief Judge,
> United States Court of Appeals,
> Third Judicial Circuit.

Wooddale
June 7, 1961

*

PREFACE TO THE REVISED EDITION

Although this book continues to be well received by both students and teachers (it is or has been the assigned text for writing courses in some seventy schools), after eighteen years some changes seem called for.

The changes made are mostly additions. A section has been added on writing law school and bar examinations. The material on sentence structure and organization has been amplified. More attention has been given to drafting principles. At least a few additions have been made to every chapter, and more than a few to the chapters on Memoranda and Briefs. The chapters on Forcefulness and Organization have been moved forward, so that they now follow the chapters on Precision, Conciseness, Simplicity, and Clarity. Suggestions were solicited from teachers who have used the book, and most of these changes were made in response to suggestions offered.

The list of "Words to Watch" has been expanded. Some newly risen questions are dealt with, such as whether we should give up using the masculine gender to include the femine, and instead, meticulously say "he or she" and "him or her," and neuter our chairmen into "chairpersons."

To keep the book from becoming too bulky, room has been made for the added materials by pruning the original text, mainly by deleting some multiple examples and a few comments that time has convinced me are not likely to be missed.

H. W.

Albuquerque, New Mexico
October, 1979

*

TO THE INSTRUCTOR

This book should be as useful to the practicing lawyer as to the student in law school. But we may as well face the fact that most practitioners (1) think they write well, and (2) at all events cannot or will not take time to learn how to write better. They may, perhaps, be glad to urge junior lawyers working under them to read a book that will teach them how to write a brief or a memorandum or an opinion. But in the main, we must pin our hopes and our efforts on the students. They, fortunately, are still young, flexible of mind and in no position to refuse.

A generation ago law school courses in writing were the exception; today they are the rule. Their content, however, varies. Some concentrate on brief-writing, others on the drafting of formal legal documents, and still others on the writing of memoranda or papers similar to law review comments. This book is intended to serve as a handbook that should be equally helpful in all such courses. Instructors or teaching fellows charged with teaching legal writing, even though they may write well themselves, may not be trained to teach students who write poorly how to improve. Trained or not, any instructor may wish to have students read a book rather than spend much class time himself delivering by oral lectures all the admonitions, exhortations, precepts and preachments contained in the following pages.

Any course in legal writing will presumably be devoted mainly to writing rather than to reading about writing. This book is not designed to substitute for or even to precede exercises in writing. The instructor need not delay assigning writing projects until after the student has had time to read and digest the book. If the instructor wishes to begin with one of the simpler forms of legal writing, such as letters, he may refer students to the chapter on Letters. Throughout the course, as students commit errors discussed in the book, the instructor can save time and effort in explaining the nature of the error and how to correct it by referring to the page in the book discussing the subject instead of spelling it out himself. To help make such references, the index has been made as full as possible.

TABLE OF CONTENTS

LEGAL WRITING STYLE

Chapter 1

INTRODUCTION

For the lawyer more than for most men, it is true that he who knows but cannot express what he knows might as well be ignorant.[1] The bricklayer, the surgeon or the cattleman who knows what he needs to know can do his work; he need not be able to explain to anyone else what he is doing or convince anyone that he is right. But in much of what a lawyer does, knowing the right answer is not enough; he must convince another lawyer, a judge or a jury, or explain to (and perhaps convince) a client. The knowledge or wisdom he has in his head is of no use to anyone unless he can communicate it to others.

Language, that greatest of man's inventions, is almost the only means we have for communicating ideas. Our subject in this book is language in its written form, but much of what is said here applies also to speech.

Writing is a skill, which like any other skill is acquired only with practice; one is not born with it. The pianist who plays Chopin flawlessly did not play Chopin the first time he sat down at the piano. The football team's star player didn't shine the first day he handled a football. You acquire skill, whether in playing the piano or in playing football or in writing, by disciplined self-critical practice. If you wish to be a good writer, said Epictetus two thousand years ago, write. Bernard Shaw, more recently, said the same thing in different words. One learns to write, he said, by making a fool of oneself until one learns how.

---

1. This is not an original thought. It was said long ago: *Qui novit* *neque id quod sentit exprimit perinde est ac si nesciret.*

It is practice, then, that makes, if not perfect writing style, at least surely and constantly improved style. You will learn to do mainly by doing, not by reading advice on how to do it. A book on how to write can be of help, just as a book on swimming can help you learn to swim. But the advice that you get from a book cannot become meaningful, cannot really be learned, except by putting it into practice.

The help that a book on writing style can give is not primarily in teaching tricks or mannerisms designed to ornament your present style. Style, said E. B. White of the *New Yorker* magazine, is not "a garnishment for the meat of prose, a sauce by which a dull dish is made palatable. Style has no such separate entity; it is non-detachable, unfilterable. The beginner should approach style warily, realizing that it is himself he is approaching, no other." [2] Buffon, the French writer, expressed the same point more epigrammatically: "Style," he said, "is the man himself."

But this is too fatalistic to be helpful; it seems to suggest that short of remaking his whole personality, a writer can do nothing to improve his style. It is perhaps more helpful to say that style should reflect the writer's mood and purpose. A lawyer sometimes will be narrating facts, at other times expounding a legal principle, at still other times arguing for a point of view. At one point, the mood he wants to convey will be one of calm impartiality, at another indignation or sympathy, stern justice or merciful pity. He does not begin by asking himself what style to use; he asks, "What point am I trying to make? What do I want the reader to see, to feel, or to believe?" If he knows what effect he wants to produce, a style will come, almost automatically. The words and arrangements of words that suggest themselves and the rhythm of his sentences will be those that most naturally express his own attitude or mood. They will convey his excitement or his calm, deliberateness or impatience, judicious equanimity or passionate conviction.

The most potent stimulus for true eloquence, of course, is a burning conviction of the righteousness of one's cause. Light

2. Strunk, The Elements of Style, with Revisions, an Introduction   and a New Chapter on Writing by E. B. White 18 (1959).

and heat, said Bernard Shaw, are the two vital qualities demanded of literature. The man who writes with light and heat can be eloquent even without the aid of rhetorical devices. This is especially true in English, because "English by its simplicity of structure permits a greater mobility of thought than other languages, and so can express subtler insinuations and more powerful thrusts of meaning." [3] This is why men without literary polish or pretensions have been able to write some very effective prose. Bartolomeo Vanzetti, an Italian-born fish peddler and anarchist, and his friend Nicolo Sacco were convicted of committing a payroll robbery and murder near Boston, on evidence the adequacy of which was the subject of widespread controversy, and were executed August 23, 1927. After receiving sentence Vanzetti wrote: [4]

> If it had not been for these thing, I might have live out my life talking at street corners to scorning men. I might have die, unmarked, unknown, a failure. Now we are not a failure. This is our career and our triumph. Never in our full life could we hope to do such work for tolerance, for joostice, for man's onderstanding of man as now we do by accident. Our words—our lives—our pains—nothing! The taking of our lives—lives of a good shoemaker and a poor fish-peddler —all! That last moment belongs to us—that agony is our triumph.

Sincere writing, then, is writing that most naturally reflects the personality, the spirit and feeling, of the writer himself.

But what is "natural"? All writing is artificial in the sense that it is something one must learn. The student who reads good writing and tries to imitate good models is learning just as naturally as the one who follows poorer models, and the style he ultimately develops is as much his own. Just as the person brought up in the backwoods, hearing nothing but the local dialect, will talk like a backwoodsman, so the student who has never read much but bad writing will write badly. The student who reads good writing will almost inevitably absorb some of its style and imitate it in his own work.

3. Robert Graves and Allan Hodge, The Reader Over Your Shoulder 37 (1944).

4. Frankfurter, Marion D., and Jackson, G., The Letters of Sacco and Vanzetti v. (1928).

How much he absorbs depends on how much conscious attention he pays to the style of what he reads and how much effort he makes to imitate it. When you read something that especially strikes you as effectively written, stop and analyze the diction, the sentence structure, the choice of words, to find out how the effect was obtained. Look for some of the devices described in this book. Learn to avoid certain practices and to cultivate others, and you will in time develop your own natural way of writing.

H. W. and F. G. Fowler begin their valuable book, The King's English, by saying:

> Any one who wishes to become a good writer should endeavor, before he allows himself to be tempted by the more showy qualities, to be direct, simple, brief, vigorous, and lucid.
>
> This general principle may be translated into practical rules in the domain of vocabulary as follows:—
>
> Prefer the familiar word to the far-fetched.
> Prefer the concrete word to the abstract.
> Prefer the single word to the circumlocution.
> Prefer the short word to the long.
> Prefer the Saxon word to the Romance.

Taken together, these rules sum up most of the advice you will find in this book. They admittedly overlap considerably. We shall rearrange them into four objectives: be precise, concise, simple and clear.

The following four chapters are devoted to the qualities of precision, conciseness, simplicity and clarity, with suggestions on how to use the elements of style, such as diction, phrasing and sentence structure, so as to attain each of these qualities. We shall deal with them separately, not because they are discrete qualities, but because it will be more orderly to focus upon each one in turn, even though they do shade into one another.

Much of legal writing is intended to convince. But conviction results not only from the intrinsic merit of the argument, but often also from the way in which it is put. A chapter on Forcefulness discusses how you can use words and phrases to give your arguments more vividness and vigor. A chapter on Organization offers suggestions for improving the structure and organization of sentences and paragraphs and for the orderly and coherent presentation of argument. Then follow chapters discussing how to attain these qualities in specific kinds of legal writing, especially letters, opinions, memoranda, and briefs. The final chapter offers suggestions for eassaying A Touch of Eloquence.

But before we get to any of these objectives, one cardinal admonition must be emphasized at the outset: REMEMBER YOUR READER.

The good writer has what Herbert Spencer called "intellectual sympathy;" he has a feeling for his reader's mental state, enabling him to adjust his phraseology and the sequence of ideas to the reader's needs. He is concerned to spare the reader doubts about his meaning and weariness from verbosity. "This is the first great principle of writing: economy of mental effort on the part of the reader." [5]

The ideal style is one that the reader will least notice. This is true even of purely literary writing; it is still more true of legal writing, which is read for its substance by people who are not inclined to spend any time admiring its artistry. What they will appreciate most is a way of writing that allows them to comprehend the substance without noticing the form. It is bad usage that is noticeable. Even if it does not mislead or confuse the reader, it calls attention to itself and away from the message.

When friends told Cicero that he was the greatest of orators, he replied somewhat as follows: "Not so, for when I give an oration in the Forum people say, 'How well he speaks!' but when Demosthenes addressed the people they rose and shouted, 'Come, let us up and fight the Macedonians!' " [6]

If the judge reading your brief is impressed merely with how well you write, you have defeated yourself. You want to make him feel that your client has a good case, not merely that he has a good lawyer.

5. Rickard, Technical Writing 11 (3d ed. 1931).

6. Curl, Expository Writing 12 (1919).

You never merely write. You write to someone. Even a novelist or a writer for the mass media does not write for everybody. An article for the *Atlantic Monthly* is written in a distinctly different style from one written for the pulps, because the readers of the one are a different group of people from the readers of the other.

The lawyer, of all writers, has the easiest task when it comes to identifying his readers. Usually he is writing primarily or wholly for an audience of one—one client, one lawyer, or one judge. In an appellate brief, he may be writing for as many as nine. The one or more persons he is writing for are usually personally known to him; he knows them much better than most writers know their readers; and he has some idea of what will appeal to them and what will not. He may know something of their several tastes and interests: their political, social and economic points of view, their hobbies and the judicial and other public figures whom they admire or seek to emulate. It is nothing less than foolish for a lawyer to fail to keep clearly before him the mental picture of the man whom he is addressing, and to measure every statement, every word he writes, with the test, what effect will this have on *him*?

A letter to a businessman and an appellate court brief are addressed to very different audiences. A letter to a businessman has a different audience from one addressed to a workman with an eighth grade education, and probably should be written differently. Language appropriate for a corporate mortgage is not appropriate for a plea to a jury. A contract, although it is usually written for only two laymen, must be drafted with a further audience in mind—lawyers and ultimately judges who will have to interpret it if it should ever become the subject of a legal dispute. The lawyer who uses for one kind of writing the style appropriate for another is likely to write poorly. But because it is difficult to develop a variety of styles, a lawyer may write a letter to a client as though he were drafting a legal instrument, or dictate the wording for a brief as though he were arguing orally in court.

The self-discipline of writing is excellent training in rigorous thinking. The lawyer who tries to be precise and clear in his writing may find that he must think a point through more thoroughly before he can make an ambiguous statement more clear. The reason he put it into fuzzy words in the first place was that the thought was fuzzy. Trying to say it clearly helps him perceive that he does not himself understand it clearly, and so spurs him to master his subject more completely. To write properly, one must both think properly and interpret properly. "In fact, expression is an essential part of truth, and the art of expression is the practical part of the art of thinking." [7]

7. Amiel, Journal, Mar. 27, 1854. Quoted in Rickard, Technical Writing 200 (3d ed. 1931).

Chapter 2

PRECISION

The lawyer must be more precise in his writing than almost anyone else. Most writers can expect their work to be read in good faith, that is, with an honest desire to understand what was meant. But the lawyer must write in constant fear of what we might call the reader in bad faith, the man looking for loopholes in the contract so as to avoid liability for his failure to perform, the disappointed heir who wants the will read in a way that would defeat the testator's intention, the criminal defendant who wants the statute interpreted so as not to cover his act, and all the others who will want to twist the meaning of words for their own ends.

Not every legal document, it is true, will be set upon by such foes. If all goes well, no question will ever arise, and fortunately most affairs run off well enough. But the lawyer never knows which of his efforts will some day be the subject of disagreement. He must therefore in all his work take pains to say precisely what he means, no more and no less—not only so that a person reading in good faith can understand, but so that a person reading in bad faith cannot misunderstand.

Saying precisely what we mean is not easy. Many of the words of our language are ambiguous, and we must know how to control them if they are not to throw us. Even experienced lawyers are thrown on occasion. In a Pennsylvania case, a farm was deeded to "Francis Lucas, a single man, and Joseph Lucas and Matilda Lucas, his wife." Francis was the son of Joseph and Matilda. Under Pennsylvania law, a conveyance to husband and wife is presumed to create an estate by the entireties. The court held, however, that the presumption does not apply when the deed is to husband and wife together with a third party; in the absence of language in the conveyance disclosing a contrary intention, such a deed is to be deemed a conveyance of one-third shares. Was there language in this deed showing a contrary intention? The court held there was; the use of the first "and" separated the grantees into two units, (1) Francis Lucas, and (2) Joseph and Matilda Lucas. Francis took a half interest and Joseph and Matilda took a one-half interest as tenants by the entireties.[1] Whether this is actually what the grantor intended we do not know. What we do know is that whoever drew the deed failed to word it clearly enough to avoid litigation over its meaning.

In an Arkansas case, a will provided that the remainder of the testator's property should be "divided equally between all of our nephews and nieces on my wife's side and my niece." Did this mean that half of the property was to be divided among the twenty-two nephews and nieces "on my wife's side," and the other half to go to "my niece," or that each person was to receive a twenty-third interest? The Arkansas Supreme Court held that the testator's niece was entitled to a full half share, and rested this largely on the fact that the will used the word "between." Literally, said the court, this word applies only to two objects. If the reference is to more than two, the preposition should be "among."[2] We can only trust that the draftsman was a lawyer of such experience and competence that we can assume he understood the distinction,[3] so that the court's interpretation left the testator resting easy in his grave. But he did cause the estate a lawsuit, which he could have avoided by saying more clearly what the testator wanted. It is surprising how often this particular form of ambiguity has been the source of litigation. An Illinois testator, for example, left instructions "to divide the remainder of my estate equally between my two sisters named above and my living nieces and nephews." There were 17 living nieces and nephews. Was each sister entitled to a third, a fourth or a nineteenth?[4]

1. Heatter v. Lucas, 367 Pa. 296, 80 A.2d 740 (1951).

2. Lefeavre v. Pennington, 217 Ark. 397, 230 S.W.2d 46 (1950).

3. "Where the will is drawn by a lawyer whose experience and competence is beyond question, the presumption that legal terms embodied in the will are used in their legal sense is all but conclusive." In re Welsh's Estate, 89 Cal.App.2d 43, 200 P.2d 139 (1949).

4. See Murphy v. Fox, 334 Ill.App. 7, 78 N.E.2d 337 (1948). See also In re Fisk's Estate, 182 Cal. 238, 187 P. 958 (1920); Courtenay v. Courtenay, 138 Md. 204, 113 A. 717 (1921).

A corporation charter required that directors "shall be elected on a vote of the stockholders representing not less than two-thirds of the outstanding capital stock of the Corporation." Does this mean that a candidate needs the votes of two-thirds of the stockholders to be elected? Or merely that two-thirds of the stockholders must be present at the meeting at which the election is held? Control of the corporation depended on the interpretation. The Louisiana court said the answer was in the word "on." If a two-thirds vote for election had been intended the charter should and presumably would have said "by a vote." "On a vote" meant that the two-thirds was only a quorum requirement.[5] Here again, careful drafting, separating quorum and voting requirements or defining terms, would have avoided this lawsuit—and perhaps prevented the client's losing control of the corporation.

An Iowa statute forbids lascivious acts with a child "of the age of sixteen years, or under." If a man commits such an act with a child who is sixteen years and six months old, is he guilty under this act? The Supreme Court of Iowa has held he is not. Taking the words "of the age of sixteen years" in their ordinary meaning, said the court, a child is sixteen only on his sixteenth birthday. Before that day, he is "under sixteen;" after that day, he is "over sixteen." [6] A careful draftsman might have foreseen that this question would arise. If all the sixteenth year was intended to be included, a clear and simple way of saying it was at hand: "under the age of seventeen years."

The qualities the lawyer must strive for in his writing condition the kind of writing he does. The situations and concepts he deals with are frequently too complex to be expressed accurately except by using qualifying phrases and clauses, or by weakening the statement with an equivocating "generally" or "as a rule." "Caution and reticence in writing," as Mr. Justice Frankfurter once said, "make for qualifications and circumlocutions that stifle spontaneity, slow the rhythm of speech, check the play of

---

5. State v. Briede, 52 So.2d 568 (La. App.1951).

6. Knott v. Rawlings, 250 Iowa 892, 96 N.W.2d 900 (1959). See also Application of Smith, 351 P.2d 1076 (Okl.Cr.1960), interpreting a statutory definition of rape "by a male over eighteen years of age."

imagination. . . . Law as literature is restrained by its responsibility."

Popular writers can get a more breezy, more colorful, style by using looser, more imaginative—but less exact—language. They can make broad generalizations that are provocative and interesting. "To philosophize is to generalize," said Mr. Justice Holmes, "but to generalize is to omit." Lawyers cannot afford to omit very much very often.

It is true that we often overdo caution; we resolve all doubts in favor of keeping every qualification that may or may not need to be expressed. The *New Yorker* magazine likes to poke fun at this penchant of ours, by reprinting, under the heading, "The Legal Mind at Work," some involved legal provision, overburdened with qualifications, cross-references, exceptions and provisos. "There is an accuracy that defeats itself by the overemphasis of details," said Mr. Justice Cardozo. "The sentence may be so overloaded with all its possible qualifications that it will tumble down of its own weight." The lawyer must exercise judgment and a sense of what is material and what is omissible —what is "over-emphasis of details" and what is useful or even necessary detail.

Law students should first concentrate on making sure that all the necessary qualifications are in, striking out later those that, on reflection, seem unnecessary. Making generalized statements without carefully considering whether qualifications are needed may have fatal consequences. Exactness must for the lawyer be the primary aim. And if constancy in this aim makes his style less graceful than he would wish it, he may be cheered by Lord Macmillan's thought, "that there are few higher intellectual pleasures than success in the task of expressing an argument or a conclusion in just precisely the right language, so that the thought is caught and poised exactly as we would have it." [7]

We shall, in this chapter, limit ourselves to imprecision resulting from the wrong choice of words. Imprecision also has other sources, such as improper word order, misplaced modifiers and

---

7. Lord Macmillan, Law and Letters, 16 A.B.A. Journal 662, 665 (1930).

wrong punctuation. But these we shall reserve for the chapter on Clarity. As already said, the elements of style overlap considerably. Here we shall restrict our discussion of precision to use of the right *word*. And that leads us to the first rule:

Choose the Right Word

Alexander Hamilton, who was not only a great statesman but a master of effective expression, said, "The selection of the right word calls for the exercise of man's greatest faculty—that of judgment." You cannot choose the right word from among several unless you appreciate the precise meaning and shading of each, any more than you can ladle out precisely a quart of liquid unless you know how much the ladle you are using holds. Students sometimes use words whose precise "size" they do not know:

> Not all vaudeville performance routines should be shrouded in legal protection.

The writer obviously does not know what a shroud is.

> Where an employee creates copyrightable material in the course of his employment, the employer accedes to the proprietorship of the copyright.

Here again, the writer uses a word whose meaning he misunderstands. He was perhaps vaguely confusing "accede" with "succeed." (The shift in subject is also a fault.)

> The Uniform Commercial Code would allow these commercial transactions to be carried on in an aura of certainty.

"Aura," which denotes a subtle, vaporous or invisible exhalation or emanation, is a most inappropriate word to depict certainty.

A New York law firm importunes a physician to serve as an expert witness in the following words:

> Your testimony is most important. Without it our position becomes extremely tenable.

These malapropisms are often the result, in Fowler's words, of "the hankering of ignorant writers after the unfamiliar or imposing." An amazingly large number of people use words they do not understand.　They have a vague general feeling about a word's connotation, which may be only a shade or two off its true meaning, or quite erroneous, perhaps almost the opposite of correct.　The backwoods preacher, spouting big, rich polysyllables without much meaning behind them, may impress his congregation, but a lawyer cannot afford to toss words around with such abandon.

It is not enough to know the approximate meaning of a word; one must also discern the shades of difference between it and somewhat similar words.　The difference between the right word and the almost right word, said Mark Twain, is the difference between lightning and the lightning bug.　Writers sometimes give a wholly wrong and even unfortunate coloration to their statements because they do not appreciate the shadings that may make an assertion intended to point in one direction actually point in the opposite.　To say that a man's acts were heroic is one thing; to refer to them as "heroics" is altogether different.

No two words are exactly synonymous.　Each has its own emotional wave length.　"Informant" and "informer" have the same meaning, but "informer" has an opprobrious connotation.　Law enforcement agencies call their sources "informants," not "informers."　Of two words denoting the same thing, one may inspire sympathetic or other favorable feeling, whereas the other evokes only ridicule or contemp.　Compare:

Boyish	Puerile
Child-like	Childish
Depreciate	Deprecate
Difference	Discrepancy
Enormousness	Enormity
Manly	Mannish
Masterly	Masterful
Travel	Junket.

Bertrand Russell years ago created a kind of game, conjugating what he called "irregular comparatives."

I am firm.　You are stubborn.　He is pigheaded.

We all play this game.　I negotiated a settlement; you worked a deal; he finagled a plum for himself.　Our purpose is to liberate the captive people behind the iron curtain; theirs is to stir up disorder and foment revolution. They use spies; we enlist counterintelligence officers. Defendants in an anti-trust suit may protest that they did not practice collusion; they merely cooperated to substitute constructive for cutthroat competition. (Anti-trust has been called "a jurisprudence of metaphor").

> In this case, the promise ran directly to the beneficiary, but the intent was the overpowering factor.

The use of a wrong word, like "overpowering" in this sentence, is as jarring as a sour note in a symphony. It diverts the reader's attention from what is being said to how it is being expressed.

What is the sour note in each of the following?

> By instigating the student loan program, the government hoped to provide an incentive for the study of science.
> It is with unbridled pride that I present
> Judge Blank deserves the most fulsome praise.
> This is to acknowledge your lengthy letter
> The proposal touched off a furore of opposition.

Even the word "precise" is sometimes used imprecisely—and by eminent writers, as when Mr. Justice Douglas writes:[8]

> . . . [T]he action of New York tends to restore some of the precise irritants which had long affected the relations between these two great nations. . . .

What was meant was not "precise" irritants, but "very" or "precisely the same" irritants.

Learn to Use a Thesaurus or Dictionary

You will, in writing, continually encounter the situation where you cannot think of the exact word you want. The only words that come to mind don't quite hit the mark. You are sure there is a better one, but you don't know it, or can't recall it at the moment. Take time to find it. Make it a practice whenever such questions arise to consult a dictionary or a thesaurus.

8. United States v. Pink, 315 U.S. 203, 232, 62 S.Ct. 552, 566, 86 L.Ed. 796 (1942).

A thesaurus serves a different function from that of a dictionary. The thesaurus gives no definitions, but only a list of synonyms and antonyms. It is useful when you know the meaning of the word at hand but are looking for another that will better convey just the right shade of meaning, or give a somewhat different nuance or a fresher way of saying it.

When you do not know the exact meaning of a word, or when you do not know the exact difference in shades of meaning between two words—between "continuous" and "continual," or between "compel" and "impel," for example—you need a dictionary.

Suppose a writer, discussing the trial of occupational disease cases, wants to say, in effect, that one picture is worth a thousand words. His first effort runs something like this:

> One concrete picture of a specific person and his condition makes more impression than a thousand-word polemic against the ravages of disease generally.

Unless the writer has at least a doubt about the correctness of his use of "polemic," he is lost. There is no hope for the person who does not know what he does not know. One who does know enough to doubt will look it up. He will find that "polemic" means an argument that makes an aggressive attack on the opinions of others. This is not precisely the thought he wants to convey, so he looks for other words. "Harangue" comes to mind, but it is not quite what he wants. But from it, the dictionary and the thesaurus lead him to others: "inveigh," "invective," "diatribe," "philippic," "declaim." He finally strikes out "a thousand-word polemic" and substitutes "a thousand words declaiming."

Sometimes, although you recognize that the word you have written is not precisely what you want, you may not succeed in finding another that will do. In such a situation, consider whether you cannot reform the whole sentence or clause, so as to put the thought in another way. Suppose you are writing a letter to opposing counsel, rejecting an offer of settlement. You write:

> My client is unwilling to accept anything less than the amount of his claim. He has asked me to file suit next Monday unless you will agree to the amount he asks.

On rereading, the last word, "asks," strikes you as weak. You cannot, however, think of a better. Resort to the thesaurus gives you a long list of synonyms, but only "request," "claim" and "demand" come close to what you need. "Request" and "claim" seem to be no better than "ask," while "demand" is too strong. Well, don't stick to that line of inquiry; when the ore begins to run thin, quit and start on another vein. Try rewording the whole last clause:

> unless the full amount is paid.

> if a satisfactory reply has not been received from you before that time.

> unless before that time we receive from you a satisfactory proposal for settling this matter.

Which wording you decide upon depends, of course, on just what thought you are trying to convey. If you are really determined to take nothing less than the full amount and want to close the door against any further offers of settlement, the first of the formulations suggested above will do it. The second is not quite so unbending; it hints that the door you have just closed is not locked, that although your client wants the full amount, it is just possible that you might persuade him to accept a little less. The third frankly invites another offer.

Don't be Afraid to Repeat the Right Word

Exactness often demands repeating the same term to express the same idea. Where that is true, never be afraid of using the same word over and over again. Many more sentences are spoiled by trying to avoid repetition than by repetition.

> The common law doctrine of *pedis possessio* was recognized both by the miners before the enactment of federal location laws and by the courts after the passage of the statutes.

Here the writer elegantly shifts from "enactment" to "passage" and from "laws" to "statutes." The last five words of the sentence should be replaced by "their enactment." The use of "their" illustrates the simplest and best way to avoid needless repetition without sacrificing exactness—using pronouns.

> Most employers would agree, but some owners have taken a contrary view.

Here, instead of hunting for a different word to avoid repeating "employers," the writer could simply have omitted it the second time: "but some have taken a contrary view."

Avoid terms such as "the former . . . the latter," "the first . . . the second," and "party of the first part . . . party of the second part." They require the reader to pause, even though only momentarily, to go back and recall who was former and latter, first and second. Don't put him to this unnecessary effort. If a short word or short phrase can be used to make the reference, the reader can move on without having to figure out who or what is meant. "Buyer" and "Seller," "the company" and "the union" are examples of such labels. Divorce settlement agreements and also other contracts sometimes refer to the parties simply by their first names.

Repeating words and phrases may impair the literary quality of your work, but as already said, legal writing must sacrifice style to precision. If, to avoid repeating a word, you substitute a variation, you may lead your reader to think that you are making a distinction when you intend none.

> Two of the seven Democratic delegates are women, whereas all of the Republican delegates are ladies.

The hapless writer merely wanted to avoid repeating the word "women," but by using "ladies," he blunderingly suggests that the Democratic women were something less than ladies.

In statute-drafting especially, the same term must be used every time the same thought or concept is referred to. This is so important that it is sometimes called "the draftsman's golden rule." No variation for the sake of mere variety is permissible. Thus what is called a "motor vehicle" in one section or sentence must not be called an "automobile" in another. Conversely, one term must not be used to refer to several ideas. "Unlawful" must not be used to mean criminal in one sentence and to include tortious in another. In drafting wills or contracts also, variation can be dangerous. If you use a different term the second time you refer to a thing, the natural interpretation is that you did it for a reason; if you had meant the same thing, you would have used the same term; since you used a different one, you must have meant something different.

> I give the farm to my brother George. If he predecease
> me, the property is to go to my sister Amy.

This invites a law-suit over what Amy is to inherit—the farm, or something more?

In telling the facts of a case, if variation is used in referring to the several parties involved, the effect may be confusing.

> Where the manager of a radio station conceived the title
> and principal characters of a program and employed another
> person to prepare the scripts and act in the production, but
> said nothing about the ownership of the program, the broad-
> caster owned the program and its title, even though the
> script writer copyrighted the first ten scripts in her own
> name without consulting her employer.

This story seems to have five people in it: the manager, another person, the broadcaster, the script writer and her employer. Actually they are only two, but the reader has to sort out the five labels and fit them to the proper persons.

Where variation is called for to avoid ambiguity or excessive repetition, the substitute should be only a substitute, and not an elegant sobriquet, such as "the weaker sex" for women, "Old Glory" for the flag, or "the staff of life" for bread. (The use of such sobriquets is a weakness of the stuffed shirts we sometimes hear at political meetings and bar association dinners, but not, it is only fair to say, of law students.)

Comply with Drafting Rules

In addition to the "golden rule," that the same term should be used every time a given concept is referred to, a few other rules followed by statutory draftsmen are useful also for legal writing generally:

The singular includes the plural. Say "any person," not "any person or persons."

The masculine includes the feminine. Say "he," not "he or she."

Prohibitions are put in the present, not the future, tense. Say "it is unlawful," not "it shall be unlawful."

Avoid Sexist Expressions (When You Can)

Does the use of the masculine gender to include the feminine invidiously imply male superiority? Some of us have become convinced that it does. Language does not only reflect reality; it also influences our perceptions of reality. Experiments have shown that generic statements about "man" evoke, to a statistically significant degree, images of males only, whereas corresponding statements that avoid using the word "man" evoke images of both males and females.[9]

But what choice do we have? The English language does not have common-gender singular pronouns. Our plural pronouns, "they" and "them," are common-gender, but for the singular we use the masculine as the unmarked gender. The clumsy effort to avoid this by saying "he or she" or "him or her" every time we need to use a pronoun would soon become a drag.

The words "man" and "men" may also include women. Although these words are sometimes used to refer only to male persons, they are also correctly used to refer to persons, without regard to sex.[10] The declaration that "All men are created equal" does not exclude women. We thus quite correctly say "Madam Chairman"; there is no need for such an ungainly neologism as "chairperson." So too, we can correctly say that a woman is "foreman of the jury," or is "a good horseman," or "a good penman." We can even correctly speak of women "manning the barricades."

But we need not always use these terms. If we are speaking of persons of both sexes, we can say "persons," or "human beings"; we can speak of "human rights" or "personal rights" instead of "the rights of man." And why not speak of a "reasonable person" instead of a "reasonable man"?[11]

---

9. C. Miller and K. Swift, Words and Woman 21–38 (1976), cited in Collins, Language, History and the Legal Process: A Profile of the "Reasonable Man," 8 Rutgers Camden L.J. 311, 322 (1977).

10. This use of the masculine, Mary Beard complained decades ago, has allowed (male) writers to engage in a kind of double talk; we cannot always tell when they are using "men" to refer solely to males and when they mean to include women. If challenged, they can explain that they mean both. M. Beard, Woman as Force in History 47 (1946).

11. See Collins, supra note 9.

If willing to make the effort, we can often find a way to avoid using "he" and "him" when speaking of both sexes. We can instead (1) use the plural, or (2) use "you" or "we" or "one," or (3) simply omit the pronoun. Thus, instead of saying "An individual taxpayer can expect to be audited at least once during his life," we can put it in one of the following ways:

1. Individual taxpayers can expect to be audited at least once in their lives.

2. You (we, one) can expect to be audited at least once in your (our, one's) life.

3. An individual taxpayer can expect to be audited at least once in life (in a lifetime).

Occupational sex-biased labels can often be avoided. Instead of jurymen, say jurors; instead of policeman, police officer; instead of workman, worker.

Above all, avoid expressions implying that a virtue is found only in men: facing danger "with manly courage," or "like a man." Things would not be easier if women endured childbirth "like a man."

Abstract Words are Inexact

Lawyers must constantly deal with abstract legal concepts— negligence, malice, consideration, intent, fraud, reasonableness, and the even wider concepts of right, wrong, property, duty, justice, and freedom. In fact, law can be said to consist entirely of abstract general principles.

While we cannot avoid using such words, we can recognize the ambiguity inherent in them. Just because they are "big" words, they do not and cannot have one exact meaning. "Justice" or "democracy" does not connote for one man quite what it does for another. A writer using such a word should pause to define the sense in which he is using it, first for himself and then for the reader; and then he should use it consistently in that sense.

Your allegation that the function of our courts is protective and corrective solely would lead to the conclusion that our courts should not be termed courts of justice but rather courts of expediency.

It would be futile to debate this proposition without first defining in what sense the words "justice" and "expediency" are being used.

> The court reached an equitable conclusion which in its essence stated that a broad principle of public policy is essential to public welfare.

What does this say, if anything?

Some writers become so addicted to the use of abstract words that they use them even for concrete things:

There are a variety of forms that the courts have approved.	The courts have approved various forms.

Abstract terms have an attraction for the writer who has not clearly thought through what he wants to say, or who is afraid that a more specific statement may be incorrect. Because these words are vague, they can be used without any precise meaning. They therefore offer an easy way out for the lazy and the fuzzy-minded. (A Birmingham, Alabama, ordinance provided that "no nude be displayed unless it is art.") The process feeds on itself: because our thoughts are fuzzy, we use woolly phrases; but the availability of these woolly phrases allows us to be content with fuzzy thoughts. A. Parker Nevin once constructed a political speech "for all occasions," made up of reverberating sentences such as this:

> The crucial test for the solution of all these intricate problems which confront and challenge our ingenuity is the sheer and forceful application of those immutable laws which down the corridor of time have always guided the hand of man, groping as it were for some faint beacon of light for his hopes and aspirations.

That this caricature is painfully true to form can be seen by picking up almost any political speech, whether made by the head of government of any great power or by a candidate for alderman. Here is a sentence from a speech by President Franklin D. Roosevelt: [12]

---

12. Both this and the next quotation are taken from Stuart Chase, The Tyranny of Words, 381, 382 (1938).

> In our inner individual lives we can never be indifferent, and we assert for ourselves complete freedom to embrace, to profess, and to observe the principles for which our flag has so long been the lofty symbol.

The example is taken from President Roosevelt designedly, not because he was one of the worst offenders but because he was one of the least. More effectively than most men, he could be vividly specific, as in the following passage:

> I have seen war. I have seen war on land and sea. I have seen blood running from the wounded. I have seen men coughing out their gassed lungs. I have seen the dead in the mud. I have seen cities destroyed. I have seen two hundred limping, exhausted men come out of line—the survivors of a regiment of one thousand that went forward forty-eight hours before. I have seen children starving. I have seen the agony of mothers and wives. I hate war.

One such concrete picture—as of men coughing out their gassed lungs—makes more impression on our imagination than a thousand words declaiming against war's irrationality, horrors, and other abstract qualities.[13]

Abstractness carried to the point of meaninglessness can be found in "new thought" magazines, "divine science" literature, and similar writings of a pseudo-philosophical sort, discussing such questions as "What is the secret of life mastery?" or "What is the unpardonable sin?" Wendell Johnson has even suggested that the most serious forms of this sort of high-level abstracting are found in patients suffering from grave mental illness.[14]

Undefined Terms may be Ambiguous

Not only abstract words, but also other terms, may need to be defined to avoid inviting disputes over their meaning. In writing contracts, terms such as "notice" or "purchase" will probably need defining. Whether "assignment" includes delegation of duties as well as transfer of rights may need to be made clear.

---

13. Now you know who it was, at page 15, that had to look for a substitute for "polemic."

14. Johnson, People in Quandaries 272–3 (1946).

In drafting a statute, regulating the operation of "vehicles," for example, that term will certainly need to be defined.

In a labor-management collective bargaining agreement, terms such as "grievance," "overtime," "emergency" and "temporary" should always be defined. So should "rate of pay" for overtime or vacations, to anticipate such questions as the correct rate of pay for an employee who works overtime on a premium shift on a contract holiday. A provision allowing the contract to be reopened "for wages only," without defining "wages," may require the company to bargain about a proposed pension plan. Even if the parties cannot agree upon a comprehensive definition, it is better to describe the effect or to give an example than merely to use the undefined term.

WORDS TO WATCH

It is not the purpose of this book to teach vocabulary or grammar. The essentials of correct English you have presumably learned before starting law school; if not, you have been ill-advised in thinking that law is your game. But experience in teaching legal writing has shown that certain words give law students especial trouble.

Aforesaid

Years ago, the Conference of Commissioners of Uniform State Laws laid down drafting rules, one of which was that the words, "aforesaid," "said," "such," and "whatever," should so far as possible be avoided. This is good advice. It does not mean that these words are bad. "Aforesaid" has a proper place in formal legal writing. But students should remember that it has a restrictive effect, and that it therefore should not be used carelessly. Examples are given under "Said."

In informal writing, such as letters to clients, it is better to say "named above" or "mentioned earlier," or, where the reference is clear without it, simply to delete it.

Alibi

When an American athlete who had confidently been expected to win his event in the 1960 Olympics was beaten by two Russians, he said, "I don't have any alibis; I was beaten fair and square." This was commendable sportsmanship but hardly commendable phrasing, unless he meant merely to admit that he had been present.

Alleged

Because the law presumes a person to be innocent until proved guilty, we should not call someone not yet convicted a criminal, not even an alleged (or accused or suspected) criminal.

And/or

Violent controversy has raged over the use of this form of expression. Judges have denounced it as a "linguistic abomination," Commercial Standard Ins. Co. v. Davis, 68 F.2d 108 (1933); State v. Smith, 51 N.M. 328, 184 P.2d 301 (1947), and "a verbal monstrosity," Employers' Mutual Liability Ins. Co. v. Tollefsen, 219 Wis. 434, 263 N.W. 376 (1935), devoid of meaning since it is incapable of classification by the rules of grammer and syntax. American Gen. Ins. Co. v. Webster, 118 S.W.2d 1082 (Tex.Civ.App.1938). It has even been held not to be "the English language," within the terms of a constitutional requirement that judicial proceedings be conducted and preserved in the English language. Tarjan v. National Surety Co., 268 Ill.App. 232 (1932).

The editor of the *American Bar Association Journal* once called it "a device for the encouragement of mental laziness," and asserted that anyone who knows the difference between "and" and "or" can take a

> contract or statute, bristling with this symbol, strike out every one of them and substitute the proper one of the words, to the great clarification of the meaning of the instrument or act.

18 A.B.A.J. 456 (1932). Some eminent lawyers promptly wrote to endorse this anti-andorian attack. One, John W. Davis, said he expected to spend his declining years in a crusade against the "bastard." Id. p. 575.

But other lawyers have defended it as a "useful abbreviation," which is "generally neither awkward nor ambiguous," and "is a perfectly legitimate offspring of the necessity for brief and precise expression." 45 Yale L.J. 918 (1936). See also 20 Marquette L.R. 101 (1936). A note in 118 A.L.R. 1367 makes the following judicious observation:

> This term is used to avoid a construction which, by the use of the disjunctive "or" alone, would exclude the combination of several of the alternatives, or, by the use of the conjunctive "and" alone, would exclude the efficacy of any one of the alternatives standing alone. It takes the place of the addition, after several alternatives connected simply by "and," of a qualifying phrase such as "or either" or "or any combination thereof," and, after several alternatives connected by "or," it takes the place of such phrases as "or both," "or any combination thereof."

> As thus used, this phrase, term, symbol, or character is a deliberate amphibology; it is purposefully ambiguous. Its sole usefulness lies in its self-evident equivocality. When the term is properly used, however, its meaning is not indefinite or uncertain. It is broad, but not indefinite; it is elastic, but within definite bounds and for a definite purpose. If the term were used in its proper place and sense, and were restricted to private contractual instruments, instead of being interpolated, with parrot-like indiscrimination, into pleadings, instructions to juries, and the like, it is probable that the courts would have accepted it without question as a useful addition to scrivener's English.

All this should warn the legal draftsman of the pitfalls that careless use of the term may lead him into. For frightening examples, he may consult "Words and Phrases," where he will find pages of digests of cases in which the court was obliged to construe its meaning—including cases in which affidavits, ballots, indictments, levies, ordinances and verdicts were held void or ineffectual, pleadings were stricken, and options, leases, pensions, insurance policies and other contracts subjected to the hazard of judicial interpretation.

As (for "for")

> Defendant's brief cites Corker v. Cram, but that is misleading, as that case does not support the contention made.

"As" in this sentence should either be replaced by "for," or it should be deleted and the comma replaced by a semicolon.

The Fowlers explain the proper, and especially the improper, use of causal "as" clauses. The subject is somewhat complex, so we shall merely quote their conclusion that "a good writer will seldom have a causal *as* clause of any kind at the end of a sentence." Fowler, The King's English (2d ed. 1908) p. 300.

Aspect

Looking out from a viewpoint (standpoint, point of view) what one sees is an aspect. A man who takes a position on a foggy viewpoint is likely to have a foggy view or aspect. What does a writer mean when he talks of "the main aspects of the case," "the most difficult aspects of the problem," or "a vital aspect of the rule"?

Case

Few words are more loosely used by lawyers than "case." The word has many correct uses: "a federal case," "a case of libel" (or of measles), "stating a case," "in case of need."

But it is often a flabby way to express what could and should be said more precisely and concisely:

In many cases	Often, frequently
It is often the case that	Often
In the case of both men and women	Of (by, for) both men and women
Few of the veniremen were willing to serve; in many cases they refused . . .	Few of the veniremen were willing to serve; many refused . . .
In any case	From any point of view

Notice that sometimes, as in the last example above, "case" must be replaced by a longer rather than by a shorter phrase. The objection to such a sentence as "The minority rule is impractical in any case" is not that "in any case" is wordy, but that it is unclear. It may mean literally that the rule would be impractical to apply in any situation (or in any litigated case?); it may mean that it is impractical from any point of view, or, coming after enumeration of other objections, it may mean "finally," or "whatever the merits of these other arguments."

Claim

"Claim" should be used to mean "lay claim to," not "assert," "declare" or "charge."

We claim that this deed is a forgery.	We charge that this deed is a forgery.

Collision

"The car collided with plaintiff's parked vehicle." No. Two things collide when they strike against one another, both being in motion. Striking or crashing into a parked vehicle is not a collision.

Compare To (With)

When one thing is likened to another, the term is "compared to." When two things are examined to find their differences and likenesses, it is "compared with."

He compared his efforts to those of his predecessor.

This bill needs to be compared with the Senate version.

Comprise

Do not confuse this word with "constitute." "Comprise" literally means "embrace." The bill of rights comprises both substantive and procedural rights, i. e., it embraces, or includes, both. The House and Senate constitute (make up) the Congress.

Contact

As a transitive verb ("Please contact me"), this has become a much-used word in businessmen's letter-writing English. Purists deplore it, not merely because it makes a verb of a noun, but because it sounds rather stuffy and because it is vague. But as it becomes more used, it perhaps will begin to sound less stuffy and self-important. As for its vagueness, this is its main excuse for being. True, it would be more exact to say, "telephone me," "write me," "meet me," "look me up," or even "get in touch with me." But "contact" is handy in the situation where the writer does not care which means are adopted and so does not want to be specific. "Get in touch with" carries the meaning, but "contact" does it in one word instead of four. Perhaps it is enough for the law student to remember that this use of the word is not in high repute, and therefore to avoid it where he can, especially where another verb better expresses his specific meaning. Thus if you mean "telephone me," there is no excuse for saying "contact me," or, worse yet, "contact me by telephone."

Contend

"Man proposes, God disposes." So litigants and their lawyers contend, but courts dispose of contentions. Writers sometimes wrongly use "contend" or "contention" when they want to refer to either a holding or a finding:

> The Board found that appellant was discharged because of his union activities. The record does not support this contention.

Datum, Data

"Datum" is a word taken from Latin which keeps its Latin plural form, "data." "The data are," not "The data is."

Other such words:

Criterion, criteria
Curriculum, curricula
Dictum, dicta
Phenomenon, phenomena

Deem

As a way to say "think" or "believe," this is a false elegancy. But it is correctly used in a technical sense to imply the inferential as opposed to the actual, as when we say that a person who does an act that he knows is likely to result in death is deemed to have intended to kill. The correct use is illustrated in a United States Supreme Court opinion [15] holding that although a corporation is not in fact a citizen, it

> seems to us to be a person, though an artificial one, inhabiting and belonging to that State, and therefore entitled, for the purpose of suing and being sued, to be deemed a citizen of that State.

15. Louisville, C. & C. R. Co. v. Letson, 2 How. 497, 555 (1844).

Disinterested

Do not use to mean uninterested. Disinterested means impartial. A judge should be disinterested, but not uninterested, in the case before him.

Due to

One of a list of terms overworked by lawyers, and too often loosely used for "through," "by," or "because of." "Due" is an adjective, which should not introduce a causal phrase.

> Due to the industry's aggressive lobbying, the bill was finally passed.

"Due to" in this sentence could be replaced with "in consequence of" or "as a result of." But such a sentence is usually better recast: "By aggressive lobbying, the industry finally succeeded in getting the bill passed."

The best practice is to use "due to" only to modify or refer to a particular noun.

> We lost due to over confidence.

> Our defeat was due to overconfidence. (We lost because of overconfidence.)

Dwell

This is now antiquated. Except when you are deliberately being formal, say "live(at)."

Fact

This word comes from the Latin, "facio," to do. It means something that has been done or that has happened. Students sometimes use it loosely when they mean idea, opinion, theory, truth, question, or any of several other words. Use it only when you are talking of that which is of actual occurrence—the reality of an event or events. If you will bear this admonition in mind, you will not be guilty of such misuse as the following:

> Section 3–415 of the Uniform Commercial Code makes clear the fact that an accommodation party is always a surety.

> The fact to be determined is whether a reasonable person would interpret the seller's words as a guarantee.

> The facts are inaccurate.

Factor

One of those terms that we reach for when we are too lazy to hunt down the right word to say exactly what we mean: "One factor in the court's opinion." One can usually find a word that is more exact and more clear.

Finding

A "finding" is the determination of an issue of fact. The word should not be used to refer to a court's *holding* on a matter of law.

Forthwith

If ordered to do something "forthwith," how promptly must you comply? Within an hour? A day? A month? The word has no fixed meaning. It must be interpreted in the light of its context in each case—and interpretation means litigation. Among the many cases that the word has spawned are some holding that two or three hours was too long, and others holding that 30 days or more was not.[16] Instead of inviting a lawsuit by using this seemingly imperious but actually ambiguous term, be specific; say "within 24 hours," or "within 30 days."

Herein

Herein means "in this." But this what? This paragraph? This section? This document?

A statutory phrase, "except as herein expressly provided," was held by the trial court in a California case to refer to the entire statute. The intermediate appellate court reversed, holding, 3–2, that "herein" meant "in this section." This holding was in turn reversed by the state supreme court, which held that it clearly referred to the entire act.[17]

To avoid litigation, be specific. Say "except as provided in this section," or "in paragraph 10."

---

16. See citations to cases, running to several pages, in 37 C.J.S. pp. 128–131; 17 Words and Phrases 605–633 (Perm.Ed.1958); D. Mellinkoff, The Language of the Law 310–312 (1963).

17. Owen v. Off, 218 P.2d 563 (Cal. App.1950), vacated 36 Cal.2d 751, 227 P.2d 457 (1951).

In legislative drafting, the term, "in this act," may invite similar doubts. If the act is later amended, "this act" may be interpreted to mean either the amendatory act or the original, excluding the amendment. Legislative draftsmen should avoid using the term whenever possible, and instead refer to either (1) the act's short title, (2) the specific behavior prohibited, or (3) specific section numbers. In bills to amend legislation that contains the term, it should be replaced with a specific statutory citation.

Individual

This word is not simply a synonym for "person." The word denotes a separate or private person as against a group of persons, or the community as a whole. It is correctly used in the following sentences:

> This assembly is a constituent body, not a mere aggregation of individuals.

> We must protect both society and the individual.

In the following sentences, "individual" is incorrectly used and should be replaced with "person":

> Any individual may be admitted to a hospital upon written application by the head of any institution in which such individual may be.

> We must protect society against such individuals.

Involve

"The foggy mind's best friend," I. A. Richards called this word (How to Read a Page 141 [1942]). Strictly, it means to roll up in itself so as to gather in or embrace; to wrap up in something; to enfold. Figuratively, it is used to mean entangle in difficulties or embarrassment ("involved in a crime"). But it is often loosely used to mean nothing more than include, influence or contain. It is good practice to use it only when you want to connote entanglement or complication.

In which of the following sentences is the word used correctly, in which should it be changed to a more exact word and in which should it be stricken out as meaningless?

The legal proceedings involved would be unduly costly.

The result would involve the overruling of a long line of cases.

The proposal would involve an increase in personnel.

My client refused to become involved in the transaction.

The delays and red tape involved make prosecution of the claim impractical.

The case involves a claim for damages involving a substantial sum.

Jury

This is a group name. Use it as a singular collective noun when you intend to refer to the jury as a unit (The jury returned its verdict). When referred to as a number of individuals, a plural verb is proper (The jury were all working men). Any question can be avoided by using "jurors" or "members of the jury" in the second situation.

Like

"Like" should not be used for "as." "Like" governs nouns and pronouns; "as" governs phrases and clauses. "Like" has long been misused by people weak in grammar. Lately it has been taken up by Madison Avenue advertising writers who use it to pander to such people. Ogden Nash paid his compliments to the trend in verses published in the *New Yorker,* entitled, "Oafishness Sells Good, Like an Advertisement Should."

Literally

"Literally" is frequently misused for figuratively—that is, for "not literally." You have perhaps seen fun poked at this gaffe, as in, "I literally sank through the floor." One way to avoid misusing this word is to avoid using it. This is not hard to do, for one will not often have legitimate use for it. A lawyer may have occasion to talk of a "literal interpretation" of a statute, that is, one adhering closely to the words. But as often used, "literally" means only that the writer means exactly what he says. This should go without saying. Counsel should no more need to protest his literalness than his truthfulness (as by interjecting, "To tell the truth").

Majority

Do not use "majority" as a grandiose synonym for "most."

The majority of the cases turned on questions of fact.	Most of the cases turned on questions of fact.

Or

In its ordinary and accurate sense, "or" is a disjunctive, marking an alternative—one or the other of two, but not both. But it is also used more loosely, and courts have held it may be construed to mean "and" where a document shows it was so intended, or to prevent an absurd result.

The Copyright Act [18] has a provision that illustrates the ambiguities lurking in the word. The act says that upon expiration of the original 28-year copyright

> the author . . . if still living, or the widow, widower, or children of the author, if the author be not living, or if such author, widow, widower, or children be not living, then the author's executors . . . shall be entitled to a renewal and extension of the copyright.

The widow of an author renewed a copyright, but an illegitimate child, by its mother, sought a declaratory judgment that the child also had an interest in the copyright. Should the court hold that the widow and the child take together, as a class, or that they take in order of enumeration, the widow first and the child only if there be no widow? And do the executors take if either widow or a child is not living, or only if there is neither widow nor child living?[19]

Personal, Personally

Both these words are overused. "My personal opinion" usually means nothing more than "my opinion." If emphasis is de-

---

18. 61 Stat. 652, 17 U.S.C.A. § 1 et seq.

19. DeSylva v. Ballantine, 351 U.S. 570, 76 S.Ct. 974, 100 L.Ed. 1417 (1956). See also Jones v. Haines, Hodges & Jones Bldg. & Dev. Co., 371 S.W.2d 342 (Mo.App.1963); Dickerson, The Difficult Choice Between "And" and "Or," 46 A.B. A.J. 310 (1960).

sired, it is simpler to say "my own opinion." "Personal" is proper, however, when it is used to distinguish private from official:

> As trustee, I am bound to refuse, but my personal opinion is . . . .

"Personally" may be correctly used in at least two senses: (1) without the use of others; and (2) as a person.

> 1. The President conferred the medals personally.
>
> 2. He is personally likable, and he is a brilliant trial lawyer.

But often, like "personal," the word is used in a way that overemphasizes the self and gives off an air of self-importance: I personally prefer tea.

Practically

As often used, this word does not mean what the writer intended. "The court practically overruled the case of Doe v. Eton" makes sense, if you mean that for practical purposes, or, so far as future practice is concerned, the case is no longer a precedent. It is not correct to say, "The court awarded practically the full amount of the damages sued for." You cannot in practice do the same things with a lesser amount of money that you can with a larger. Try paying a hundred dollar debt with $99.50. The smaller sum is almost as much, but it is not practically the same.

Presume, Assume

Although much alike in meaning, these words are not interchangeable. When you merely mean to "take for granted," or "suppose," in the ordinary layman's sense, use "assume." "Presume," because of its relation to "presumption," carries more technical legal connotations.

Proven

As a past participle of "prove," this form is archaic; modern usage favors "proved." But "proven" is still used as an adjective: "This is a proven fact;" but "We have proved our case."

Rule, Ruling

Like "find" and "finding," these words are sometimes used by law students when they mean "hold" or "holding."

> The Supreme Court ruled that the state court's failure to allow reasonable time to secure counsel was in violation of the 14th Amendment.

A rule or ruling is an order or direction of a court or tribunal on a point of law, regulating practice or the action of parties in the case. The judge *rules* on motions and on objections to evidence; ultimately he *holds* for the plaintiff or for the defendant.

Said

This word means afore-mentioned; it therefore confines the meaning of the word with which it is used to something that has been mentioned before.

In a pleading, a prayer for relief against "said defendants hereinafter named" was construed not to include a defendant who had not been previously named. Wheeler & Wilson Mfg. Co. v. Filer, 52 N.J.Eq. 164, 28 A. 13, 14 (1893). In that case, the word "said" was obviously thrown in without any purpose. Many lawyers get into this habit. The following excerpt from a complaint shows how seriously addicted some of them become:

> . . . [B]eginning at a point on said railroad track about a half mile or more north of a point opposite said curve in said highway, large quantities of highly volatile coal were unnecessarily thrown into the firebox of said locomotive and upon the fire contained therein, thereby preventing proper combustion of said coal. . . . [Defendant] knew said smoke would fall upon and cover said curve in said highway when said engine reached a point on said railroad tracks opposite said curve, unless said smoke was checked in the meantime.

Exposure to this language apparently infected the court. After quoting this passage, the court's opinion continued with a sentence starting, "Said paragraph of the complaint . . ." and containing seven more "said's." Button v. Pennsylvania Ry. Co., 57 N.E.2d 444 (Ind.App.1944), quoted by Evans, "Words, Words, Words," 2 Ky. State Bar J.No. 1, p. 19 (Dec. 1946).

Writers other than lawyers get along without using "said" at all. We could get along at least as well if we eliminated most of our use of it.

Same

Used as a pronoun, "same" is another example of the "heavy footed jargon" used by some lawyers. Discriminating readers will think it offensive.

> The plaintiff took the note for value and endorsed the same over to the bank.

> Please sign the enclosed releases and return same to this office.

Shall/May

In drafting, "shall" imposes an obligation to act. When conferring a privilege or a discretionary right, use the indicative or "may," not "shall": "The owner has the right" or "The owner may," not "The owner shall have the right." Using "shall" states the right as if it were a duty.

When a right or privilege is being denied or abridged, use "may not" or "No . . . may." With a negative subject, use "may," not "shall": "No person may," not "No person shall."

In giving directions or conferring authority, do not use the passive. Do not say "is directed"; say "shall." Not "is authorized" or "is entitled," but "may."

Since

In origin, this word refers to time; it means "subsequent to the time that." But it is also used as a causal conjunction, meaning "because." Avoid using it in a way that leaves the reader in suspense as to the sense in which it is being used.

> Since the statute, following protracted litigation in both the state and federal courts, was finally upheld and enforcement vigorously initiated . . . .

At this point, the reader still does not know whether "since" here means "after" or "because."

State

Most students seem to think it beneath a court's dignity for it to "say" anything. It must always "state." Even Jesus Christ was content merely to "say unto you." It is not contempt of court to have judges do the same.

Strictly, "state" means to express fully or clearly. The word is correctly used in the following sentences:

> The precise terms and conditions of every new appointment shall be stated in writing.

> I shall proceed to state my reasons.

Such

The adjective "such" sometimes serves a useful purpose, as where it saves having to repeat a concept that cannot be referred to in a word or two. In statutes and regulations, for example, it may be necessary to make clear that the second reference is to exactly the same concept mentioned previously. The word "such" is the simplest way to do so.

> Whenever application is made to a judge of any district or county court stating under oath that a person found in the judicial district or county is in need of hospital care and treatment, such judge may order such person. . . .

But some lawyers get into the habit of tagging "such" on to almost any noun they have already used in the same passage.

> A contract of insurance is void ab initio if such a contract.
>   . . .

In this sentence there is no reason for not saying "the contract," or better yet, "it."

> The 1959 Act is an attempt to remedy the situation in the building industry already described, but such attempt can succeed only if such situation. . . .

This would read more naturally if "such attempt" read "the attempt" or "this attempt," and if "such situation" read "that situation" or "the situation."

That, Which

Many people in writing use the word "which" when in talking they would use "that"—probably because they have a vague feeling that "which" is the more literary word. More often than not, "that" is really the word they want. Or they shift from the one word to the other without any reason other than a desire for variation, and perhaps without even noticing.

> The parties are compelled by the agreement to engage in practices that they would rather avoid, and to refrain from activities which they would like to undertake.

The two clauses in this sentence are quite parallel, and the shift from "that" to "which" is wholly without reason.

Generally, we should use "that" as the defining or restrictive relative pronoun, and "which" as the non-defining or non-restrictive. That is to say, if the clause being introduced could be omitted without changing the meaning of the noun it modifies, we should use "which." If omitting the clause would change the meaning, we should use "that."

> The Eighth Amendment, which defendant relies upon, forbids cruel and unusual punishments.

The subject is "The Eighth Amendment," and omitting the clause would not change it. We therefore use "which."

> The constitutional provision that forbids cruel and unusual punishments is the Eighth Amendment.

Here, the subject is not "The constitutional provision," but a certain provision, namely, the one that forbids cruel and unusual punishments. The clause is thus a restrictive one, introduced by "that."

This distinction is not always observed, however, and we therefore cannot assume that others will read it into our own writing. If a clause is intended to be purely descriptive and not defining, it is well not only to use "which," but also to set the clause off with commas, or to recast the sentence.

Though, Although

"Though" and "although" are synonymous, but "although" is preferable at the beginning of a sentence, "though" for introducing short supplementary clauses or phrases.

> Although the court accepted the principle, it refused to apply it in this case.
>
> The plaintiff was careless, though not willfully so.

Otherwise, choose the one word or the other depending on the rhythm and on the formality of what you are writing. "Although" is the more formal.

To Wit

This is legal jargon. "Namely" sounds simpler and more natural, and should be preferred in all but the most formal legal documents.

Unto

Lawyers, especially in writing wills, still seem to think they must talk in King James English: "I give unto my son John. . . ." Why not "to"?

Various

"Various" means "differing from one another," or "of several kinds." It should not be used to mean "several" or "many." It is correct to say, as Mr. Justice Curtis said in Cooley v. Board of Port Wardens, 12 How. 299 (1851), "Now the power to regulate commerce embraces a vast field, containing not only many, but exceedingly various subjects, quite unlike in their nature." It is incorrect to say, "These laws gave birth to a problem that has plagued various courts."

Viz.:

An abbreviation for *videlicet*. Since not one lawyer (or judge) in a hundred knows enough Latin to translate this, it would seem sensible to stick to English instead. Say "namely," or "that is to say."

Where

Strictly, "where" denotes *place* only. One can speak of "states where the rule is followed," but "cases where the rule is followed" should be changed to "cases in which the rule is followed" or "cases that follow the rule."

Crops and animals are not the only property where an after-acquired property clause may be used.	Crops and animals are not the only kinds of property for which an after-acquired property clause may be used.

Whereas

This word has spawned litigation for two centuries. Sometimes it means nothing; sometimes it has meaning, but that may be any of several meanings. To take just one example from Mellinkoff:[20] if a contract of sale reads, "Whereas there are 4,000 square feet of floor space in Seller's house," does it mean that Seller warrants? Does it mean that the parties have examined the house and agreed that whether it has more or less than 4,000 square feet of floor space will not affect the contract? Or does it mean that if it has more or less than 4,000 square feet the price will be adjusted?

When you find yourself about to indulge in a "whereas," consider whether it means anything. If not, delete it. If you intend to say something meaningful, say it in clearer language.

While

In origin, this word is related to the notion of time, and means "during the time that." But it has come to be used also as an adversative conjunction, meaning "although," "but," or "whereas." It is better to avoid such use, especially where it leaves the meaning unclear.

> While such combinations were expressly prohibited by statute, this venture flourished.

Does this mean the venture flourished during the time it was prohibited, or although it was prohibited?

20. Mellinkoff, The Language of the Law 324 (1963).

Chapter 3

CONCISENESS

If the first aim in writing is to communicate our thoughts with accuracy, the second is to do it with dispatch. As one unusually successful writer, Antoine de Saint-Exupéry (*Wind, Sand and Stars*), said, "perfection is finally attained not when there is no longer anything to add, but when there is no longer anything to take away, when a body has been stripped down to its nakedness."

Conciseness is particularly important for lawyers. Lawyers, more than most writers, must say exactly what they mean, no more and no less. Every additional word is one more potential source of ambiguity. "He that useth many words for the explaining of any subject," said John Ray, "doth, like the cuttlefish, hide himself for the most part in his own ink."

Some of a lawyer's most important writings—briefs, for example—are written for busy men. If, remembering the injunction to keep your reader in mind, you will picture the judge reading your brief in his study late at night, it will help spur you to say what you have to say in the fewest possible words. Doing so will not only spare the time and energy of your reader, but also increase the readability of your material.

In our busy age a leisurely style, adorned with rhetorical fretwork, is more likely to arouse impatience than admiration. We like a writer who can communicate his thoughts in a straightforward way, without circumlocutions or redundancies.

We need not strip our writing down to the irreducible minimum that Judge J. Edgar Murdock of the United States Tax Court achieved in a case in which a taxpayer testified, "As God is my judge, I do not owe this tax." The judge's answer was, "He's not, I am; you do." But we can profitably try to be less wordy than most of us are.

41

A master of English style, Sir Winston Churchill, said "Give us the tools and we will finish the job." Sir Anthony Eden expressed the same thought thus: "We shall not let go until we have done the job, and we welcome all those who will give us a hand to finish it." Eden's sentence is certainly not verbose. But Churchill's is clearly better. It is the one that sticks in our memory. It illustrates what is generally true: the briefer form is the livelier and more forceful.

Good style conveys meaning directly, with a minimum of interference or excursiveness. Circumlocution—taking the long way round to say what you have to say—slows you down. That is why all writers on writing warn against it. "Circumlocutions are tedious," say Bergen and Cornelia Evans. "Prefer the single word to the circumlocution," say the Fowlers. "Use no more words than are necessary to express your meaning," says Gowers, "for if you use more you are likely to obscure it and to tire your reader." "In particular," he adds, "do not use round-about phrases where single words would serve." In short, get to your point. Get there as directly and quickly as you can.

Eliminate Unnecessary Words

One simple way to reach your point more quickly is to cut out unnecessary words that clutter up the path.

"Vigorous writing is concise. A sentence should contain no unnecessary words, a paragraph no unnecessary sentences, for the same reason that a drawing should have no unnecessary lines and a machine no unnecessary parts. This requires not that the writer make all his sentences short, or that he avoid all detail and treat his subjects only in outline, but that every word tell."[1]

We all tend to use unnecessary words. If you reread your writing looking for words you can strike out, you will probably be astonished to find how many never would be missed. Trimming away the fat gives you a leaner, more muscular style.

---

1. Strunk, The Elements of Style, with Revisions, an Introduction and a New Chapter on Writing by E. B. White 18 (1959).

Some words and phrases that often can be deleted as unnecessary are listed below:

Any and all. Say "any" or "all," but not both.

As to. The words, "as to" in phases such as "as to whether," "as to what," "as to who," and "as to how" are almost always superfluous. The Fowlers[2] called "as to whether" "a hideous combination." Yet it and other "as to" combinations pervade legal writing. A favorite phrase in lawyers' briefs and judges' opinions is "There is no question as to." Here are six passages taken from one United States Supreme Court opinion:[3]

> If, however, the above-quoted provision of § 380a as to docketing is a prerequisite. . . .

> . . . As to dismissals the first sentence of Rule 47 requires. . . .

> The assumed controversy between affiant and the Civil Service Commission as to affiant's right to act. . . .

> We can only speculate as to the kinds of political activity appellant desires to engage in. . . .

> . . . There is no question as to the exhausting of administrative remedies.

> . . . There is no problem of judicial discretion as to whether to take cognizance of this case.

In some of these passages, "as to" means "concerning" or "about;" in others it means "of," and in the last it is merely superfluous.

Character, nature, type, sort. As often used, these words are wholly unnecessary.

Contracts of an immoral character (nature, type, sort)	Immoral contracts

Fact, the fact that. Of the phrase, "the fact that," it has been said, "It should be revised out of every sentence in which it

---

2. Fowler and Fowler, The King's English 333 (1908).

3. United Public Workers v. Mitchell, 330 U.S. 75, 67 S.Ct. 556, 91 L. Ed. 754 (1947).

occurs."[4] This is probably too lofty an ideal for lawyers to attain, but simpler and better wording can usually be found.

Due to (Owing to) the fact that	Because
Notwithstanding the fact	Although
The fact that defendant was negligent	Defendant's negligence
The fact that this contention ignores is that	This contention ignores

Of, (in "all of"). What does the word "of" contribute in the following passages?

A pardon restores all of his civil rights.
All of the world is sad and dreary.
In all of these cases.
All of Hell broke loose.

With a pronoun, "of" is needed: all of us; all of them. But elsewhere it is not.

That. In a long sentence, it is easy to forget that one has already used "that" as a conjunction and to repeat it, as in the following sentence:

The court held that if the statute is interpreted in accordance with the intent of Congress as reflected in the committee reports and the debates in both houses, that the Board's decision must be upheld.

Even where the repetition is not erroneous, "that" can often be omitted, especially when it appears more than once in a sentence. Train your ear to sense when a statement sounds better without it. In each of the following sentences, which of the two "that's" should be deleted?

It was only reasonable to suppose, as the evidence shows that he did suppose, that a felony was being committed.

---

4. Strunk, op. cit., p. 18. The same can be said of "as a matter of fact."

Whether this is a provision that should be retained is a question that the committee ignored.

There are, there is, it is. Starting a sentence with "There are," "There is" or "It is," is a word-wasting habit. It is good practice, whenever your find yourself writing such a sentence, to consider whether you should not revise it. (That was such a sentence; did you notice? Wouldn't it be improved if revised to read, "Whenever you find yourself writing such a sentence, consider whether you should not revise it"?)

The following examples show that eliminating these introductory words often makes the sentence both shorter and stronger.

It is the contention of the petitioner	Petitioner contends
It is not necessary for you to	You need not
There are a few states that have rejected the rule	A few states have rejected the rule
There can be no question but that	Unquestionably
It has been held by most courts	Most courts have held
There is uncontradicted evidence to support this finding.	Uncontradicted evidence supports this finding.

Who, which, who is, that is, which were. These words can often be deleted as unnecessary.

This case, which was the first one decided in this state,	This case, the first to be decided in this state,
John Doe, who was the first witness to testify,	John Doe, the first witness to testify,
Neutronics, Inc. is a company that is engaged in processing	Neutronics, Inc. is a company engaged in processing (or, is engaged in processing; or, processes)

Many of our wordy phrases consist of compound prepositions and conjunctions. Often these two- or three-word combinations can be replaced by a single word. Prepositions encumbered by nouns can be unshackled and allowed to stand alone.

At the present time	Now
At the time at which	When
Be of help to	Help
By means of	By
During the course of	During
During the time that	While
For the purpose of	For
Have the desire to	Want
In back of	Behind
In favor of	For
In order to	To
Notwithstanding the fact that	Although
Subsequent to	After
The manner in which	How
Until such time as	Until
With the exception of	Except
With the result that	So that

Other compound phrases ("as to how long," "in relation to," and "with a view to," among the many), are also all too popular. These forms are not often used in talk. That alone should make them suspect of pomposity. A law student may feel impelled to use them because he is impressed with the formality of legal writing. "I am writing a legal opinion," he says to himself, "so I must try to sound like a lawyer, not like an ordinary Joe." But a lawyer is not required to be a stuffed shirt. His sentences need not be padded with windy words. The student should learn to distinguish a style that is dignified and formal from one that is merely overstuffed and flabby.

Other writers may have no conscious purpose in using these compound phrases. Because they have no precise meaning, they can be used without much thought of what one is trying to say. Like abstract words (see Chapter 2), they therefore have a strong attraction for the hazy and the lazy writer.

Prepositions often can be omitted:

Climb up	Climb
Explain about	Explain
Join together	Join
Start in (off, out)	Start

Prepositions and conjunctions are what one writer calls "glue words," words that hold together the "working words," mainly nouns and verbs, which carry the meaning. One gains conciseness by cutting down on the number of glue words, so as to have a higher proportion of working words.[5] Clauses in this way can sometimes be cut down to phrases.

While the trial was going on	During the trial
The court decree which was handed down in July ordered that payments be made each month on the mortgage.	The July court decree ordered monthly mortgage payments.

A phrase or clause can sometimes be replaced by a single adjective or adverb:

The fact that defendant was present at the meeting of June 10, which cannot be denied . . .	The undeniable fact that defendant was present
Plaintiff testified in a frank and unhesitating manner.	Plaintiff testified frankly and unhesitatingly.
Plaintiff accepted the offer that the defendant had made to settle the case for $7,500.	Plaintiff accepted the defendant's $7,500 settlement offer.
There can be no doubt but that	Doubtless, no doubt

Participles are useful for making "which" clauses more concise.

Courts which follow the majority rule	Courts following the majority rule
The measures which were enacted in 1961	The measures enacted in 1961

Sometimes a whole phrase can be replaced by less than a single word, namely, by a colon or a dash. One example must suf-

---

5. Wydick, Plain English for Lawyers, 66 Cal.L.Rev. 727 (1978).

fice here; the point is discussed at greater length in the chapter
on Organization.

The convention now faced its most serious crisis, in the form of a threatened walk-out by the labor delegates.	The convention now faced its most serious crisis: a threatened walk-out by the labor delegates.

Some sentences are so marbled with verbal fat that instead of
trying to delete superfluous words, one had better start over and
recast the sentence.

The particular weakness of the defendant's argument arises in connection with its basic premise relative to the primary purpose of the legislature.	Defendant's argument is weak because its basic premises is fallacious. It assumes that the primary purpose of the legislature was . . . .

Conciseness can sometimes be aided by combining sentences,
as by reducing one sentence to a subordinate clause.

The first case to pass on the issue was Dow v. Dow. In that case, the court held . . .	In Dow v. Dow, the first case to pass on the issue, the court held . . .

Adjectives and adverbs can often be deleted. They are relatively ineffective, especially for most lawyers' purposes. A lawyer who wants to convey the idea that his conclusion clearly follows had better present his material in such a way that his reader can quickly and easily come to that conclusion, and not merely tell him that it is clear. The objection to such conclusion-beg-
ging words is similar to the pleading objection of "pleading a
conclusion." Don't demand that the reader take your word that
something is "clear," "reasonable," or "essential." Demonstrate
that it is. Other adjectives and adverbs overused by lawyers include: completely, definitely, obviously, perfectly, quite, and
very. Instead of trying to strengthen a statement with such
hackneyed intensifiers, try to find a stronger noun, that will get
the effect you want without any qualifier.[6]

6. See Chapter 6, on Forcefulness,
post, at p. 107.

Changing from a noun or adjectival to a verb form will often make the wording both more concise and more forceful.

Are in need of	Need
Comes into conflict	Conflicts
Make an attempt	Try
Reach a decision	Decide
Take into consideration	Consider

Conciseness in its finest sense is obtained by hitting upon just the right word or phrase. When Thoreau said, "The average man lives a life of quiet desperation," he expressed a thought that might have sounded commonplace if put in other words; "quiet desperation" made it memorable. (Thoreau also said, "Some circumstantial evidence is very strong, as when one finds a trout in the milk.").

Eliminate the Long Wind-Up

A weed-patch of useless words is the long-winded introductory phrase. Nothing tends more to slow down the pace of one's writing than the habit of introducing each new point with one of these hackneyed phrases:

The next question that must be discussed is

It is also of importance to bear in mind that

Another significant point that we wish to call to the court's attention is

Consideration should be given to the possibility of

It should be noted in this connection

It is our contention that

It is unnecessary to point out how important it is . . . (Writers who say this always go on, however, to point it out).

Another important issue that has loomed large during the trial of this case is the question of whether . . ..

Few, if any, of the issues in this case were the subject of more conflicting testimony than that of whether . . ..

Someone once said of such woolly phrases, "There is less here than meets the eye." Most of them are mere padding. They can usually be replaced by a word, or omitted.

This applies not only to introductory words or phrases, but sometimes to entire sentences and even paragraphs. Here is a sentence that seems to consist almost wholly of empty words:

> It may be stated without fear of successful contradiction that although our opponents have filed a replication relative to the proposals made in connection with the several issues in dispute, the clearly apparent conflict as to basic philosophy and approach in regard to the concept of management prerogative remains wholly unresolved.

If on reading what you have written, the introduction seems weak or slow, see if it cannot be cut down or eliminated. Usually the best introduction is one that moves at once into the development of your subject—the assertion of a significant fact or proposition that serves as a base on which to build your argument.

Wordy introductions are often nothing but warming-up motions. The best advice we can give writers addicted to them is to cut out the wind-up and start pitching.

Avoid Pointless Repetition

One kind of unnecessary words and phrases comprises those that needlessly repeat an idea already expressed. The simplest form (called a pleonasm by grammarians) is one to which lawyers are much addicted, the use of two or more words, conjoined, when any one of them would serve the purpose.

> Authorized and empowered
> Confessed and acknowledged
> Free and clear from
> Intents and purposes
> Mutually understood and agreed
> Null and void and of no effect
> Of any sort or kind
> Part and parcel
> Quiet and peaceable possession
> Ratifying and consenting
> Reputation for truth and veracity
> Save and except
> To have and to hold
> True and correct
> Undertakes and agrees

Unless and until [7]
Various and sundry
Ways and means

No less redundant are pairs of words one of which includes the other, such as "authorize and require," or "request and demand." Instead of tossing in both of such pairs, use the broader or the narrower, as the context requires. A gaseous verbosity such as, "is hereby vested with power and authority and it shall be his duty in carrying out the provisions of this act to," can be reduced to one word, "shall."

Pointless repetition flourishes most luxuriantly in deeds and wills. In deeds, the granting clause sometimes "witnesseth" that the grantor "has granted, bargained, sold, remised, released, conveyed, aliened, and confirmed, and by these presents does grant, bargain, sell, remise, release, convey, alien, and confirm." The warranty provisions in some states recite that the grantor and his heirs

". . . all and singular the hereditaments and premises, hereinabove described and granted, or mentioned and intend-

---

7. Some readers may argue that "unless and until" is not tautological, because the two words express different meanings. True; but Gowers seems to be right when he says, "I have not been able to find (or to imagine) the use of *unless and until* in any context in which one of the two would not have sufficed alone." Plain Words: Their ABC 102 (1957).

"If and when" has more to be said for it. Take this sentence: "If and when a complaint is filed, I shall order a more thorough investigation." Here, "if" alone would not suffice, you may argue, because you want to say not only that if the event does happen, you will act, but also that you will act promptly; "When" alone will not do, because it seems to assume that the event will happen, whereas you want to imply that it may not. Very well then, use both. No

one would urge you to cut out words that serve a purpose. But when you find yourself writing both, ask whether they do serve a purpose, or whether you are using both merely because you have fallen into the habit of treating them as a team that must always be hitched together.

Ernest Weekley suggested a historical origin of some paired legal phrases: "After the Conquest, the language of the law was for centuries a barbarous form of French. As this was unintelligible to the conquered English, the practice gradually prevailed of coupling two words, one French and the other native, with the result that such pairs may now be counted by the dozens." Weekley, Cruelty to Words 43 (1931). See also Mellinkoff, The Language of the Law 38–39, 121–122 (1963).

ed to be so, with the appurtenances, unto the said grantee, his heirs and assigns, against _____, the said _____, his heirs, and against all and every other person or persons whomsoever lawfully claiming or to claim the same, or any part thereof, shall and will warrant and forever defend."

Statutory short forms today allow all this to be said in the words, "conveys and warrants."

In wills, many legal draftsmen, and perhaps their clients, like the sonorous and rolling repetitiveness of the old stock phrases: "sound and disposing mind and memory," "not acting under duress, menace, fraud or undue influence of any person whomsoever," "to make, publish and declare," "hereby expressly revoke and cancel any and all other wills, codicils, legacies, bequests and testamentary dispositions heretofore at any time made by me." A past president of the Illinois State Bar Association, Mr. Thomas Edmunds, estimated that from 25% to 40% of the words used in a simple will are meaningless or redundant.

A lawyer has reason to be especially careful in wording a will. It is a mournful characteristic of probate cases that the testator is always dead, and so is not available to explain what he meant. The draftsman should therefore take care to express his client's wishes without ambiguity.

In contracts, such introductory words as "whereas" and "Now, therefore," add nothing. "It is agreed" need usually be said only once, and not repeated in every paragraph. The consideration clause can often be less wordy than formulations frequently used. If the undertakings of the parties are well stated, no recitation of consideration may be needed. The common but false statement, "in consideration of the sum of one dollar and other good and valuable consideration, the receipt of which is hereby acknowledged," is in most states ineffective[8] and should be avoided. Whatever recitals of agreement and consideration you write into the contract should be expressed only once; do not repeatedly say that in consideration of so and so, X agrees to do this and that. "X will" is just as effective as "It is further understood and agreed that X will" or, "In consideration of the

___

8. Restatement of the Law of Contracts 2d § 244.

aforesaid . . . X hereby undertakes and agrees that he will."

Mr. Walter P. Armstrong, when president of the American Bar Association, suggested that one reason why lawyers so often write jargon incomprehensible to laymen is "sheer mental laziness:"

> Old forms, couched in longiloquent phraseology, are followed because of an unwillingness to make the effort to create something simpler and better. The other reason is the feeling that there is safety in following language that has stood the test of litigation. There is some reason for this in the drafting of wills and conveyances, and occasionally in drawing other documents, but its importance is vastly over-emphasized. That a document has to be construed by a court is some evidence that it was imperfectly drafted. If its meaning had been perfectly clear there would have been no need for construction. When it is sustained this usually means not that it has been approved but that it has escaped condemnation.[9]

Statutes today are usually written or edited by legislative drafting counsel, yet many still on the books are grievously verbose. To take only one example, the New York Domestic Relations Law, § 24, subd. 1, says:

> A child heretofore or hereafter born of parents who prior or subsequent to the birth of such child shall have entered into a civil or religious marriage, or shall have consummated a common-law marriage where such marriage is recognized as valid, in the manner authorized by the law of the place where such marriage takes place, is the legitimate child of both natural parents notwithstanding that such marriage is void or voidable or has been or shall hereafter be annulled or judicially declared void.

That this can be said more concisely and clearly is shown by the fact that most states have done so. Ohio, for example, says it in less than half as many words:

> When a man has a child by a woman and before or after the birth intermarries with her, the child is legitimate. The

9. Armstrong, The Bar and the Schools, 28 A.B.A.J. 93, 96 (1942).

issue of parents whose marriage is null in law are nevertheless legitimate.[10]

Lawyers are not alone in having a weakness for repetitive
phrases. The same penchant is revealed in scores of such phrases
in common use among people in all walks of life: each and every,
first and foremost, one and the same, over and above, really and
truly.

Many of these repetitions are alliterative. We use them because they give a sense of balance and rhythm. Old folk verses,
magic formulas and sayings were often given in rhymed or alliterative forms. So were old legal rules.

When you find yourself writing one of these tandem phrases
out of mere habit, stop, and look for a single word (one of the
series or a wholly new one) that is clear and strong enough to
carry the meaning by itself.

Some redundancies are the result of grammatical carelessness
or failure to notice that the word already appears in the sentence:

> Its avowed object is to prevent, not the carrying of intoxi-
> cating liquors *out* of the State, but to prevent their manufac-
> ture, except for specified purposes, *within* the State.[11]

> In determining whether a child is dependent and neglected,
> the treatment and care received by it from persons other
> than its natural parents are irrelevant to such determination.

Ignorance of a foreign language may lead to redundancy:

The La Fonda Hotel
A matinee performance
The Rio Grande River
The Sahara Desert
Sierra Mountains

10. Ohio Rev. Code Ann. § 2105.18
(Page 1972). Many other examples
of verbose language in statutes,
contracts, wills and other documents, with suggested simplifica-
tion, are provided in Biskind, Simplify Legal Writing (1975).

11. Kidd v. Pearson, 128 U.S. 1, 22,
9 S.Ct. 6, 10, 32 L.Ed.2d 346
(1888).

Tautologies

Less excusable than pairs or series of synonyms is the tautological phrase, used by unthinking writers who do not notice that they are expressing the same idea in two ways. (Tautology is defined by Bergen and Cornelia Evans, A Dictionary of Contemporary American Usage, as "a form of redundancy, consisting of the needless repetition of an idea, especially in other words in the immediate context, without imparting additional force or clearness.").

A real basis in fact (a basis in fact is necessarily real)

Actual fact; true fact (all facts are actual and true)

Advance planning (all planning is for the future, and so always in advance)

Consensus of opinion (a consensus is an agreement of opinion)

Contributing factor (a factor is something that contributes to produce a result)

Mutual friends (mutual implies an action or relation between two or more persons or things—that A is to B as B is to A. "Mutual benefits" (obligations, abettors or respects) makes sense, but since it takes two to make a friendship, to say that A and B are mutual friends is no more than to say they are friends. To say that they have a mutual friend in C is meaningless; they have a common friend, or a friend in common)

A panacea for all ills (a panacea is a remedy for all ills)

Surrounding circumstances (circumstances means surroundings, or surrounding conditions)

With the consequent result that (all results are consequent)

As one example, for instance

Both equally illegal

Continue to remain

During the daytime

Equally as good

Evidently seemed

Further, as a second requirement

Give all possible assistance that I can

He died of a mortal blow

In the meanwhile

Just exactly

Many similar cases of the same general nature

Nearly approximate
On the other hand, however
Paid the total amount in full
The basis of the plaintiff's claim rests on
The exception is limited only to
The reason was because (due to)
Universally popular with all the people
While at the same time

The "tautological phrase of specification" is the name that has been given to such a phrase as "red in color," or "young in age." To say that a person is "young in appearance" is meaningful, but to say that he is "young in age" is only to say that he is young. Other phrases in which the specification is merely tautological are the following:

Earlier in date
Few in number
Friendly in character
Narrow in width
Invisible to the eye
Square shaped

You can probably think of others. Try it—as a game, and as a way to help remember not to use them.

We sometimes see the adjective "successfully" tacked on to a verb (such as avoid, conquer, prevent or withstand) that itself expresses success:

She successfully withstood cross-examination.

Did the writer think he had to make clear that she didn't withstand cross-examination unsuccessfully?

Except for emphasis or other good reason it is a waste of words to say that something is "objective rather than subjective," "valid rather than invalid," or "the majority rather than the minority rule." As often used, this inclusion of both a positive and negative way of saying the same thing is as unnecessary as "guilty rather than not guilty."

Not only words and phrases but whole clauses or sentences are sometimes repetitious.

This is a comparatively minor point, and one that is of little importance.

The intention of the parties is found by looking to the instrument to determine what was intended.

Psychiatrists agree that one way to avoid mental illness is to have a healthy mind.

The last-quoted sentence is more sententious than repetitious. Sometimes the sententiousness is not so obvious; the statement may even seem learned, until we think about it a bit. The late Professor Thomas Reed Powell once told us [12] that the rule on state taxation of interstate commerce could be "lucidly and delusively" stated as follows:

> "State taxes on interstate commerce are an invalid regulation thereof; whether a tax is one on interstate commerce depends upon whether such commerce is the subject that is taxed."

Courts solemnly manipulate some circuitous formulations that are just as delusively lucid as Powell's. Examples are the requirement that the defendant shall have been under a duty towards the plaintiff to take care, as a prerequisite of liability towards him in respect of negligence ("an outstanding example of the circuitous reference"); and the rule, as sometimes stated, that "all injuries done to another person are torts, unless there is some justification recognized by law." [13]

Ordinarily, if an idea can be expressed in one sentence, say it in one sentence and move on. Don't say it over again in different words. Inexperienced writers sometimes fail to follow this advice. After wording an idea one way, they think of another way to put it, so they add that. Now, second thoughts are sometimes better, and there is no reason why, if a good alternative sentence or phrase comes to mind, you should not promptly get it down on paper before you forget it. But don't keep them both. Choose between them, or, what will probably be better, combine them into one, using the most effective words and phrases of each.

12. Powell, Contemporary Commerce Clause Controversies Over State Taxation, 76 U.Pa.L.Rev. 773 (1928).

13. Julius Stone, The Province and Function of Law 181, 185 (1950).

Not All Repetition is Pointless

What this chapter has been criticizing is pointless repetition or redundancy. But repetition can serve a purpose. The chapter on Forcefulness will show how it can be used to lend emphasis. Even verbiage that on its face is redundant or unnecessary may have its purpose. The lawyer who includes a direction that the testator's debts be paid probably knows quite well that the law will see that debts are paid without specific direction. But he may have learned that his clients expect and want the express provision. Perhaps they have seen other wills and noticed that they contain such a provision (just about every will does) and if their lawyer omits it, they may ascribe the omission to ignorance or carelessness. Confronting such deep-rooted preconceptions, counsel may agree with Goethe that against ignorance, even gods fight in vain.

In an instrument appointing a trustee or an executor, the draftsman may want to use words that will give the agent adequate discretion to act, and also give confidence to others with whom he will have to deal. The draftsman must therefore use words that will encourage a timid agent to act where action is called for, and assure third parties that he has the necessary authority. One way in which this perhaps can be done is by one broad "necessary and proper" clause similar to that used by the Framers of the Constitution to make sure that Congress was given all the power it needed. But another way is to multiply descriptions, using a long list of specific words instead of one general one. Thus a power of attorney will usually confer power not merely to "receive any of my property" but "to receive and take possession of any or all moneys, stocks, bonds, securities, goods, chattels, land, buildings, and other property, belonging to me." The justification for this has been well explained by the late Charles P. Curtis:

> Here we are dealing with documents which are addressed on their face to the agent, but really they are addressed to everyone with whom he is going to transact business, who also will have to accept some responsibility, and liability, and none of them will have the least obligation or interest to act. The draftsman, therefore, must be thinking of people who are not only indifferent but meticulous. Do not precipitately blame the draftsman whose duty it is to indulge their doubts

and anticipate their hesitations. Good round words are what they want. A foresighted draftsman will give them as many as they want, unless he can find a better way to encourage them.[14]

Rewrite

The advice to cut out unnecessary words is not easy to take. Even though we may not think ourselves great writers, once we have composed something, we quickly come to love it. As a mother loves her child, we love this brain child of ours. We cannot easily bring ourselves to carve off parts of it. We certainly cannot expect to do it in the warm flush of writing. Let your work get cold, then read it the next day—and try, when you read it, to forget that it is *yours*; pretend you are instead the person for whose eye it is intended, reading it for the first time. And as you cut, remember that you are not hurting the composition, but only your parental pride of authorship. Only by a conscious and resolute act of will can you even come close to attaining the coldly detached attitude you need to carve out unsparingly every bit of fat.[15]

This advice, to cut out unnecessary words, is only a specification of a broader admonition: rewrite. No one writes so well that he cannot, if he reads critically what he has written, find ways of saying it more concisely and more precisely. If you will reread your work after allowing a day or two for the warm glow of composition to cool, you may find that the arrangement is poor, or that a sentence needs to be made clearer, smoother, or more readable. A word may not carry quite the nuance you want, and need to be replaced by one that says it better. If possible, have someone else read your draft, and don't be defensive against criticism. Plato, it is said, rewrote the first paragraph of The Republic about twelve times. If his first drafts needed reworking, ours presumably do too.

14. Curtis, A Better Theory of Legal Interpretation, 4 Record of N. Y.C.B.A. 321, 355 (1949).

15. In an earlier draft of this sentence, the last clause read, "to root out ruthlessly every luxuriating verbal weed." That sounded mighty fine when I wrote it, but it went out under the spur of Dr. Johnson's only rule for writing: "Read over your compositions, and when you meet with a passage which you think is particularly fine, strike it out."

Exercises

1. Rewrite the following sentences to eliminate redundancies:

The court held that the statute was not merely for the protection of third parties only.

The purpose of the act was declared to be "for the encouragement of learning . . .."

The court construed the act to require that all conditional sales contracts must be in writing and acknowledged.

We shall attempt promptly upon the issuance of the court's decree to try to arrange a meeting with the defendant's counsel.

The reason for the complexity and specificity of the legislation is due to the complexity of the modern labor-management problems of today.

Although both men belonged to different parties, they both knew each other well.

It is only ten years ago since the act was passed.

Many lawyers procrastinate until the compulsion of the court rules compels action. Actually, there is no real excuse for such procrastination.

2. Rewrite the following passage to gain conciseness:

Prior to recent years, it was generally held that hospitals were to be deemed to be immune from lawsuits based on negligent injuries which had been incurred by patients under the doctrine of charitable immunity. However, nowadays more and more of the courts are inclined to accept the view that the reasons and arguments that have been advanced in support of said immunity can no longer be considered persuasive. As a consequence, they have therefore been starting to impose liability in tort actions. And it has been discovered that the imposition of said tort liability on the hospitals has effectuated a prophylactic result in that there has been an introduction of new procedures and precautions, and there has as a result been a dramatic decline in the rate of "accidents" so-called. Thus it is interesting to note that after the addition of new procedures and precautions following the outcome of a malpractice case, there was a reduction of 70% in the sponge-count problem in hospitals.

Chapter 4

SIMPLICITY

The main objective in writing, as already said, is to make oneself understood. Simple, everyday words are more likely to be understood than strange or unusual ones, and they are more likely to sound sincere than are the flowery or high-flown. "If men would only say what they have to say in plain terms," wrote Samuel Taylor Coleridge, "how much more eloquent they would be!"

Even in poetry, where many of us are disposed to assume that the effect is to be attained by luxuriant verbiage, poignant emotion can be evoked with extreme simplicity. Greek verse was almost epitaphic. And A. E. Housman[1] could word his salute to young men who died in war almost wholly in words of one syllable:

> Here dead lie we because we did not choose
>> To live and shame the land from which we sprung.
> Life, to be sure, is nothing much to lose,
>> But young men think it is, and we were young.

Achieving a simple style is no simple matter. On the contrary, it is extremely difficult. One cannot say anything simply and clearly unless one first understands it clearly. Clarity of thought, especially about inherently complicated matters such as lawyers constantly have to discuss, takes hard mental labor. Many of us feel impelled to start writing without first expending the effort necessary to understand clearly the principles we are trying to explain or to perceive clearly their application to the problem. In consequence, our writing is designed, consciously or unconsciously, not so much to convey ideas as to conceal the fact that we have not cleared our own minds about them. The ponderous and abstract words and phrases that we tend to reach for

1. Housman, More Poems, XXXVI, from The Collected Poems of A. E. Housman, published by Holt, Rine-hart and Winston, Inc. Copyright 1940 by Henry Holt and Co., Inc.

in such a situation may seem profound. But if the reader looks below the surface for the underlying sense, he discovers that the water is murky not because it is deep but only because it is muddy.

Some legal writers actually seem to try to be unclear, apparently under the delusion that their ideas will seem more learned if cloaked in obscure and pretentious prose. Merely to make an ostentatious display of vocabulary, they sacrifice clarity, emphasis and conviction. Of all vanities, this is surely one of the most self-defeating. Some years ago, a book on constitutional law was published whose opening words were:

> From time to time with varying tempo the call goes around to "get government out of business" .   . . . Probably no problem of such political and economic proportions has suffered so much from anamorphosis and has been so constantly subjected to acetic enfilade. Before we can hope to decorticate the issue of its partisan and selfish aspects we must bring our minds to orthoptic view-point of the political nature and function of government.

Words or phrases that the reader does not understand are to him what Stuart Chase called "semantic blanks." What comes through to him can only be something like this:

> Probably no problem of such political and economic proportions has suffered so much from blah-blah-blah-blah-blah and has been so constantly subjected to blah-blah-blah blah-blah-blah.

And he is left not only uninformed but resentful. Throwing words at him that he doesn't understand, without explanation, implies that you think he ought to be able to understand them. If he doesn't, his self-esteem is hurt. And a wounded reader—even if pinked only in his pride—is a resentful one.

Studies made some years ago of the readability of union-management collective bargaining agreements showed that more than 90 per cent of them were written at a readability level adapted to persons who had attained a high school or college education.[2] Yet only 14 per cent of American adults have a col-

2. Tiffin and Walsh, Readability of
Union-Management Agreements, 4
Personnel Psychology 327 (1951).

lege education and only 24 per cent have completed high school and had some college education. This means that most of these agreements are very difficult for the rank-and-file worker to understand, and probably almost as difficult for many shop stewards and foremen. These agreements set out the rules that are to govern the behavior of men and women during their working hours. Unless written in language that these workers understand, they may foment more bad feelings, grievances, disputes and strikes than they prevent.

Simplicity of style has nothing to do with simplicity of the ideas presented. Never "talk down" to your reader—any reader, whether a bench of appellate judges or the least learned client. "Talking down" means simplifying your ideas so as to make them comprehensible to a person of a lower level of intelligence. The reader who finds it difficult to comprehend writing that is replete with pretentious jargon and technical phrases is not necessarily obtuse. He can probably grasp complex concepts well enough if you will explain them in plain English. If you cannot do so, you probably do not comprehend them adequately yourself.

How to Gain Simplicity

Benjamin Franklin gave us the first and most important rule for attaining simplicity: never use a long word when a short one will do. This was also the advice of the Fowlers, quoted in our first chapter. Their other rules also make for simplicity no less than for the other essential qualities of style: prefer the familiar to the far-fetched, the concrete to the abstract, the single word to the circumlocution.

Law students sometimes assume that legal writing should be characterized by big words. There is an element of soundness in the notion. Most legal writing is formal writing and should use language suitable for public exhibition. Colloquialisms or slang impair the dignity that should be maintained in addressing a court. But this does not mean that a lawyer must shun simple, everyday words and look for pompous polysyllables. Below is a list of some overused formal or stuffy words and phrases, and their simple equivalents.

Formal, stuffy	Simple
Advert	Refer
Apprise	Inform
Cease	Stop
Commitment	Promise
Communicate	Write, Telephone
Consummate	Bring about, Complete
Demonstrate	Show
Desire	Wish
Donate	Give
Edifice	Building
Effectuate	Bring about
Eliminate	Remove, Strike out
Elucidate	Explain
Employ ("Employ certain words")	Use
Employment	Work
Endeavor	Try
Ensue	Follow
Expedite	Hasten, Hurry
Expiration	End
Facilitate	Make easy
Initiate	Begin, Start
Interrogate	Question
Locality, Location	Place
Locate	Find
Objective	Aim
Peruse	Read
Prior to	Before
Proceed	Go
Remuneration	Pay, Wages, Salary, Fee
Render	Make
Reside	Live
Respecting, Regarding	About
Retain	Keep
Terminate	End
Transmit	Send
Utilize, Utilization	Use
Visualize	Imagine
Afford an opportunity	Allow
Experience has taught that	I have learned
In order to insure	To make sure
In process of preparation	Being prepared

Formal, stuffy	Simple
Interpose an objection	Object
Is predicated on the assumption	Assumes
Raise the question	Ask
With a minimum of delay	As soon as possible

None of the formal expressions listed is wrong. At times, for one reason or another, the simpler term will not serve. But if you fall into the habit of always choosing the formal, without valid reason and even without thinking, your style will become that much more ponderous. Some people have the habit so badly that even when a simple word is at hand, they pass it by to reach for a grander one. They reject "see" and choose "visualize" or "envisage." They reject "land use" in favor of "land utilization." Pronouncements of political personages are replete with neologisms like "actualize," "inferiorize," "prioritize," and of course "personalize." An advisor to the governor of New York complained that legislators working on New York City's financial problems "overstrategize themselves." Izationism is a sure sign of literary edematization.[3] Moreover, using so many words that sound alike tends to make one's style dull and monotonous.

Devotees of the ponderous and turgid style favor "-wise" almost as much as "-ize." "Taxwise" has a certain usefulness, but a speaker is just too wised up when he says, as Senator Birch Bayh said in 1975, that "energywise, economywise and environmentalwise, we have become obsessed with the problems." This is a maladroit way of saying "We have become obsessed with the problems of energy, the economy, and the environment." Why add a wise to the word?

Cousins to the fatties ending in -ise and -wise are words ending in -ive such as promotive, supportive, and eradicative. The chairman of a presidential election campaign said that a cabinet ought to be made up of people who are qualified, "but who are totally supportive of the President." "Who support the President" would be simpler. But simplicity is exactly the quality that people who issue such statements do not want. They want

3. Izationese for bloat.

to sound pontifical. And words like "supportive" do sound pontifical, and ponderous.

In Writing For Laymen, Avoid Technical Jargon

The stock caricature of the lawyer is a man whose every sentence is loaded with legalistic terms. In that unkind poem of Carl Sandburg's, "The Lawyers Know Too Much," "the higgling lawyers" are guilty of

> Too many slippery ifs and buts and howevers,
> Too much hereinbefore provided whereas

We need not go so far as to say that a lawyer should not sound like a lawyer, but at least he should try not to sound like the popular stereotype of a lawyer.

In writing for other members of the profession, as in an office memorandum or a brief, the use of technical terms is appropriate and even necessary. Every profession, science, art and trade has its own technical jargon, a lingo that serves as a form of shorthand to describe concepts or processes that do not occur outside the specialized field and for which there is therefore no name in ordinary English.

But the lawyer must remember that a technical term that may be the most correct and most precise way of expressing his thought when speaking to another member of the profession may be meaningless to a layman. The reader, like the customer, is always right. If the person for whom you are writing cannot understand you, you have not written clearly. The fact that your words would be clear to someone else is irrelevant.

Some technical terms the lawyer can hardly avoid using even though they may be unfamiliar to the lay reader: tort, consideration, negotiability, mandamus. Even these can and should be explained in plain English when writing for a layman, as in a letter to a client. But unnecessarily technical terms should be avoided, and so should the hereinbefores, hereinafters and theretofores, the saids and the aforesaids, the whomsoevers and the whereases. To any educated person with an ear for prose all these are dull and heavy sounds that make for that "heavy-footed jargon," as John Mason Brown called it, "which so many lawyers are persuaded by the pressure of their duties and their

deafness or indifference to language to mistake for English."
Many of them have found their way into laymen's English by
way of legal instruments; thus we have contaminated the entire
language. Even in strictly professional writing, their use could
profitably be reduced. Law students may be impressed with
them because they seem to sound professional, and may take
them up on the innocent assumption that this is the way lawyers
are expected to write. No!

Certain Latin terms are still used in formal writing, perhaps
more by lawyers than by others. At least in writing to laymen,
it is better to translate such terms as the following into English:

A fortiori	Per annum
Ad hoc	Per se
A priori	Pro rata
De facto	Qua
De jure	Sine qua non
Inter alia	Status quo
Non sequitur	Viz.

The Latin abbreviations i. e. and e. g. are also better translated into the English "that is" and "for example."

If you do use Latin or other foreign words or phrases that
your reader may not understand, give the definition. But do it
unobtrusively, not in a way that says, "I know you are not well
enough educated to translate this, so I'll do it for you." If you
use the term in pari materia, for example, do not say, "This is a
Latin term meaning 'on the same subject matter.'" You can be
less obvious by running the definition in with the use of the
term:

> When a number of statutes, whenever enacted, relate to the
> same subject matter, they are in pari materia and are to be
> construed together.

Certain legal concepts bear Latin designations, with no English equivalents: habeas corpus, in personam, in rem, res ipsa loquitur, res judicata. In writing to laymen, these must be not
only translated but explained. Explaining legal concepts to laymen is difficult, whether the shorthand label is a Latin term like
res ipsa loquitur or an English one like contributory negligence.
But it is good practice for developing a clear and simple way of
writing.

Avoid Gobbledegook

"Gobbledegook" is a word coined by former Congressman Maury Maverick of Texas, to describe "talk or writing which is long, pompous, vague, involved, usually with Latinized words. It is also talk or writing which is merely long, even though the words are fairly simple, with repetition over and over again, all of which could have been said in a few words."

The term was invented to describe a style too often adopted by government officials, but it flourishes in law offices too. The New Yorker magazine likes to cull specially turgid specimens and reprint them under the heading, "The Legal Mind at Work."

Government jargon is often loaded with piled up modifiers. Instead of "a policy meeting of the Drainage Control Commission for the Second District," bureaucratic style is likely to write, "a Second District Drainage Control Commission policy meeting."

Many persons have been moved to satirize this style. A. P. Herbert, a British humorist who was also a member of Parliament, exasperated by governmental jargon, governmentalized Lord Nelson's immortal words, "England expects every man to do his duty," as follows:

> England anticipates that, as regards the current emergency, personnel will face up to the issues, and exercise appropriately the functions allocated to their respective occupational groups.

But Herbert was too good a writer to be able to do full justice to this style, even when he tried. No true practitioner of gobbledegook would allow himself even so mildly colloquial a phrase as "face up to."

The King James version of the Bible is a model of simple style. We may take just one line from the Lord's Prayer, "Give us this day our daily bread"—only seven words, all but one of them one-syllable—and see what legal jargon might make of it:

> We respectfully petition, request and entreat that due and adequate provision be made, this day and date first above inscribed, for the satisfying of petitioners' nutritional requirements and for the organizing of such methods of allocation

and distribution as may be deemed necessary and proper to assure the reception by and for said petitioners of such quantity of cereal products (hereinafter called "bread") as shall, in the judgment of the aforesaid petitioners, constitute a sufficient . . ..

This could go on quite a bit longer.

The frustration of laymen trying to comprehend such language in government regulations, or in insurance policies or installment loan agreements, has vented itself in protests loud enough to spur official efforts to do something about it. President Carter in 1978 ordered that regulations of federal agencies be "written in plain English" that is "understandable to those who must comply" with them.[4] New York has enacted a "plain language law" requiring residential leases and consumer agreements in transactions primarily for personal, family, or household purposes to be written in "non-technical language and in a clear and cogent manner using words with common and everyday meanings."[5] These mandates may help to reduce the quantum of obfuscation and verbosity in legal writing.

If we are to avoid gobbledegook in our own writing, we must recognize its peculiar vices. We have already mentioned them in a general way. Let us now point them out more exactly:

1. It uses round-about rather than direct ways of expressing the thought.

2. It prefers pompous or pretentious to simple expressions.

3. It makes excessive use of nouns.

4. The nouns it uses tend to be abstract ones rather than concrete.

5. It has a penchant for compound prepositional phrases.

6. It makes much use of the passive instead of the active voice.

Most of these shortcomings we have been inveighing against throughout this book. Others we shall discuss in later chapters. Thus the use of abstract words will be covered in the next chapter, on Clarity, and the use of the passive in the chapter on

---

4. Exec. Order No. 12044, 43 Fed. Reg. 12661 (1978).

5. New York Gen. Obligations Law § 702 (McKinney Supp. 1978).

Forcefulness. Here, we want to give special attention to the habit of overusing nouns.

Don't Overuse Nouns

Style can be made simpler by eliminating excessive use of nouns and using more verbs.

There has been a complete absence of any attempt at reconciliation of differences between the parties.	The parties have never even tried to reconcile their differences.
We inaugurated the practice of making cross-indexes to the files.	We started to cross-index the files.
For many years prior to my retirement	For many years before I retired
Perhaps the failure of bankruptcy trustees to attempt to use § 67d against pre-bankruptcy transfers of exempt property has been based on the theory that § 1 (30) defines "transfers" for all purposes under the Act in terms of "property."	Bankruptcy trustees have not tried to use § 67d against pre-bankruptcy transfers of exempt property, perhaps because they have assumed that § 1(30) defines "transfers" for all purposes under the Act in terms of "property."

Sometimes the density of nouns is too great to allow any meaning to come through.

In Durnherr v. Rau, the lack of a creditor-beneficiary existence was the detriment to recovery.

The overstuffed style often resorts to the use of a verb, a noun and a preposition when a verb alone would serve.

Exhibits a tendency to	Tends
Make an adjustment in	Adjust
Make provision for	Provide for
Serves the purpose of	Will
Provides evidence of the truth of the allegation	Shows

The noun is often formed by adding "tion" or "ization" to the verb. Thus "capitalizing" becomes "capitalization," "consider" becomes "give consideration to," and "This implies" becomes "The implication is."

This form of expression robs the sentence of its key verb by using it as a subject nominative, with the result that the writer has trouble finding a suitable predicate-verb.

Confirmation of the offer was obtained	The offer was confirmed
Reversal of the judgment was handed down	The judgment was reversed
The compilation of the statistics was done in 1960	The statistics were compiled in 1960

The noun-addict will often use a noun form when all he needs is a simple adjective or adverb.

Of great importance	Important
Of an indefinite nature	Indefinite
Of an unusual kind	Unusual
In a negligent manner	Negligently
The question that is in doubt	The doubtful question
In size, in length	Long
In height	High

Even two-letter prepositions are encumbered with nouns by devotees of this viscid style.

In order to	To
By means of	By
In the event that	If

Other examples of some of these faults are given in the chapter on Conciseness.

Using too many nouns may produce not only a heavy style, but grammatical error:

The secret of the attainment of a cultivated literary style is difficult and elusive. The observation of the style and manner of expression of those judges and authors endowed with a gift of literary expression may be a helpful suggestion.

"The secret" is "difficult"? "The observation" may be a "suggestion"? Grammatical correctness as well as simplicity and vigor could be gained by cutting out nouns:

> A cultivated style is an elusive goal, difficult to attain. Observing the style and manner of expression of judges and authors who have a gift of literary expression may be helpful.

Prefer Concrete to Fuzzy Nouns

Gobbledegook has a penchant not only for nouns, but for fuzzy, woolly nouns, such as "case," "situation," "factor," "basis" and "problem." In the chapter on Precision, we discussed the imprecision that comes from using abstract terms, such as "justice," "right," "responsibility" and "democracy." What is said there is relevant here, but we may take note of certain less pretentious words, addiction to which also makes for an abstruse, inflated style. There are passing fashions in jargon as in other things. We shall focus attention on some terms which are much in vogue today.

"Basis" is a current favorite. A writer may fail to remember the word's literal meaning, of a base or foundation, and may speak of a "fragmentary basis" or a "fleeting basis." A New Jersey prosecutor's report of some years ago said that the number of cases pending and the increase expected "cry out for a third judge to sit in Passaic County on a rotating basis between the criminal and the civil side." But who wants a dizzy judge?

More precise wording can usually be found.

The plant is working on a 24-hour basis.	The plant is working 24 hours a day.
All these arrangements are on a temporary basis.	All these arrangements are temporary.
We are located here on a temporary basis.	We are here temporarily.

Sometimes it is impossible to tell just what the phrase means.

> We are trying to put the organization on a legal basis.

"Based on" is equally woolly. Moreover, it is sometimes used in a way that is not only unclear, but ungrammatical.

> Based on the preceding two decisions, it is apparent that the courts have been unable to decide whether the N.I.L. intended accommodation parties to be treated as sureties.

"Based on" should read "from."

"Case" and "instance" are also gobbledgook favorites. "Case" has been discussed in our list of "Words to Watch." "Instance" also is often mere stuffing.

This is the only instance of such a holding in Ohio.	This is the only Ohio case so holding.
The verdicts were for large amounts in most instances.	Most of the verdicts were for large amounts.

"Position" is often another empty word.

Our position will be more favorable	We shall be better off
Our position in regard to the claim for damages is that this should	We think that the claim for damages should

So is "situation."

We should like to be informed in regard to the present situation.	We should like to know how things stand.
The situation in regard to revenues is alarming.	The shortage in revenue is alarming.

"Breakdown" (statistical, not mental), is highly popular with certain writers who seem to think it sounds more scientific than "division," "classifying" or "change." When used in referring to things that can actually break down, either mentally or physically, the word is not only pretentious but inept:

> The breakdown of mental patients into psychotic and nonpsychotic

> The breakdown of motors according to

> A population broken down by sex

"Ceiling" is much used currently, to mean maximum or limit. There is no objection to such use, but frequent repetition may lead a writer to forget that it is a metaphor, and to speak of "increasing" the ceiling. One may raise or lower a ceiling, but "increasing" gives no clear picture of the operation being described.

Other words beloved by writers of the stuffed-shirt school include:

> Ideology (for creed, faith)
> Implement (used as a verb)
> Level ("on the local level")
> Over-all (for aggregate, comprehensive, complete, supreme, total, whole, and other words)
> Proposition (for plan, proposal or project)
> Reaction (for impression, opinion)
> Viable (for feasible, practical)

Avoid Outmoded Wording

A writer should develop an ear for wording. In reading old literary works and old cases one may pick up certain words and phrases, and fail to notice that they are not used in present-day writing. They are dated, and when used today they sound bookish. A few examples follow:

Albeit	Oft times
Betoken	Partake (of a dinner)
Erstwhile	Peruse
Of late years	Save (for except)

Fashions change, in writing as in other things. Writing that echoes the literary fashions of a past age sounds insincere. This is unfortunate, because the writer usually is not insincere; he is merely a bit quaint.

The simple direct term is sometimes avoided because it is too blunt. Politeness or tact may dictate using language that is less outspoken, and we therefore turn to a euphemism. This is justified when done to avoid vulgarity or grossness, but not merely to evade facing stark reality. Legal statements of facts, pleasant or unpleasant, must be set forth dispassionately, and not softened merely to save emotional distress.

Humanitarianism and an increasing concern for human dignity has given us a whole new vocabulary of what we may call sociological euphemisms. The jobless are now unemployed; the poor are underprivileged; and the work of the old "overseers of the poor" is now performed by the department of public welfare. The former "insane asylums" are now "mental hospitals," or merely "hospitals." They house not inmates and guards, but patients and attendants.

Terms like idiot, imbecile, moron and feeble-minded, formerly accepted, have been replaced by "mentally retarded," which in turn is giving way to "developmentally disabled." The progression from the older and cruder to the newer and more refined ways of thinking and therefore of talking is reflected in the progression of usage: alms, charity, philanthropy, relief, rehabilitation, casework, family welfare.

This delicacy was carried to an extreme, we now think, in the reign of Queen Victoria, when all legs were "limbs" (even chicken legs), breasts were "bosoms," and only horses sweat (men perspired and young ladies got all glowy). All these are now outmoded genteelisms. In today's writing, even young ladies are permitted to sweat.

But there are still people for whom the homely incidents of life are too coarse to mention. In their vocabulary, "stink" becomes "smell" and "smell" becomes "odor;" "belly" becomes "stomach" and "stomach" becomes "tummy." They do not take a job; they "accept a position." "Man" and "woman" are for their taste not elegant enough labels for members of the human species; they prefer "gentleman" and "lady" and would see nothing incongruous in speaking of "the gentleman who struck the saleslady on the posterior." In their language, the town drunkard is never carried home drunk; he is "conveyed to his place of residence in an inebriated condition." When they need to use toilet facilities, they look for a "rest room." (And we laugh at the Victorians!) Even death and dying, dignified and decent words though they be, are too melancholy to be allowed. Their loved ones therefore never die, they always "pass away."

Such genteelisms are objectionable because (1) they are usually roundabout ways of expressing the thought, and so take more time to write and to read than do the plain direct words for which they stand; (2) they require the reader not only to read more words but also to translate the circumlocutions into the direct meaning; and (3) they cheat reality; by trying to pretty-up the image, they blur or discolor it.

Saxon versus Latin Words

In our introductory chapter, we listed Fowler's advice, including the rule, "Prefer the Saxon word to the Romance." We have said nothing about this rule so far, and we need not say much now.

The reason for the rule, we can guess, was that Romance words are usually the more pretentious. The Saxon words in the English language are usually the homely ones. After the Norman Conquest, the Saxons were the conquered, the peasants. The Normans were the overlords. The peasants talked of simple and homely things, and their words for them endured. More abstract or more technical subjects were discussed by the ruling classes, who spoke Norman-French. The big words, the abstract and the vague words in English are usually of Latin or Romance origin. Their incessant use therefore gives a ponderous and pretentious tone to one's style.

But many English words of Latin or Romance origin are now just as "ordinary" as Germanic ones, and some of them are just as vigorous. Beef, bill, brave, bribe, face, fact, vote and veto are examples. So the rule to prefer the simple or familiar to the more pretentious word is not always the same as saying prefer the Saxon to the Romance.

There is another reason why we may ignore the latter rule: it is for most people impractical. Latin is so little taught these days that it is no reflection on a person as an educated man to say he has not even a little Latin at his command. Most students probably could not with any certitude choose between commence and begin, or between cease and stop, assist and help, purchase and buy, render and make, by identifying the one as Latin in origin and the other as Anglo-Saxon.

Although our subject in this chapter is simplicity, we must remember that simplicity is not our only aim in writing. When other ends are more important, Latin or other elaborate words may be appropriate. You may want a long Latin word for its sonorous or majestic effect, or for conveying an important emotional idea, or simply because the number of syllables gives better rhythm. Lincoln's "four score and seven years ago" has better cadence than "eighty-seven years ago," and was magnificently successful, even though most writers might have feared that it would sound affected (notice also that the longer phrase is just as Anglo-Saxon as the other). The line between the felicitous and the overblown is sometimes so fine that only the writer with a good ear for the sound of words can make a reliable choice. This "ear" can be developed, simply by listening to how your words sound, even when they are not intended to be spoken aloud.

We are fortunate in English to have words stemming from both Latin and Germanic roots. By carefully choosing between them, we can get not only the word that best expresses our meaning, but also the precise nuance [6] and the most attractive rhythm or cadence to the sentence. We can also get emphasis by a change of pace: we can enrobe the product of our cogitation in sonorous Latin polysyllables judiciously selected for their pontifical tone, and then clinch it with a short Germanic punchline.

Should You "Write as You Talk" ?

In urging law students and lawyers to try not to sound pompous, we sometimes compare written with spoken language, and suggest that they would develop a better and more "natural" style if they would "write as they talk." Within limits, this advice is sound. Writing is essentially a device for putting speech into more lasting form. However much it may depart from the spoken word, "there still inheres in it as it were the vibration of a voice." [7] Good writing therefore aims for the simplicity and buoyancy of good conversation.

But we cannot write exactly the way we talk. In talking, we can (and do) repeat ourselves and use loosely organized, disjointed and fragmentary phrases that would be intolerable in

6. "*Juvenile* does not signify the same thing as *youthful, ponderous* as *weighty, portion* as *share, miserable* as *wretched. Legible* means 'that can be read,' *readable* generally 'worth reading'. Sometimes the Latin word is used in a more limited, special or precise sense than the English, as is seen by a comparison of *identical* and *same, science* and *knowledge, sentence* and *saying, latent* or *occult* and *hidden.*" Jesperson, Growth and Structure of the English Language 139–40 (9th ed. 1955).

7. Genung, The Working Principles of Rhetoric 119 (1900).

print. Moreover, we use other contrivances besides words. We use our voice for intonation, emphasis, pauses. We laugh, shout, whisper. We use our hands to gesture; we use facial expressions; we lean forward and back or move about. Speaking always involves personal interaction between two parties. This is true not only of conversation or debate; it is also true of the speaker addressing an audience: if he is any good as a speaker, he is attuned to his audience and he and the audience react to one another as human personalities. He veers and tacks in response to the reactions of his listeners. His sentences may be long and even rambling, with footnotes and parenthetical asides interjected as he goes, but intonation enables his listeners to follow without difficulty. A similar sentence in print, without the guiding voice, might be utterly confusing. Read a reporter's verbatim transcription of spoken English, and you will quickly see this; no one would write that way. Even a President of the United States, speaking "off the cuff," may turn out sentences such as these:

> In our efforts throughout the world, on outpost positions, I mean positions that are exposed to immediate Communist threat, physical threat, if we will help those people hold out and get ourselves back where we belong as reserves to move in to any threatened danger point if they carry it to that point, carry it to that level, then what we will be doing it will be taking these 22 million South Koreans, pushing programs for getting them ready to hold their own front line.

> Well, I would think that this plan would appeal to any thinking American and so I would—if I have—now I would like to get it done better, of course—quicker, but always as I think it's a soldier's attitude, if you know what you want to do, get it done in a hurry.

A speaker can repeat himself, and still get variety in expression by stressing a different word or phrase the second time, or by varying the inflection or the tempo. Even the speaker who merely reads from a manuscript and does not depart from it can project his personality to some extent through his voice.

The written page has none of this help. It must make what impression it can on the personality of the reader without any help from the personal presence of the writer. How much that personal presence contributed we may sometimes realize when we read in print a speech we heard delivered. The most fiery and moving oratory may now seem bloodless and inane. What has changed? In substance, nothing; only the magnetic personality of the speaker is missing.

This difference explains why the dictated brief is likely to be a literary failure. A paper intended to be absorbed through the eyes and not through the ears must be composed in a wholly different way. It must have a style that is comprehensible without intonation (underlining or italics is typically the device of those who try to imitate in writing their oral style). It must move smoothly. It must move rapidly; the eye runs over the words at two or three times the normal talking speed. The speaker can pause or speak slowly when he wants to give his audience time to grasp or think through the point he is making, or to feel it emotionally. But the writer has no control over the speed at which the reader's eyes move. All he can do is to use more punctuation and more words to phrase and perhaps rephrase his thought, so as to give it the time it deserves.

If a person forms orally sentences that are intended to appear as writing—as when a lawyer dictates a letter or a memorandum to his secretary—using the style that is his normal speaking style, he may find that it does not read well in type. This is equally true the other way around. A speech that was written, and never tried out orally, is likely to sound stilted. As Charles James Fox once put it, a speech that reads well is a damned bad one when spoken. The inexperienced speaker who has carefully written out his speech, and perhaps polished it up carefully by several rewritings, may be surprised to find when he delivers it that it does not sound right. His natural way of writing is not his natural way of speaking. One should never undertake to prepare in writing something to be delivered orally without speaking it out loud. Almost always one will find passages that looked well on the page but do not sound right when spoken.

How Simply Should You Write?

A lawyer must develop several levels of formality in his writing, the highest for such technical instruments as deeds, statutes and pleadings, followed closely by briefs, through opinions and office memoranda to letters addressed to clients who are also friends. Moreover, he must know how to stay on the proper level, and not inject some stuffy legalism into a friendly letter, or on the other hand drop a discordant colloquialism into formal discourse. A sudden lapse distracts the attention of the reader from the substance and also reflects unfavorably upon the writer. The following are examples of idiomatic expressions that are acceptable in speech and in informal writing but out of place in a brief:

Idiomatic	Formal
get used	become accustomed
a good deal	much
get out of the way	avoid, escape
pretty well	fairly well
get off work	quit work

In an early draft of this book, a sentence in Chapter I read as follows:

> Because so much of a lawyer's writing is for the purpose of convincing, and because conviction is often the result not alone of the intrinsic merit of the argument, but also of the way in which it is stated, a chapter on Forcefulness is included, discussing ways to use words and phrases so as to give your arguments more vividness, more emphasis, more punch.

This was later revised to read:

> Some of these [kinds of writing], notably briefs, are typically intended to convince, and conviction is often the result not only of the intrinsic merit of the argument but also of the way in which it is put. A chapter on Forcefulness is therefore included, discussing how you can use words and phrases to give your arguments more vividness and vigor.

It should not be difficult for you to figure out which changes were made to get more simplicity, and which to get more formality.

Even in addressing laymen, a lawyer may in certain circumstances want to affect a tone of extreme formality or magisterial impressiveness—for example, in a letter threatening a delinquent debtor with dire consequences. Even if the words are beyond the recipient's comprehension, the effect may be good, even as the Latin words of a Catholic mass may be the more impressive just because they are incomprehensible.

Legal writing may have other purposes than merely to inform. Law is a command. Imposing patterns of behavior on people is not easy. To make its statutes, decrees and other legal commands impressive, society has traditionally called upon formalism and ritual to lend their sanction. We make use of archaic and stately phraseology, more imposing, we hope, than the homely language of everyday life. Animating all such ritual is perhaps the ghost of a primitive belief in word-magic.

Simplifying is Painstaking Work

As said earlier in this chapter, achieving a simple style is no simple matter. It can be done only by painstakingly revising your first drafts, changing long words to short, fuzzy abstract words to concrete, round-about wordings to direct ones, replacing "raise the question" by "ask," "stated" by "said," "employ" by "use." Each little change may seem inconsequential. Standing alone, it probably is, but the cumulative effect of scores of such little prunings is appreciable.

Students often assume that their first formulation will be too simple, and that in reworking it they should strive for more lofty prose. Some crude colloquialisms and even slang may find their way into one's first draft and need to be eliminated, but much more likely to appear are the kind of inflated phrases criticized in this chapter. Many of them are already so habitual with us by the time we get to law school that only by sharp watchfulness can we hope to eradicate them.

Simple style does not mean using the first word that comes to mind, but the best one for the purpose, not loose, slipshod allusions, but clear-cut ones. Finding words twice as big as the thought requires is easy. What is hard is to come upon the one word that will look tailor-made for the thought.

This "right" word may not quickly come to mind. Two or three words may occur to you, but not quite fit. This is when you need a thesaurus. Look up every word that comes close;

from the synonyms listed, you will almost certainly find the word you want. The shade of difference between its meaning and that of any of the others may be so slight as to be almost imperceptible, yet the difference may be decisive. This is the only way to achieve a simple, "easy" style—the way a dancer finally comes to do a difficult step with apparent ease—by rigorous practice.

Chapter 5

CLARITY

Ambiguous wording has been and continues to be the source of innumerable lawsuits. And in conducting those lawsuits, lawyers too often write briefs containing further ambiguities. There is a certain impertinence in submitting to a busy court pages of words that have to be read twice before meaning can be got from them.

The chapter on Precision discussed such causes of ambiguity as ignorance of the correct meaning of words and carelessness in choosing words. Here we shall discuss how to put words together so as to enable the reader to grasp their meaning with a minimum of effort.[1] We shall examine such faults as misplaced modifiers and other defects in sentence structure, the use of pronouns without antecedents and of comparisons that do not compare. Certain other causes of ambiguity we shall reserve for the chapter on Organization.

Think About What You Are Saying

Much fuzzy writing is the result of fuzzy thinking. The writer may know his subject, but he is not thinking about the way he is expressing himself.

> It could not have been done except at a prohibitive cost.

This seems to say that it could have been done at a cost that would have prohibited its being done.

> We make no such claim. Much less do we claim. . . .

How much is less than none?

> The court did not allow recovery on the ground that it did not want to extend the liability of companies supplying necessary public services.

1. Classical rhetoricians might include most of what we have discussed in the preceding three chapters under the heading of diction, the selection of words (*electio ver-* *borum*), and place the subject of this chapter under sentence structure, or the arrangement of words in sentences (*compositio verborum*).

This sounds as though the court did allow recovery on some other ground. But what was meant was that the court *denied* recovery, and the ground mentioned was the ground for the denial.

> The term "third party beneficiary" refers to that type of contract wherein two people contract for some kind of performance to be rendered to a third person.

Even a moment's thought should have made the writer realize that these words say something he does not mean; a "third party beneficiary" is not a "type of contract."

Careless, blundering wording may lead you to say things you do not intend. Here is a passage from an appellee's brief, objecting to appellant's statement of facts:

> Appellant says Dr. Peterson testified that "It is unlikely that the knee injury sustained in October, 1959, could have caused the back condition, which did not manifest itself until 1961." This is an accurate statement made by Dr. Peterson, but appellant makes no reference to additional statements made by the doctor concerning the back injury.

Whether the 1959 knee injury caused the injury to the back was the sole issue in the case, so the appellee certainly did not mean to admit that the doctor's adverse opinion was "an accurate statement."

> He testified that he remembered being in the lobby when he saw a young woman carrying a baby and her husband enter.

One does remember sights like that.

> Under the law, the board must approve any award recommended by the arbitrator.

"Must" is sometimes used in this misleading way. The writer does not mean that the board must approve. He means that "before an award can become final the board must approve it," or that it "does not become final unless approved by the board."

Be on guard against slipping into what we may call ex post facto construction.

> The doctor persuaded the deceased to submit to the operation.

Did he manage to persuade a corpse? No. Because the writer has been referring to the person as "the deceased," he here mistakenly uses that term in narrating something that happened before the person became deceased.

Such fumbling approximations of what we are trying to say frequently show up in our first drafts. This is the way we might talk if we had to do so extemporaneously. You need have no feelings of inferiority or guilt because you find such blunders in your writing. You do deserve blame if you fail to find them because you fail to read your early drafts critically.

A final examination question in the course in Constitutional Law concerned a state statute requiring all contract carriers using state highways to obtain a state permit, and providing not only for criminal penalties for failure to comply with load limits and other restrictions, but also for suspension of the permit. A student answering the question meant to say that as applied to interstate carriers operating under certificate from the Interstate Commerce Commission, the state could impose criminal penalties but probably could not completely prohibit the operation by suspending the permit. What he wrote was:

> A state may subject interstate commerce to reasonable regulations designed to protect public safety and preservation of the roads. However, a certificate from the I.C.C. preempts much of the field, and it may be that the state can only impose a fine when the carrier has an I.C.C. permit.

What is the error in sentence order that allows a wholly unintended meaning to be given the second sentence?

Follow Normal Sentence Order

To be clearly understood, you must not only know what words denote and how to choose the right words for your purpose; you must also know how to put them together into sentences.

The normal English sentence order is: (1) subject, (2) verb, (3) object. Write all your sentences in this order, except when you may want deliberately to depart from it in order to get a particular effect, such as emphasis on a certain word or phrase.

A manual for United Press reporters written years ago [2] gave this advice:

> Direct approach is the best way of starting a story; do not begin sentences with participles, subordinate clauses, and the like. Make your statements in the natural order of subject first, then the verb, etc.

In each of the examples below, if the writer had followed normal sentence order by starting with his subject, instead of with "There have been" or "Because," his difficulty would have vanished.

There have been many solutions to this problem advanced.	Many solutions to this problem have been advanced.
Because a rule is old does not prove it is sound.	A rule is not sound merely because it is old.

Legal writing so frequently calls for complex sentences containing many qualifying clauses and phrases that adhering to normal sentence order whenever possible is not likely to oversimplify one's style.

Put Modifiers With the Word or Phrase Modified

One big source of ambiguity is the careless placing of modifiers:

> The district game warden filed four complaints, charging illegal fishing in Judge J. J. Padgett's court.

"In every sentence," said Herbert Spencer, "the sequence of words should be that which suggests the constituents of the thought in the order most convenient for the building up of that thought." This requires that the words and expressions most nearly related in thought be brought closest together—modifiers of the subject with the subject, modifiers of the verb with the verb, modifiers of the object with the object. Spencer explained why this is important.[3]

---

2. Quoted by Walter B. Pitkin, The Art of Useful Writing 185 (1940).

3. Economy Applied to Words, reprinted in Brown, The Writer's Art 105 (1921).

> The longer the time that elapses between the mention of any qualifying member and the member qualified, the longer must the mind be exerted in carrying forward the qualifying member ready for use. And the more numerous the qualifications to be simultaneously remembered and rightly applied, the greater will be the mental power expended, and the smaller the effect produced. Hence, other things equal, force will be gained by so arranging the members of a sentence that these suspensions shall be at any moment the fewest in number; and shall also be of the shortest duration. . . .

Legal propositions may have to include a number of modifying phrases or clauses. Fitting them all into the sentence without making it clumsy or unclear is sometimes difficult. Usually, the best places to put these phrases and clauses are (1) before the subject, or (2) after the predicate. Conditions or exceptions modifying the subject should generally be placed before the subject. Those qualifying the predicate should generally be placed after the predicate. A short modifier of the subject may be placed (3) after the subject; but a long string of words defining or otherwise qualifying the subject may make the sentence hard to follow because the whole thought is kept hanging until we reach the verb. The least desirable place to put modifiers is (4) between the verb and its object or predicate noun.

The complaint was, in the court's opinion, both in form and in substance, seriously defective.	In the court's opinion, the complaint was seriously defective both in form and in substance.
A petition by property owners in Paving District No. 21 protesting the board's order of June 17, 1961, calling for reassessment was filed yesterday.	A petition was filed yesterday by property owners. . . .

Although it is not usually good practice to place modifiers between the verb and its object or predicate, an indirect object may sometimes be put before the direct object, where the latter is long.

The lessor conveyed all the minerals of whatever kind that lay on or below the surface of the tract to lessee.	The lessor conveyed to lessee all the minerals . . . .

"The lessor conveyed all the minerals to lessee" is proper and normal sentence order. But when one word or phrase in the sentence carries with it a long string of qualifying words, as "minerals" does here, it is better to get the indirect object, "to lessee," into the sentence before starting the long clause describing the minerals.

Clumsy word-order impairs reading efficiency by requiring undue mental effort on the part of the reader.

> In the Buchannon case, the promisee procured money to prosecute a claim to a will which would benefit his wife.

What would benefit the wife—the will, or prosecution of the claim?

> The exclusion of implied warranties under the common law is more readily accomplished than under the provisions of the Uniform Commercial Code.

The subject under discussion is "The exclusion of implied warranties," not "The exclusion of implied warranties under common law." This exclusion, the writer wants to say, is more readily accomplished under common law than under the Code; "under common law" therefore belongs after "is more readily accomplished."

> The court's holding that the lessee's right to use the underground tunnels was terminated when the coal was exhausted is inconsistent with the holding that the estate in the coal is perpetual in Attebery v. Blair.

> The court's holding that the lessee's right to use the underground tunnels was terminated when the coal was exhausted is inconsistent with the holding in Attebery v. Blair, that the estate in the coal is perpetual.

> There was probable cause to believe that an illicit still was being operated only after there had been an illegal trespass by the federal officers.

> Only after there had been an illegal trespass by the federal agents was there probable cause to believe that an illicit still was being operated.

Even judges may on occasion arrange words so carelessly that they fail to say what was intended, as when Mr. Justice Murphy begins a dissenting opinion by saying: [4]

> It is disheartening to find so much that is right in an opinion which seems to me so fundamentally wrong.

What disheartened the Justice was surely not to find so much that was right in the opinion; rather, it was to find the opinion reaching a conclusion that seemed to him so fundamentally wrong: It is disheartening to find an opinion containing so much that is right come to a conclusion that seems to me so fundamentally wrong.

Misplaced modifiers or other clumsy word-order may not only impair reading efficiency but leave the meaning ambiguous:

> When Brown was arrested by Sheriff Ramsey, on May 10, the sheriff testified he told Brown the reason for his arrest.

Did the sheriff testify on May 10?

> The promise to pay a liquidated sum due and owing at a later date needs consideration.

What the writer was trying to say was that a promise to pay at a later date a liquidated sum that is due and owing now, is insufficient consideration for a promise by the creditor to extend the time for payment.

> Unfortunately, the eastern operators have taken advantage of this provision but our organization has not.

The writer did not really regard it as unfortunate that the eastern operators had acted. What he meant to say was:

> The eastern operators have taken advantage of this provision, but our organization, unfortunately, has not.

A misplaced modifier may make a statement ludicrous.

> The federal officers arrived at the conclusion that a felony was being committed by the odor of moonshine whiskey.

4. Wolf v. Colorado, 338 U.S. 25, 41, 69 S.Ct. 1359, 1372, 93 L.Ed. 1782 (1949).

Even an offensive odor should not be dubbed an offender.

> There are millions of children who do not go to school in Asia.

Yes: yours and mine, among others.

A common form of misplaced modifier is the dangling participle. When a participle begins a sentence, it must modify the subject of the main clause that follows it. If the subject noun is placed in some subordinate position, or is omitted entirely, the participle is left dangling.

> Notwithstanding its many shortcomings, this court has adopted the Missouri rule.

The writer does not mean that the court had shortcomings; he means the rule had. He should either (1) keep the participle construction but make the rule his subject (Notwithstanding its many shortcomings, the Missouri rule has been adopted by this court), or (2) leave his main clause as it stands but abandon the participle construction (This court has adopted the Missouri rule, notwithstanding its many shortcomings).

> Overcome with emotion, the defendant's eyes filled with tears.

His eyes were not overcome with emotion; he was.

> Having borne him two sons, Mrs. Abney and her husband were hoping that this would be a girl.

Without disparaging Mr. Abney's contribution to the birth of his sons, he was not an equal partner in bearing them. (See how easy it is to dangle a participle? What needs to be done to straighten out that sentence?)

Single words as well as phrases and clauses are sometimes misplaced. Adverbs are especially likely to get lost, and certain adverbs more than most. "Only" is perhaps the most footloose. Unthinking writers tend to put it next to the verb whether it belongs there or not. "Both," "even," "alone," "at least" and "merely" are other words often mislaid. Usually the best place for these and similar modifiers is immediately before the element they modify.

What is the difference in meaning between the following two sentences?

He agreed only to play the following week.

He agreed to play only the following week.

Modifiers preceding or following a series are likely to create ambiguity. Suppose a regulation says that it applies to "all domestic corporations or partnerships engaged in intrastate commerce." Does it apply to all domestic corporations, or only those engaged in intrastate commerce? All partnerships engaged in intrastate commerce, or only domestic ones?

It will sometimes happen that your efforts to rearrange a poorly constructed sentence seem futile; the revision is no better than the original. The reason probably is that you clung too closely to the original, changing only words here and there, when the defect lay in its basic structure. Ask yourself whether you are not violating one or more of the guides laid down in this book. Does the sentence follow normal sentence order? Does it attempt simultaneously to make two or three statements, which had better be made in two or three sentences instead of one? Are modifying phrases and clauses next to the words modified? With perhaps some clues from these guides, start over, and hammer out a properly organized sentence.

Avoid Ambiguity by Association

The accidental placing of two words next to one another may lead the reader down a false trail.

> Federal laws directed at the control of an evil thought by
> Congress to require regulation have been upheld.

When we have "an evil" followed by "thought," we have, alas, "an evil thought." The writer, knowing what he means, may not notice that his words are subject to such "ambiguity by association," as we may call it, but the reader will probably notice and be momentarily confused by it.

This kind of ambiguity can result when an introductory word may be read as one of a series that follows:

> To policemen, migrants, bikers, and vagrants are suspicious
> characters.

Be Sure Your Pronouns Have Antecedents

The chapter on Simplicity pointed out that we can make our writing less clumsy by using pronouns to avoid repeating nouns. The repetition of nouns is one big reason for the cumbersomeness of legal writing. We can therefore make good use of pronouns.

But pronouns carelessly used can make trouble. We may laugh at the poor social-agency client who wrote, "In answer to your question, I gave birth to a boy, weighed ten pounds. I hope this is satisfactory." But law students are sometimes guilty of the same fault. They will discuss a case or a rule of law, and then start a new sentence with "this:" "This is also true when . . .." The reader may not be able to discover whether "this" refers to an entire preceding paragraph or only to a specific thing or idea previously mentioned. Sometimes, it seems to refer to something not mentioned at all.

> There has been dissatisfaction with what appears to be a tendency on the part of courts not to disturb Board findings. This has been true even where such findings are based on questions of mixed law and fact.

What the writer meant was that this *tendency* was true (existed) even where, etc. But what his words say is that the *dissatisfaction* existed. One way to avoid falling into this error is to avoid using "this" as a demonstrative pronoun, and to use it instead as an adjective by adding the noun identifying what is referred to: "this tendency," or "this dissatisfaction."

A book on Brief Writing argues for brevity in the following words:

> It is a pity that so many, often justifiably, consider lawyers to be "slaves of verbosity." Actually, such should not be the case.

What should not be "the case?" Does the writer mean: (1) it should not be a pity (but a good thing, perhaps?) that many people consider lawyers to be "slaves of verbosity; " (2) lawyers should not be such slaves; or (3) people should not consider them to be?

The word "it" is particularly easy to misuse in this way. It is so convenient that writers often use it without making clear what "it" refers to.

> In order to exclude the warranty of merchantability, it must be mentioned expressly, and if in writing, it must be "conspicuous."

The word "it" in this sentence, both times it is used, refers grammatically to "the warranty of merchantability." But that is not what the writer intended; what he meant to say is that the exclusion must be mentioned, and if in writing, the exclusionary provision must be conspicuous.

"He" and "him" are also often used without clear antecedents.

> Defendant killed the deceased when he thought he was raising his gun to shoot him.

Who thought who was going to shoot whom?

Similar to the fault of using pronouns that lack antecedents is that of using nouns with demonstrative adjectives that lack referents, as by referring to "this" item when no such item has been mentioned.

> From the dicta in Daly v. Palmer, it might seem that a choreographic work would be held registerable as a dramatic composition, but this hope was quickly dispelled.

No such hope had been mentioned.

> The defendant was indicted for unlawful possession of marihuana. This indictment was based on evidence obtained by a search warrant improperly issued.

Because he has said that the defendant was indicted, the writer mistakenly assumes he is free to refer to "this indictment."

> The majority view is found in Lill v. Gleason, 92 Kan. 754, 142 P. 287 (1914). This court declares that. . . .

Because he has cited a Kansas case, the writer assumed (if he was thinking at all) that "This court" is sufficient to refer to the Supreme Court of Kansas.

> The Company must bargain with the union for a period of
> one year. At this time, if the situation still exists, the com-
> pany may file a petition for determination of representation.

At what time? For referring to a past occasion, "at that
time" is better; "at this time" can then be reserved for referring to the present.

Use Hyphens Where Needed

Compound adjectives may need to be joined with a hyphen, to
show that they are to be read together as one word.

> The program is designed to help small businessmen.

"Small-business men" would make clear that it is not a program for five-footers. Other compounds where hyphens would
help:

> A general rule making process
>
> The court appointed experts
>
> Our work oriented curriculum
>
> The full time staff

Beware of Double Negatives

If you want to be clear, avoid double negatives; they are confusing.

> We do not deny that immoral works should not receive
> copyright protection.

> No valid distinction can be drawn between this case and
> Wolf v. Colorado on the ground that here the evidence has
> not already been brought under control of the state.

Even a United States Supreme Court justice may on occasion
produce a glut of negatives:

> This is not to say, however, that the prima facie case may
> not be met by evidence supporting a finding that a lesser de-
> gree of segregated schooling in the core city area would not
> have resulted even if the Board had not acted as it did.[5]

5. Mr. Justice Brennan in Keyes v.   211, 93 S.Ct. 2686, 2698, 37 L.Ed.2d
School Dist. No. 1, 413 U.S. 189,   548, 564 (1973).

The worst kind of double negative is that created by adding a redundant negative in a subordinate clause, making the sentence say the opposite of what was intended.

> We would not be surprised if investigation did not ultimately prove the signature to be a forgery.

> I do not know how many times I haven't checked this item.

> We do not contend that no case may ever arise in which an exception to the rule would not be justified.

To avoid confusion of all concerned, it is good practice when possible to convert double negatives into affirmative statements.

Distinguish Between the Conjunctive and the Disjunctive

If either fact A or fact B will suffice to produce a legal result, it is obviously wrong to say that the law requires A *and* B. Put in this bare form, the error is obvious; but it may not be apparent when swathed in many words. Even courts occasionally trip over the distinction between "and" and "or." In a New York case,[6] the trial court instructed the jury that a mere false belief would not excuse a woman accused of murdering her child "unless it was the result of some mental disease which prevented her from knowing the nature and quality of the act and that it was wrongful." On appeal, this was held to be erroneous; it should have been made clear "that a defect of reason which inhibited a knowledge *either* of the nature and quality of the act *or* that the act was wrong excused a person from criminal liability." In states recognizing both the right-and-wrong and the irresistible impulse test of insanity, courts sometimes carelessly say that the test is ability to distinguish between right and wrong *and* ability to resist the impulse.[7]

Whether to use "and" or "or" may in some situations be difficult to decide. Suppose a law licensing cleaners and dyers defines a cleaning establishment to mean "any place where cleaning and dyeing is done." Use of the word "and" requires that

6. People v. Sherwood, 271 N.Y. 427, 3 N.E.2d 581 (1936).

7. See Howard v. United States, 232 F.2d 274 (C.A.5, 1956); State v. Beckwith, 242 Iowa 228, 46 N.W.2d 20 (1951); Com. v. Smith, 374 Pa. 220, 97 A.2d 25 (1953); Weihofen, Mental Disorder as a Criminal Defense 75 (1954).

both be done. Substituting "or" would cover places where either is done, but might in some situations be interpreted to exclude places where both are done. The safe way to cover all the possibilities is to say "any place where cleaning or dyeing, or both," are done.

A contract between a professional research man and an industrial corporation provided:

> Bonger will assign to the corporation all right, title and interest to any invention he makes during the period of his employment if:
>
> a. Such invention relates to any method of transmitting handwriting specimens by wire;
>
> b. Such invention is made by using or with the aid of corporation materials or property.

What ambiguity do you detect in this statement?

The Former and the Latter

"Former" and "latter" are sometimes used to distinguish between two things previously mentioned, especially when those subjects have no names or short descriptive labels. Arguments, theories or points of view are examples. But "former" and "latter" are rather stiff, and should be avoided if possible.

The two significant dates are 1820 and 1857, the former because it is the date when the act was passed and the latter because it is the date when it was held unconstitutional.	The two significant dates are 1820, when the act was passed, and 1857, when it was held unconstitutional.

When you do use these terms, if the two subjects occurred at different times it is well to make "former" refer to the earlier in time as well as first mentioned, and "latter" to the later.

> In Grovey v. Townsend, 295 U.S. 45, 55 S.Ct. 622, this Court had before it another suit for damages for the refusal in a primary of a county clerk, a Texas officer with only public functions to perform, to furnish petitioner, a Negro, an absentee ballot. The refusal was solely on the ground of race. This case differed from Nixon v. Condon, supra, in that a

state convention of the Democratic party had passed the resolution of May 24, 1932, hereinbefore quoted. It was decided
that the determination by the state convention of the mem-
bership of the Democratic party made a significant change
from a determination by the Executive Committee. The
former was party action, voluntary in character. The *latter,*
as has been held in the Condon Case, was action by authority
of the State. The managers of the primary election were
therefore declared not to be state officials in such sense that
their action was state action.[8]

In this passage, determination by the Executive Committee
was the earlier device; determination by the state convention of
the party members was adopted later. Clarity is not aided by
referring to the earlier device as the "latter" and the later as
the "former."

"Former" and "formerly" occasionally confuse writers, including the New York Times reporter who wrote:

Leon H. Keyserling was a former government economist.

Has Mr. Keyserling ceased to be a former government economist? No, he still is. "Still is" applies also to the baseball
trainer who, a sports commentator told us, "used to be a former
major leaguer."

The Passive Voice is Sometimes Ambiguous

In the chapter on Forcefulness, we shall point out that the
passive voice is a weaker way of saying things than the active.
It is also sometimes less clear. When, instead of saying that
someone did something, you say that something was done, you
may leave it unclear *by whom* it was done.

The cotenant can either develop the property himself, or, in
some cases, force the other cotenants to join with him in leasing or operating. The problems arising from unilateral action will be discussed first and then the circumstances under
which joint leasing or developing are ordered.

8. Smith v. Allwright, 321 U.S. 649,
659, 64 S.Ct. 757, 762, 88 L.Ed. 987
(1944).

"Are ordered" by whom? Presumably by a court, but use of the active voice would save the reader from having to figure this out for himself.

A complainant in a suit for the value of plumbing work done by him in a building of which defendant was a tenant worded it as follows:

> That the work was authorized because of defendant's immediate pecuniary interest in the transaction, knowing that no water could have been furnished the store unless said work was done.

Does this allege that the work had been authorized by defendant?

In another case, plaintiff was attempting to charge defendant company for work ordered by X, defendant's manager. Plaintiff's contention was that X acted as agent for the company. But its complaint merely alleged that X "was authorized" to enter into contracts—without saying by whom he was authorized. Does this allege authority from defendant?

Do not shift without reason from active to passive voice or vice versa.

Plaintiff signed the contract on March 1 and it was mailed to defendant the same day.	Plaintiff signed the contract on March 1 and mailed it to defendant the same day.

Somewhat akin to the ambiguity of the passive voice in failing to identify the actor is the presentation of an assertion without identifying the asserter, that is, without making clear whether the writer is speaking for himself or is attributing the assertion to someone else (a court, for example):

> Though this ambiguity concerning the doctrinal basis of the constitutional holding exists, the decision fortifies the proposition advanced by some writers that the only effective restraint on the commerce power resides in the political processes rather than the judicial process. The term "interstate commerce" no longer presents a constitutional problem, but only raises a problem of statutory construction to determine the scope of federal regulatory power authorized by Congress in any particular statute. The Court was faced with this

> problem in the instant case, not only in connection with the phrase "or the doing of any other act," but also in the construction of the clause "while such article is held for sale after shipment in interstate commerce."

In the second sentence in this paragraph, is the writer speaking for himself, or is he merely enlarging on "the proposition advanced by some writers"?

An employer, during negotiations with a labor union over rates of pay, was asked by the union to supply certain financial information. He consulted his attorney, who wrote an opinion containing the following paragraph:

> The union has stated to you that the information requested is necessary for administering the existing contract and for bargaining in good faith. For these purposes, they need to know your net profit for last year, the number of hours worked by each of your employees and their total pay.

The second sentence was intended merely to state the union's position—not the lawyer's own. But the client may read it literally, and he may resent his lawyer's saying something that he strongly feels is wrong.

Compound Prepositions Are Often Vague

The chapter on Conciseness pointed out that compound prepositional phrases are wordy. Sometimes they are also ambiguous.

> The appellant argues that he was incompetent to stand trial in view of an earlier adjudication as insane by a West Virginia court in 1955.

"In view of" befogs the statement so that we do not know what appellant argued: (1) that the earlier adjudication conclusively established appellant's incompetency at the time of trial; (2) that it created a rebuttable presumption of such incompetency; or (3) that it was evidence tending to show such incompetency.

Other prepositional phrases, such as "with reference to," "as to," and "in this connection," also often cloak ambiguity of meaning:

> By 1950, 37 states had adopted the Uniform Sales act, and the remaining jurisdictions formed their law with reference to it.

The seller must know the purpose to which the goods are to be put, and the buyer must rely on the seller's judgment as to the selection of the goods.

Besides the problem of whether a newsboy is an independent contractor, other questions have come before the Board in this connection.

Clarity in Presenting Statistics

Statistical data that may be hard to comprehend when presented in one way may be quite plain when presented in another. Do not normally bury copious statistics in the text. Do not write:

> In the federal courts, 32% of the defendants whose bail was fixed at $500 could not raise bail. When bail was set at a higher amount, the proportion of offenders who could not put up bond rose. When the bail was $1000, 50% could not raise bail; when the amount of bail was $1500 to $4000, 67% could not put up bond; and when the amount was $5000 or over, 87% could not put up bond.

Instead of being put in solid paragraph form, this sort of data may be set out in a table; but tables, if long, are themselves difficult to read, and the trend or point you want to demonstrate may not be apparent. One way to meet the problem is to state the point you want to make and then support it with a table, perhaps in a footnote.

When You Do Not Want to be Clear

Occasions will arise when you do not want to be clear. Stuart Chase, in The Tyranny of Words, tells of a distinguished and astute Senator skilled in political management, who announced that Americanism was to be his campaign issue. When asked what Americanism meant, he said he did not know, but that it was a damned good word with which to carry an election.

A lawyer will often have more legitimate reasons for using ambiguous language. He may not want to take a firm position or make a firm commitment, thinking it wiser or at least more prudent to express only a vague assurance that he will take some favorable action or a vague threat to do something adverse.

> Unless this account is paid within the next ten days, it will
> be necessary to take appropriate action.

Certainly the writer could have found more specific wording
—"start legal proceedings" or "bring suit," for example. He
uses the vaguer wording precisely because he does not want to
make such a specific threat at this time.

Because law is an imprecise science, a lawyer often cannot be
sure of the soundness of his position, and he may therefore not
want to expound it with any air of assuredness.

> In view of the fact that payments had been so erratic, my
> client exercised his right to cancel the contract.

"Because" would be both more precise and more concise than
"In view of the fact that." And "erratic" does not state a legally recognized objection to the way payments had been made.
But perhaps counsel was not sure that the way payments had
been made gave legal cause for cancellation, or that he wanted
to rest on the manner of payment as *the cause* of his client's
cancelling. He therefore preferred not to state baldly what the
deficiency was, nor to use a word asserting that it was cause.
"In view of the fact that," a phrase that suggests a broad-mind-
ed perspective, therefore replaces a narrower word implying a
causal relation.

"Seems" or "it seems" is a phrase often useful for hedging.
The variation, "it appears," the American College Dictionary
tells us, is less desirable: "SEEMS is applied to that which has
an aspect of truth and probability . . . APPEAR suggests
the giving of an impression which may be superficial or illuso-
ry." But this distinction is probably too refined to be appreciated by most readers. At all events, it does not imply that you
should avoid "appear;" superficiality or illusoriness may sometimes be exactly what you want to suggest. Your opponent's argument, you may want to say, "appears, until one examines it,
to have some validity."

"It seems to me" adds nothing except to focus the spotlight on
the writer instead of on his subject. Never interject yourself
needlessly between your writing and your reader.

Putting a question commits one less than suggesting an answer, no matter how tentatively. In a book review, discussing

the difference between the Russian inquisitorial and the American accusatorial system, the reviewer wrote:

> What the distinctions are, and wherein the Russian procedure is more effectively designed to obtain confessions, Rogge does not tell us. Does the answer perhaps lie not in the procedure as laid down in the books, but in its abuse? And if so, is the distinction that deserves emphasis not so much the virtues of the accusatorial system as against the inquisitorial, but rather the virtues of the rule of law as against the rule of men who are above the law?

The editor suggested changing both questions to declarative sentences, the first, for example, from "Does the answer perhaps lie," to "The answer perhaps lies." But even with the word "perhaps," the statement would have been more assertive than the writer wanted to be.

In writing an affidavit in support of a motion some lawyers make it very tight and short, so as to reveal as little as possible of the thrust of the motion. When counsel then submits his copious supporting papers, his opponent is ill-prepared to reply.

Because, as already said, the passive voice is sometimes less clear than the active, it may be useful where ambiguity is desired. In saying that certain discreditable acts have been committed, we may not want to name the actor. By using the passive, we avoid pointing the finger at any particular person.

> Certain rumors have been circulated.
>
> The gun was fired at close range.

One reason for ambiguity is courtesy. When your answer must be a refusal or other disappointment, a vague expression is usually less harsh than a bluntly direct one. Since such refusals are more often expressed in letters than in other forms of legal writing, this subject is discussed in Chapter 8, Letters.

Even in drafting projects in which clarity is ordinarily a prime requirement, its opposite may be called for on occasion. Although the legislative draftsman should normally do his best to make his meaning clear, occasions will arise when he will deliberately be vague—perhaps because specificity would raise doubts or opposition in committee or on the floor and precipitate a fight that would jeopardize the basic program; or because it seems wise or expeditious for the legislature to lay down only a broad policy, leaving the task of determining specific issues to administrators or courts. The Federal Trade Commission Act, for example, deliberately uses a broad concept in forbidding "unfair methods of competition," leaving it to the Commission to determine what practices should be held to be unfair. Mr. Justice Brandeis later [9] explained the reason for adopting this device:

> Experience with existing laws had taught that definition, being necessarily rigid, would prove embarrassing and, if rigorously applied, might involve great hardship. Methods of competition which would be unfair in one industry, under certain circumstances, might, when adopted in another industry, or even in the same industry under different circumstances, be entirely unobjectionable. Furthermore, an enumeration, however comprehensive, of existing methods of unfair competition must necessarily soon prove incomplete, as with new conditions constantly arising novel unfair methods would be devised and developed.

Collective bargaining agreements provide another example of documents in which the draftsman must sometimes tread a fine line between unnecessary or unintended ambiguity on the one hand and embarrassingly naked clarity on the other. Such agreements are frequently negotiated by representatives on both sides whose prestige is at stake. "Face-saving is an important interest which can be ignored at the risk of cessation of operations, or served by statement less than bitingly clear." Or specific provisions are avoided because they would be targets for objections, each of which may have little power behind it but which cumulatively might endanger acceptance of the agreement. The union may look with suspicion on any proposal by the company to clarify an existing provision, fearing that it may "take something away." Or, as with legislation, the parties may not be able or willing to spell out the details of how a general principle should be implemented, and so prefer to leave the specific questions unresolved—perhaps hoping that they will not arise during the life of the agreement.[10] The employer's right

---

9. Dissenting opinion in F. T. C. v. Gratz, 253 U.S. 421, 436, 40 S.Ct. 572, 64 L.Ed. 993 (1920).

10. Shulman, The Settlement of Labor Disputes, 4 Record of N.Y.C.B. A. 12 (1949).

to discharge, for example, is typically restricted in such agreements, but the restriction is usually put in general terms: employees are not to be discharged except for "cause" or "just cause." The general term is made to suffice because it is almost impossible to foresee all the situations that might warrant discharge. One device for gaining somewhat greater specificity is adding to the general term some of the more common specific grounds. The specification eliminates disputes over whether a named ground is sufficient, not only for some sort of discipline but for discharge.

Judicial opinions are sometimes deliberately imprecise, and on rare occasions frankly so. Mr. Justice Frankfurter, dissenting in a case on property taxation of airplanes, said, "I am not unaware that there is an air of imprecision about what I have written. Such is the intention." Imprecision may be better than giving an illusion of exactness by attempting to lay down absolutes or generalizations in an area where particulars are so various that any generalization is sure to be either unsound or too vague to be useful.

Even the Founding Fathers thought it wise not to give specific answers to all the questions that they knew would arise under the Constitution they were drafting. In Article IV, section 3, they provided that "new States may be admitted by Congress into this Union." They recognized that this gave no answer to a question sure to arise: were new states to be admitted as equals, or was Congress to have power to attach conditions to admission? The delegates debated this question, but in the end rejected an addendum that "the new States shall be admitted on the same terms as the original States." They left the question unresolved, and so it remained for more than a hundred years.[11]

11. Coyle v. Smith, 221 U.S. 559, 31
S.Ct. 688, 55 L.Ed. 853 (1911).

Chapter 6

FORCEFULNESS

The subjects of most legal writing are typically complex enough to demand concentrated attention in reading. But a reader tires and his attention flags. Writing thus becomes a psychological campaign, an exercise in arousing and holding the reader's interest. The writer must continually spur him on, now tickling his fancy with a neat turn of phrase, now stirring or shocking him with a moving or vivid word, constantly stimulating him to think more keenly, see more clearly or feel more strongly. Especially in presenting argument, the lawyer will want to make the impact of his points on the reader strong and indelible.

Before considering how forcefulness can be attained, let us make clear how it cannot.

I. HOW NOT TO DO IT

Force or emphasis is not rightly conveyed to a word by mechanical contrivances such as underlining or italics. The practice of putting single words into italics, said one authority, is vulgar; "a well-constructed sentence should be able to carry a stress on any of its words and should show in itself how these stresses are to be compounded." [1]

Attention is not effectively directed to a particular statement by saying, "It is important to bear in mind," "We should like to point out," or "It is to be noted." Nor by adding intensifying adjectives or adverbs such as "very," "clearly," or "certainly." Adjectives and adverbs are indispensable parts of speech and can lend character and color. They are valuable and even necessary when you want to characterize the nature of the thing you are

---

1. William Empson, Seven Types of Ambiguity 34 (3d ed. reprint, 1955).

talking about, but not when you merely want to intensify the degree. It is proper to refer to a "financial crisis" or a "procedural point," but when you find yourself writing about a "serious crisis" or a "very important point" it is time to reach for the blue pencil. Avoid extreme or exaggerated adjectives or adverbs, such as absolutely, completely, perfectly, utterly.

Much use of such extreme terms gives an air of school-girlish hyperbole ("Utterly divine!") Any intensifying effect they may have quickly wears off, leaving them as weakeners rather than strengtheners. "The adjective," said Voltaire, "is the enemy of the noun."

> I find the arrangement of the opinions to be terribly unimportant.

This was written by a law professor. "Terribly" is a poor word to modify "important." It is worse for modifying "unimportant." Was the writer really terrorized by the unimportance of the arrangement? This question may strike you as cavilling; any sensible reader, you may say, should understand that the writer was not using the word "terribly" to mean "exciting terror." Yes, but what the defense amounts to is that any sensible person will understand that this writer does not always mean what he says. It is better to try to build the opposite kind of reputation.

> Four witnesses testified that the foreman's account was accurate in every particular.

The reader's suspicion is aroused by such an extreme claim. Did all four witnesses really testify that the account was accurate "in every particular"? If they did, weren't they overdoing it, and aren't we justified in wondering whether they themselves were being accurate in their testimony?

Exaggeration destroys the reader's confidence not only in the particular statement but in everything you say. A lawyer has a special responsibility to be trustworthy and reliable. If he hopes to gain and hold respect, he must be careful to avoid reckless superlatives and unrestrained generalizations. Otherwise he shows himself to be a person whose judgment, or even veracity, is not to be trusted.

When you feel that the noun you are using is not strong enough, instead of trying to intensify it by adding an adjective find a stronger noun. If "accident" doesn't seem strong enough, don't call it a "terrible accident." Look for a stronger synonym for "accident," such as "disaster," "catastrophe," "calamity," or "tragedy." So also:

Instead of Saying	Say
Grave error	Blunder, botchery, bungle, folly, lubberliness
Great malice	Hatred, malevolence, spitefulness, venom
Great pain	Agony, anguish, torment
Great wrong	Evil, iniquity, outrage, villainy, wickedness
Very negligent	Heedless, mindless, rash, reckless

That adjectives and adverbs may weaken rather than strengthen was forcefully affirmed in the House of Lords two centuries ago. Sir George Savile in 1770 made certain blunt accusations against fellow members of the House. Lord North the next day tried to soften his words by saying that he was sure "Sir George had spoken in warmth." "No," said Savile, "I spoke what I thought last night, and I think the same this morning. Honorable members have betrayed their trust. I will add no epithets, because epithets only weaken. I will not say they have betrayed their country corruptly, flagitiously, and scandalously; but I do say they have betrayed their country, and I stand here to receive the punishment for having said so." [2]

Certain adjectives look too small and lonely to some writers to stand unaccompanied by an adverb. These writers never describe a thing as merely "far" or "near," "long" or "short"; it must always be "very far," "quite near," "fairly long," "relatively short."

One of the most overused adverbs is "very." In its original meaning of "truly" this was a word of some force, but it has become so worn out from overuse that it no longer packs even a

2. Trevelyan, Early History of
Charles James Fox 199 (1880).

powder-puff punch. When you catch yourself using it, stop to ask whether it ever would be missed if you deleted it. The answer will almost always be no. To say that a point is "very clear," a speech "very good" or "very convincing" and its defects "very few," does not add anything to the same statements without "very." On the contrary, "clear," "good" "convincing" and "few" without the qualifying adverbs are stronger.

The way these intensifiers are sometimes used suggests that the writers do not know what they mean. They say "quite" when they mean "not quite"—as in "The citations were quite complete." They say "literally" when they mean "figuratively" ("We were literally thrown out of court"). They will say that one thing is "incomparably better" (or worse) than another, and then proceed to compare them. They use comparatives with qualities that have no degrees, as "very (or most, more) essential," "most perfect," or "more unique." All these are as inane as "very dead." It may help drive home the point to recall the jests about the girl who was just a little bit pregnant, or the salesman who wanted to be transferred to a more virgin territory.

If you say, "It is impossible to contend   .   .   ." in answering an opponent who does so contend, you are obviously wrong. If you mean that it is illogical or unsound so to contend, say so. If you mean it is stupid to do so, say that (but suaviter!).

"Unthinkable" is another intensifier that overshoots the mark. Things that are really unthinkable can hardly be talked about, so when a speaker or writer calls something that he is thinking and talking about "unthinkable," we know that he does not mean what he says.

Saying that something is "undoubtedly" true suggests doubt. Introducing a sentence with "To tell the truth" or "To be frank" merely prompts the question, "Haven't you been, so far?" "I am sure that" is so often used to bolster an assertion the writer is unsure about that we have come to expect anything introduced by these words to be questionable. To say that a contention is "clearly" unsound, that it has been "practically" overruled, or that "no thinking man" would accept it, is more likely to lead an intelligent and critical reader to question and perhaps reject the view that is thus being forced on him than it is to induce him to accept it. There is a streak of contrariness in human nature that prompts us to reject peremptory assertions; and judges and lawyers are generally no less contrary than most people.

"I am only too glad" is weaker than "I am glad." (This peculiar use of "too" is not only weak but fatuous). The same can be said of "not too," as in, "His feelings toward defendant were not too friendly," or "the decision is not too clear." "This kind of misrepresentation is not to be taken too lightly" implies that it may be taken somewhat lightly. Omit "too."

Comparatives are weaker than unqualified statements. "Let us die to make men more free" is weaker, not stronger, than "Let us die to make men free."

Sometimes these supposed strengtheners weaken the statement to the point of carrying the opposite meaning from that intended. If you want to tell your client not to be alarmed over certain developments, you do not add reassurance by adding the word "unduly." "There is no reason to be unduly alarmed" means that there is reason for a certain amount of alarm but that he should not be more alarmed than the circumstances justify.

"With all due respect" does not imply more respect than the word "respect" standing alone; it implies less. Since the phrase is usually used to introduce a critical statement, what it says is, "with all the respect that is due to someone holding such an unsound view."

The point of all this is that restraint is more effective than exaggeration, just as the low growl of a mastiff is more persuasive than the vehement yipping of a terrier. The right noun or verb, unqualified, is more forceful than the wrong one arrayed in superlatives. Deliberate understatement, relying on the reader's intelligence to supply the more appropriate expression, is more complimentary and often more successful in inducing the desired emotional response than overt urging.

Having dismissed these mistaken expedients, let us see what more effective ways we can suggest for gaining forcefulness. We can group our suggestions under two main headings: choos-

ing the forceful word or expression; and arranging words for
emphasis.

II. CHOOSING THE FORCEFUL WORD OR
EXPRESSION

"Be precise, concise, simple and clear." The qualities of precision, conciseness, simplicity and clarity, discussed in Chapters II
through V, are not only virtues in themselves, but also means
for making one's style more forceful. One way to make a sentence stronger is to make it shorter, plainer and clearer. A short
word is ordinarily more forceful than a long, the homely idiom
than the elaborate or bookish. In this chapter we shall examine
certain other devices for increasing forcefulness.

Use Verbs

We have just warned against overusing adjectives and adverbs. In the chapter on Simplicity, we said that overusing
nouns makes for an overstuffed, pretentious style. Verbs are
the muscular words, the words of action. It is verbs that give
vitality and vigor to style.

When we say "use verbs," we don't mean the colorless little
auxiliary verbs, like "be," "give," "have," "hold," "make" and
"take," which seduce you into using nouns that derive from
verbs and sap their strength. Use the direct verb itself.

Have knowledge of	Know
Held a meeting	Met
Is binding upon	Binds
Made the decision	Decided
Make a payment	Pay
Took notice	Noticed
Was suitable	Suited

Before a state will be al-lowed so to impair a person's liberty, it will be required to show a "compelling justifi-cation."	Before a state may so impair a person's liberty, it must show a "compelling justifica-tion."

The auxiliary little verbs encourage making nouns out of verbs by adding endings like -ion, -ation, -ment, -ence, -ancy and -ent. Thus "examine" becomes "make an examination;" "act" becomes "take action," "encourage" becomes "give encouragement;" and "appear" becomes "make an appearance."

Transitive verbs, that aim at an object, are more forceful than intransitive ones.

Participles can often be substituted for nouns.

Upon performance of certain minimum conditions, the lessee	Upon performing certain minimum conditions, the lessee

The active voice is normally more concise and more forceful than the passive. "The verbs you want to use," says Flesch, "are those that are in the active business of doing verb work." Sir Arthur Quiller-Couch similarly said, "The first virtue, the touchstone of a masculine style is its use of the active verb and the concrete noun." More recently, a writer on legal style has said, "An excellent rule-of-thumb, especially for legal writing is: active voice, indicative mood, present tense." [3]

The passive is not only weaker; it may be so indefinite as to leave the statement ambiguous. It may, for example, leave uncertain who the actor is. Even when the actor is known, the passive takes the spotlight away from him and leaves him in the shade.

The measure was approved by the President in his State of the Union message.	The President in his State of the Union message approved the measure.

Passive is sometimes piled on passive to produce graceless constructions such as the following:

A favorable atmosphere was hoped to be created

The decision was attempted to be taken to the Supreme Court

The question that is proposed to be discussed

3. Miller, On Legal Style, 43 Ky.L.J. 235, 242 (1955).

If you find you have written such a sentence, you can (and should!) recast it, by identifying the actor (unnamed in any of the specimens above), and starting your sentence with him as your subject:

> The proponents hoped to create a favorable atmosphere
>
> Defendant attempted to take the decision to the Supreme Court
>
> We propose to discuss the question of

Make Assertions in Affirmative, Not Negative, Form

The lawyer who wants to make a strong assertion should put it in affirmative form. He should avoid using "not" except to make a denial. Telling us that something "is not" only denies the existence of some thing or quality. It does not posit anything. Language is more forceful when it is positive—that is, when it posits, or affirms something. Even negative ideas can often be expressed in positive form, and thereby given greater forcefulness.

Did not give any consideration to	Ignored
Did not remember	Forgot
Did not take care	Neglected
Not important	Trivial, insignificant
Not very often	Seldom

Not only words and phrases, but sentences, can often be changed from a negative to a positive form.

This provision does not apply to lessees who do not reside on the premises.	This provision applies only to lessees who reside on the premises.

Remember that we are here speaking of how to achieve forcefulness. There may be times when a lawyer does not want to be forceful or positive, when he has reason for saying "not unlawful" instead of "lawful."

Use Specific and Concrete Rather than General and Abstract Terms

Specific terms, we have said, are more precise and clear then general ones; concrete terms more than abstract. They are also more forceful.

The ineffectiveness of general words lies not in any incorrectness. What they say is true, but it is also true of so many other things that they tell us nothing very helpful about their subject in particular. That is why there is no vividness and so no force in words like large, small, fast, slow, good or bad, adequate, reasonable, sufficient. Other words are vague mainly because they are almost wholly subjective: interesting, attractive, inspiring. Abstract words are vague because of their "size;" they are so inclusive that they have no precise boundaries: law, right, wrong, idea, property, equity, reasonableness, fairness, due process, justice. Writing that is stuffed with broad and general nouns is hard to read, mainly because such nouns tend to lack color and life. They also tend to call for equally colorless verbs. They never run, jump, grasp or scratch; they produce, comprise, or refer to. What is worse, they demand mental effort of the reader, to translate the generalities into concrete propositions. The reader who doesn't invest that much effort finds his eyes moving over words that leave no impression. Legal writing deals with complex matters difficult enough to comprehend without being made more difficult by being swathed in fuzzy verbiage.

Lawyers, continually discussing general principles and propositions, are particularly subject to the danger that their discourse may soar to such a high level of abstraction that even judges or other fellow members of the profession will find it difficult to follow. Even more than most writers, therefore, lawyers should work to make their writing specific and concrete, by using examples, details, similes and metaphors that call up vivid and clear-cut images in the reader's mind. They should talk of automobiles rather than "means of transportation," and of green Buick sedans rather than automobiles. They should refer not to a "noise," but to a "crash," "roar," "shriek" or "hum;" not merely to a "traitor," but to a "Judas" or a "Benedict Arnold."

Herbert Spencer said we should avoid such a sentence as:

> In proportion as the manners, customs, and amusements of a nation are cruel and barbarous, the regulations of their penal code will be severe.

Instead we should write:

> In proportion as men delight in battles, bull-fights, and combats of gladiators, will they punish by hanging, burning, and the rack.

A famous sentence of Mr. Justice Holmes [4] illustrates this advice:

> The most stringent protection of free speech would not protect a man in falsely shouting fire in a theater and causing a panic.

In relating facts, do not rest content to say, for example, that "the boy was often beaten by his father." Give us concrete details: "The father often lashed the boy's back with a leather strap that cut the flesh and left permanent scars."

A lawyer should have at his command some tough, hard-hitting words he can call upon when he wants to shock, surprise, or express strong feeling. But he must sense the line between toughness and crudity. Tough words can be found that are not crude or offensive.

Do Not Qualify Unnecessarily

When you can make an absolute statement, do so. You can hardly make a stronger statement than that something is *always* or *never* so; that every A is always B, or that no A is ever B. Unqualified assertions such as the following are very effective:

> We have been unable to find a single instance of a criminal trial conducted in camera in any federal, state or municipal court during the history of this country. Nor have we found any record of even one such criminal trial in England since abolition of the Court of Star Chamber in 1641.

> Every other state in the union has found it possible to regulate the professions of architecture and engineering without being nearly as indefinite as Arizona. Assuming for the sake of discussion that these professions are constitutionally subject to some regulation, it would be easy to do better than Arizona has done, and hard to do worse.

4. Schenck v. United States, 249 U. S. 47, 52, 39 S.Ct. 247, 63 L.Ed. 470 (1919).

Unfortunately, in our world of relativity, a lawyer can seldom make an absolute statement. When he thinks he can, he had better examine it to make sure it is really true. More often than not, it will have to be qualified. But because the need for exactness so often calls for qualifications, lawyers are likely to fall into the habit of qualifying everything they say. They put "it seems," "apparently," or "it is indicated that" even into the most innocuous sentences. They timidly back away from saying that B is "as good as" A, and prefer B "compares favorably with" A. They may even say:

> The report you filed does not seem to include a statement of your income for the past year.

Either it does or it doesn't. Why not omit "seem to"?

> An impression is being gained, however, of how things should *not* continue. This concerns the way in which community facilities have had the dangerous tendency to view man and his problems in a fragmented, overspecialized, and jealously institutionalized way.

The writer of these lines was not trying coolly and impartially to narrate facts. He was arguing for a program. Why then doesn't he put his argument to us in a strong and positive way? Instead of saying, impersonally and passively, that "an impression is being gained," he should tell us in direct and forthright words what he wants us to believe or to do:

> One thing we do know, however: we should stop doing some of the things we now do. We should stop looking at man and his problems in a fragmented, overspecialized and jealously institutionalized way.

The last words, "in a fragmented, overspecialized and jealously institutionalized way," should also be rephrased to say more vividly what the writer means. We cannot do that for him because the words are too amorphous for us to translate into anything specific.

Law students may hesitate to be positive, because they think that these wordy circumlocutions are more formal and dignified than plain talk. But dignity does not demand a debilitating verbosity.

Use Figures of Speech

The most vivid way to make a point is by using a figure of speech. Similes, metaphors and other figures are a kind of shorthand. They enable us to say more in fewer words, and to say it with vitality and color.

Mr. Justice Harlan in 1896, arguing that the Constitution forbids any distinctions based on race or color, said, "Our Constitution is colorblind." Chief Justice Stone, in a memorandum to his associates on the subject of dissents, suggested that it was not necessary to play every fly speck in the music. Oliver Wendell Holmes, in The Common Law, written before he became a judge, argued that the distinction between intentional and unintentional wrongs must have been recognized even in primitive law. "Even a dog," he wrote, "distinguishes between being stumbled over and being kicked." On another occasion he said that "Deep-seated preferences cannot be argued about—you cannot argue a man into liking a glass of beer." Illustrating a general proposition with a specific symbol in this way is a highly effective stylistic device.

An apt illustrative statement is likely to impress the reader more than anything else you say on the subject. We all like analogies, and indeed are often willing to accept them too readily and extend them too far. The analogy is such a delightfully easy device to use that the writer who discovers it may be tempted to use it to oversimplify intrinsically difficult concepts. Nothing in law is so apt to mislead, said Lord Mansfield, as a metaphor. From the proposition that free speech "would not protect a man in falsely shouting fire in a theater," the conclusion may appear all too obvious that free speech does not protect a man who criticizes government policy in the conduct of a war.

In law, figures of speech are sometimes used to refer to legal doctrines, rules or theories. Conflicts of laws has a "bootstrap doctrine" and a "center of gravity" theory. An important provision of the Bankruptcy Act, giving broad powers to the bankruptcy trustee, is called the "strong-arm" clause. In constitutional law we had, years ago, the "silver platter" concept; when it was repudiated, we had law review comments with such titles as "The Tarnished Silver Platter."

Simile

The most obvious figure of speech is the simile, which describes or illustrates one thing by saying that it is like another: "The brain is like the hand," said Mr. Justice Brandeis. "It grows with using." A good simile portrays some striking, concrete or picturesque aspect of the subject. It lends vividness to abstract subjects. Conjuring up a good simile calls for imagination. The comparison should be between objects of such different classes that the reader gets a slight shock of surprise that things so unlike should have one point in common. We find pleasure in resemblances we had not seen before. Mr. Justice Jackson made much use of simile: [5]

> There is no such thing as an achieved liberty; like electricity, there can be no substantial storage and it must be generated as it is enjoyed, or the lights go out.

> Unless this Court is willing to say that citizenship of the United States means at least this much to the citizen, then our heritage of constitutional privileges and immunities is only a promise to the ear to be broken to the hope, a teasing illusion like a munificent bequest in a pauper's will.

> We granted certiorari, and in this Court the parties changed positions as nimbly as if dancing a quadrille.

> If ever we are justified in reading a statute, not narrowly as through a keyhole, but in the broad light of the evils it aimed at and the good it hoped for, it is here.

> The principle then lies about like a loaded weapon ready for the hand of any authority that can bring forward a plausible claim of an urgent need.

When you use a simile, use it without apology. Don't qualify it with "as it were," or "so to speak," or—worst of all—"if you please." Don't say the thing you are discussing is "somewhat like" your simile; say it is "like."

---

5. The quotations are from: The Task of Maintaining Our Liberties, 39 A.B.A.J. 962 (1953); Edwards v. California, 314 U.S. 160, 186, 62 S. Ct. 164, 86 L.Ed. 119 (1941); Orloff v. Willoughby, 345 U.S. 83, 87, 73 S.Ct. 534, 97 L.Ed. 842 (1953); dissenting opinion in United States ex rel. Marcus v. Hess, 317 U.S. 537, 557, 63 S.Ct. 379, 87 L.Ed. 443 (1943); dissenting opinion in Korematsu v. United States, 323 U.S. 214, 246, 65 S.Ct. 193, 89 L.Ed. 194 (1944).

Metaphor

A metaphor is stronger than a simile; it not only compares one thing with another but identifies the two. The simile pictures and illustrates, and so makes for clarity, but the metaphor is more striking in effect and so is more forceful. The ability to create metaphor, said Aristotle, is the surest sign of originality. It is as useful a gift for the legal writer as for any other.

When we say that nominal damages are "a peg" on which to hang costs, we are using a metaphor. Abraham Lincoln was doing the same when he said that the patent system "added the fuel of interest to the fire of genius." He also used earthy metaphor to express himself on responsibility at the polls:

> It is the people's business. The election is in their hands. If they turn their backs to the fire and get scorched in the rear, they'll find they have got to sit on the blister.

Mr. Justice Clark used the device to criticize a decision from which he dissented: [6]

> Although there are many ways to kill a cat, drowning remains the most favored. The Court applies this method to this conviction—drowning it by watering down the Findings of Fact and Conclusions of Law. By attributing to them a diluted meaning, the judgments of the District Court and the Court of Appeals are rendered insupportable.

Metaphors take several forms. One of the most common is that which takes the part for the whole, the thing for its use, or the effect for the cause.[7]

> The pen is mightier than the sword.
>
> The battle of Waterloo was won on the playing fields of Eton.

---

6. Jones v. United States, 357 U.S. 493, 500, 78 S.Ct. 1253, 2 L.Ed.2d 1514 (1958).

7. Although these figures of speech may be regarded as aspects of metaphor, rhetoricians usually classify them as different. A reference to part for the whole is technically called synecdoche; effect for the cause, container for the thing contained, etc., is metonymy.

The purpose of the federal Filled Milk Act, said one court,[8] is "to forbid the competition of a cocoanut grove with the American cow."

A trope is a one-word metaphor. "The bite of law," said Mr. Justice Frankfurter, "is in its enforcement." He also spoke of "the slippery slope of due process," and referred to an easy case as "a horse soon curried." Mr. Justice Holmes told us that when he began, the law was "a ragbag of details."

There are dangers in using figures of speech. They must be used with discrimination and restraint. One good one is better than several mediocre ones—or even several good ones. Too many mental pictures flashed before the reader in rapid succession become wearying. Rudolph Flesch says, "Do not use metaphors without an explanation."[9] Lawyers write for persons who can usually understand a metaphor, if it is apt, without any explanation. But Flesch's advice should be taken as a warning. Ask yourself whether the reader is likely to misunderstand your reference. If there is any danger that he may, better make it clearer.

In using metaphors one must pay attention to their literal meaning. Failure to keep this literal meaning in mind leads to ludicrous metaphors:

> Only a handful of spectators
> Our biggest bottleneck

Failure to remember the literal meaning also leads to ludicrous mixing of metaphors, such as that of the speaker who said, "We build castles in the air, the bubble bursts, and leaves naught but ashes in our hands." Or the state official who said that the record in his case spoke "louder than any smoke screen."

> Though often the target of storms of criticism, the Supreme Court has been the keystone of our constitutional system.

8. Carolene Products Co. v. Wallace, 27 F.Supp. 110, 113 (D.C.D.C.1939).

9. Flesch, The Art of Plain Talk 105 (1946).

Storms do not have targets and keystones are not targets of storms, nor of anything else.

Mr. Justice Harlan, dissenting in a leading case on the constitutionality of obscenity statutes, expressed the fear that the majority opinion "paints with such a broad brush" that "it may result in a loosening of the tight reins" that courts should hold on enforcement of such statutes.[10]   Two good metaphors, but badly mixed.

Metaphors fade fast.   A hackneyed comparison, faded from overuse, calls up no mental image, but slides unnoticed through the mind.   "To wrestle with a problem" no longer makes us think of a man wrestling;   neither "saddled with debts" nor "debt-ridden" makes us think of a man with a saddle or a rider on his back.   To convey strong feeling we need strong words. But words that once were strong but now are weak from age and overwork won't do.   We need words that have the strength and freshness of youth.

Clichés and Platitudes

A good figure of speech is likely so to take the popular fancy that it becomes worn out from overuse.   Such a faded expression we call a cliché.   A cliché is a word or phrase that once was a fresh or novel way of expressing a thought, which has lost its freshness and perhaps even precise meaning from being overworked.   A platitude is simply a dull or insipid remark.   If a cliché is a has-been, a platitude never was.   It is and always was "weary, stale, flat and unprofitable," and when uttered with an air of solemn importance is annoying.   "Poeta nascitur, non fit" was an original remark, once.   But over the centuries, so many kinds of people have been said to be born, not made, that the expression has long ago lost its bloom.   "To make the supreme sacrifice" was a moving and effective way to refer to dying for a cause, the first time it was used.   Today, it is so hackneyed that one uses it only to evoke derision.

10.   Roth v. United States, 354 U.S. 476, 496, 77 S.Ct. 1304, 1 L.Ed.2d 1498 (1957).

Thousands of these stale expressions still pass as currency in our language. Here are only some of many that turn up frequently in legal writing:

Acid test, the
Add(ing) insult to injury
Agree to disagree
All things to all men
All walks of life
Armed to the teeth
Auspicious occasion
Be that as it may
Beat about the bush
Birds of a feather
Bitter end
Blessing in disguise
Blind leading the blind
Bone of contention
Built upon sand
Burning question
By no manner of means
Call a spade a spade
Can safely say
Cold light of reason
Considered opinion that
Conspicuous by its absence
Courage of his convictions
Damn with faint praise
Deadly earnest
Death's door
Devoutly hope
Distinction without a difference
Do a good turn to
Draw to a close
Every effort is being made
Far be it from me
First saw the light of day
Follow in the footsteps of
Force to be reckoned with
Foregone conclusion
From the bottom of one's heart

Go to the other extreme
Good men and true (of a jury)
Grievous error
Height of absurity
If the truth were known
Ill-gotten gains
Implicit confidence
In no uncertain manner (terms, voice)
In the last analysis
In the affirmative (negative)
Incontrovertible fact
Inevitable conclusion
Irony of fate
It stands to reason
Kill two birds with one stone
Know full well
Last but not least (this is *not* freshened up by changing it to "last but by no means least")
Law-abiding citizens
Lay down the law to
Light on the subject, to shed
Long arm of the law
Look facts in the face
Make a clean breast of it
Make a mountain out of a molehill
Matter of life and death
Might and main
More dead than alive
More in sorrow than in anger
Needs no introduction
Neither rhyme nor reason
New lease on life
Not a shadow of doubt
Not wisely but too well

Of the first magnitude
On the right side of the law
Path of least resistance
Pious fraud
Pure and simple; purely and
     simply
Put all one's eggs in one basket
Sanctity of the home
Step in the right direction
Stern reality

Thing of the past
Throw the baby out with the
     bath
Time and time again
To all intents and purposes
Weigh in the balance
Wholesome respect
Worldly wisdom
Year in, year out

Some common expressions do not even make sense. "Dead as a doornail" is meaningless. "Happy as a lark" is not much better. What we mean is happy as a lark sounds (to us). Others once had meaning, which, however, has been lost to most people who use them today:

At first blush
A great deal
At one fell swoop
At loggerheads
A windfall

In the lurch
Rack and ruin
Salt of the earth
In a trice
Turn the tables

Some writers stumble into these clichés without thinking about what they are saying. They start to say "safe," and "safe and sound" rolls out, by free association. They say "pomp" and for no good reason add "and circumstance." That's the trouble with habit; it makes us bring up the same response with little concern for sense.

> After Nebbia v. New York, due process as a restraint on legislative experimentation in economic matters was dead "ere its prime."

Nothing the writer had said before this sentence indicated that he thought the concept he was discussing deserved to live and grow in vigor. It apparently had reached "its prime." The writer added the words in quotation marks apparently merely because they came to mind and their sound pleased him. The fact that they made no sense in the context seems not to have occurred to him.

The good writer tries to stay away from these faded phrases. It isn't easy. They are so much in use that we sink unnoticingly into the habit of echoing them without thinking what they mean, if anything. In infancy, we learn to say many words before we understand the ideas for which they stand; we repeat them without much more thinking than a parrot's. The habit persists into later life; we continue to pick up words from others, and we assume that because they have become familiar to us they are proper, even though attention to their literal meaning would make us see that they are empty or fatuous. We could eliminate a vast amount of verbiage if we would only consider what we are saying, and ask whether it has any clear meaning—or any meaning at all. And if we would pull out the hackneyed, foolish and vacuous stereotypes and use fresh and meaningful words instead, we would add vividness and vigor to our style.

Of course, if one can give a new twist to an old saw, that is quite different. "Not worth the paper it's written on" is a drab cliché; but it sports a bright new coat of paint when, for example, Judge Biddle of Philadelphia tells us that in his court, " 'the unwritten law' is not worth the paper it isn't written on."

Vogue words are faddish clichés, words that allure people who think they are modish terms for the newest concepts in scientific or other thinking, but who are insensitive to the fact that overuse has already robbed them of any freshness they may have had. Feedback, input, interface and viable are examples.

Use Reiteration

One of the most obvious ways of getting emphasis is to repeat a word or phrase that you want to stress. "Repetition," said Sir Walter Raleigh (The Oxford professor of English, 1861–1922, not the explorer, 1552–1618), "is the strongest generator of emphasis known to language."

President Lincoln wrote a letter to Horace Greeley in 1862, outlining the policies he was pursuing in the conduct of the Civil War. In the course of it he said:

> My paramount object in this struggle is to save the Union, and not either to save or to destroy slavery.
>
> If I could save the Union without freeing any slave, I would do it; if I could save it by freeing some and leaving others alone, I would also do that.

What I do about slavery and the colored race, I do because I believe it helps to save the Union; and what I forbear, I forbear because I do not believe it would help to save the Union.

I shall do less whenever I shall believe that what I am doing hurts the cause; and I shall do more whenever I shall believe doing more will help the cause.

I shall try to correct errors where shown to be errors, and I shall adopt any new views as fast as they shall appear to be true views.

Many other examples of the use of reiteration to get emphasis could be cited. A few follow:

Men are born into the State, are members of the State, must obey the laws enacted by the State, in time of danger must come to the defense of the State, must, if necessary, hazard their lives for the State.—Lyman Abbott.

[The forefathers] knew what emergencies were, knew the pressures they engender for authoritative action, knew, too, how they afford a ready pretext for usurpation. We may also suspect that they suspected that emergency powers would tend to kindle emergencies.—Mr. Justice Jackson.[11]

Somewhat akin to reiteration is the use of several words in place of one. Eliminating unnecessary words is a virtue, but whether certain words are necessary or not may depend on the context. The three words, "but only if" say no more than the word "if" alone. "If," however, is a very short word and one that carries no emphasis. In a sentence where it seems likely to be overlooked, and where the writer considers the word so important that it should not be overlooked, he can underscore it for the reader by saying "but only if." Similarly, while "but" means the same as "however," the latter may be preferable for emphasis, simply because it is a longer word.

11. Concurring in Youngstown Sheet   579, 650, 72 S.Ct. 863, 96 L.Ed. 1153
    & Tube Co. v. Sawyer, 343 U.S.   (1952).

III. ARRANGING WORDS FOR EMPHASIS

Put Words to be Stressed at the Beginning and End of Sentences

Emphasis is largely determined by the placement of words within the sentence, and of sentences within the paragraph. The positions that carry the most emphasis are (1) the end, and (2) the beginning. At the beginning, we are attentive to see whether the new thought promises to be interesting; as we near the end we look forward to seeing it brought to its completion. Professor Barrett Wendell, endeavoring to express this point, wrote: "Be sure that your sentences end with words that deserve the distinction you give them." Only after writing it did he notice that his sentence violated the rule it laid down; it placed in the positions of distinction the unimportant words "be" and "them." What were the most important words? Clearly, "end" and "distinction." He therefore rearranged his sentence to put these words at the beginning and end respectively: "End with words that deserve distinction." [12]

Sometimes, of course, this cannot be done without doing violence to the natural word order. But if you try, you will be surprised to see how often you can find an arrangement that puts the words to be stressed in their proper places and sounds better than your first version. Consider the words, "Faith, hope and charity, and the greatest of these is charity." The emphasis would be lost if written, "and charity is the greatest of these."

In a sentence made up of parallel members of different values, they should be arranged so as to progress from the lesser to the greater.

He is a murderer, a liar and a thief.	He is a liar, a thief and a murderer.
Their only choice was to be killed or to obey.	Their only choice was to obey or be killed.

The part of a sentence that carries the least emphasis is the area between the beginning and the end. That is where to put terms like "however," "nevertheless," "for example," and "of

12. Wendell, English Composition 102–103 (1918).

course." If you want to emphasize such a term, put it first, but otherwise put it somewhere in the middle.

However, personal belongings are exempt.	Personal belongings, however, are exempt.
Nevertheless, defendant continued with the work.	The defendant nevertheless continued with the work.
For example, a summer cabin is considered a residence.	A summer cabin, for example, is considered a residence.
Of course, this rule is subject to exceptions.	This rule is of course subject to exceptions.

The middle is also the place to bury subordinate thoughts— and those you do not want to emphasize.

A grammatically subordinate clause may nevertheless contain the thought you want to give most emphasis. If so, put it at the end. Compare the shift in emphasis in the following two sentences. Which is the more optimistic? Which the more doubting?

This, if the jury believes it, is a perfect defense.	This is a perfect defense, if the jury will believe it.

A restrictive phrase or clause, such as one beginning with "at least," is almost sure to make a weak and anti-climactic ending:

Such an interpretation of the statute would render it grossly unjust, at least in some cases.	At least in some cases, such an interpretation of the statute would render it grossly unjust.

Phrases or clauses beginning with "not" also make weak endings:

The rule we ask the court to adopt would promote corporate responsibility, not recklessness as plaintiff contends.	The rule we ask the court to adopt would not encourage recklessness as plaintiff contends, but would promote corporate responsibility.

As the illustration above shows, ending with a "not" clause may give the place of greatest emphasis not to your own contention but to your opponent's.

Weak words make a weak ending. A monosyllable is usually a weak word.

As a result, a donee beneficiary may recover in an action today.	As a result, a donee beneficiary (in an action) today may recover.
A creditor beneficiary may recover also.	A creditor beneficiary may also recover.
We have had no success as yet.	As yet, we have had no success.
We have been disappointed ever since.	Ever since, we have been disappointed.

To put emphasis on a modifier, put it after the term modified:

He deliberately committed this crime.	He committed this crime deliberately.

Unemphatic words at the beginning of a sentence get you off to a weak start:

By such a rule, the court could establish the means by which businessmen could find what their rights were in such transactions.	This rule would enable businessmen to find what their rights were in such transactions.
Because the judgment was affirmed it does not follow that this particular contention was sound.	Affirmance of the judgment does not mean that . . . .

Chapter 3 pointed out that introductory terms such as "there are," "there were" and "it is" are wordy. They are also weakening, because they are unemphatic and because they often lead to overuse of nouns and weak verbs.

There are more men killed by relatives or acquaintances than by strangers.	More men are killed by relatives or acquaintances than by strangers.
It is the contention of the petitioner	Petitioner contends

In a two-part sentence, the natural emphasis falls on the part that comes at the end. That therefore is the place to put the more important proposition. A lawyer can minimize his opponent's argument and emphasize his own by putting the rule or proposition that is against him in a subordinate clause and ending with the limitation or opposing principle that he wants to emphasize. Mr. Justice Douglas did this when he said: [13]

> And while a search without a warrant is, within limits, permissible if incident to a lawful arrest, if an arrest without a warrant is to support an incidental search, it must be made with probable cause.

This puts the emphasis on the point he wanted to make: that arrest without warrant must be on probable cause. Consider also these two arrangements of the same words:

> The prosecutrix, although she testified that her assailant had worn a blue sweater, could not give any description of his features and failed to identify defendant in the line-up.

> Although the prosecutrix could not give any description of her assailant's features and failed to identify the defendant in the line-up, she testified that her assailant had worn a blue sweater.

The left-hand wording is obviously more favorable for the defense. The right-hand version emphasizes the sweater, and would be appropriate for introducing an argument showing, for example, that defendant was in fact wearing a blue sweater at the time in question.

Suppose your opponent's brief has argued that a certain rule of law established by case A (which you rely on as a precedent) has been weakened if not largely overruled by case B. You want to rebut that assertion and argue that the cases can be reconciled. Which of the three following ways of saying it is best for your purpose?

> The two cases can be reconciled, although they differ somewhat on their facts.

13. Henry v. United States, 361 U.S. 98, 102, 80 S.Ct. 168, 4 L.Ed.2d 134 (1959).

> Although they differ somewhat on their facts, the two cases can be reconciled.
>
> Although the two cases can be reconciled, they differ somewhat on their facts.

Inversion of the natural order of a sentence is an effective way to get emphasis by position. The normal English sentence order is (1) the subject, preceded or followed by its modifiers; (2) the verb; (3) the object; and (4) the predicate modifiers. Changing this order emphasizes whatever words you remove from their normal position. Since the normal place for the subject is at the beginning, putting it there gives it no special emphasis. It can be given such emphasis by moving it to the end:

> The greatest man I ever met was Franklin D. Roosevelt.

Conversely, if the end of the sentence is the natural place for a word, it is not emphasized by leaving it there, without using some contrivance such as interpolating phrases or clauses to build suspense. It can be given emphasis by moving it to the beginning:

> Liberty he seeks.
>
> Courage it is that sustains a man.

Phrases can be given emphasis in the same way:

> With malice toward none; with charity for all; with firmness in the right, as God gives us to see the right, let us strive on . . ..

As is true of other devices, this should not be overdone. Used too much, it becomes a rather boring mannerism and ceases to achieve its purpose.

Emphasis can be given a word by setting it off with an interpolation following it.

> You, being a businessman, recognize better than most men the value of a good credit rating.

If no such heavy accent is intended to be put on the word "you," it is poor writing to use this form by mere blundering. Thus:

> You, being a businessman, recognize the value of a good credit rating.

> Being a businessman, you recognize the value of a good credit rating.

Even subordinate clauses can be improved by putting important words in the important positions:

In the absence of a show-ing of the essential nature of the information you have asked for,	In the absence of a showing that the infor-mation you have asked for is essential,

Although the passive is usually less emphatic than the active
voice, the passive may sometimes supply a way to get emphasis
where you want it. You may, for example, want to emphasize
the name of the doer by putting it at the end of the sentence:

> Some labor legislation has been enacted by the states, but
> the more important controls are those enacted by the Federal
> Government.

> The gun could only have been fired by this man.

You may want to emphasize the deed rather than the doer or
the recipient:

> For many are called, but few are chosen.

> All four were indicted, but only one was convicted.

When you want to put emphasis on the object or recipient,
and cannot do so by putting it at the end, you can move it to the
second most emphatic position in the sentence, the beginning:

> The fallacy of defendant's argument was pointed out by
> this Court in Patton v. Peck.

In the sentence above, the word desired to be emphasized is "fallacy." But it cannot be put at the end, for it is followed by "of
defendant's argument." With the aid of the passive, it is therefore put first.

The periodic sentence is a device by which the normal sentence order is distorted or interrupted for the sake of emphasis.
Completion of the thought, to prevent the reader's attention
from wandering and to heighten the dramatic effect, is suspended, through subordinate clauses, adverbial modifiers and participial or adjective phrases, until the end.

In periodic and other long sentences, emphasis can be obtained by developing a good ear for sentence rhythm.[14]   By observing where the cadence of the sentence causes the verbal emphasis to fall, the writer with a sense of rhythm can use this natural stress to emphasize his key words.

The periodic sentence is a stylized device that may tempt students into fine writing.   Is the following a successful or an unsuccessful specimen?

> I resent the apostles of punishment-for-its-own-sake arrogating to themselves words like "moral" and "justice," and implying that those who scorn their metaphysics are unconcerned with moral values.   Surely the feeling of concern for the offender as a human being, the desire to save him from a criminal career and to help him redeem himself as a member of the human family, the even wider concern to prevent others from falling into criminality by searching out the influences and conditions that produce those frustrating and embittering defeats, degradations, and humiliations of the human spirit that turn a man against his fellow men, the effort, therefore, to give men the advantages that will help them keep their feet on the right path—better education, more healthful dwellings, readier aid for the casualties of sickness, accident, and failures of employment—surely this is not a less moral ideal than that which knows only one measure of morality, an eye for an eye and a tooth for a tooth.

An important means for gaining emphasis is moving to a climax.   Arranging words, phrases, clauses or sentences in an ascending series causes a continual heightening of interest.   The novelist Thomas Wolfe (1900–1938) used this device in *Of Time and the River*:

> If a man has a talent and cannot use it, he has failed.   If he has a talent and uses only half of it, he has partly failed. If he has a talent and learns somehow to use the whole of it, he has gloriously succeeded, and won a satisfaction and a triumph few men ever know.

So much do we like things to wind up with a grand finale that we are disappointed and a little annoyed when they end not with a bang but a sputter.

---

14. On sentence rhythm, see post,
pp. 314–316.

Anti-climax can, however, be used to gain emphasis by reverse English, so to speak. You may want to use anti-climax deliberately, to shock or amuse your reader by the unexpected or the incongruous: "The chief justice," wrote Macaulay, "was rich, quiet, and infamous."

Use Parallel Construction

Parallel sentence structure is a kind of repetition, in which the pattern or arrangement of words in one sentence or part of a sentence is repeated in another. The expressions so balanced are thereby strongly accented.

> First in war, first in peace, first in the hearts of his countrymen.

Students frequently fail to make use of balanced sentences, perhaps because their attention has never been called to the form, or because they mistakenly think they should avoid such reiteration. They write sentences such as those in the left-hand column below, which obviously should be put into parallel form, as at the right.

The buyer must be reasonable and act in good faith.	The buyer must act reasonably and in good faith.
In the former situation, the courts have held for the defendant, while in the latter the plaintiff has been successful.	In the former situation, the courts have held for the defendant; in the latter, for the plaintiff.
Filing under the Uniform Commercial Code is not designed to give detailed information, but only that some of the debtor's assets are already encumbered.	Filing under the Uniform Commercial Code is designed to give, not detailed information, but only information that some of the debtor's assets are already encumbered.
Plaintiff contends that he had no duty to exercise the option but that the duty was on the transferee.	Plaintiff contends that the duty to exercise the option rested not on him but on the transferee.

In enumerating or listing a series of points or items, parallel construction is needed not only for emphasis but also for grammatical consistency.

The amendments include a new penalty clause, additional remedies for individual members and create a wholly new category of offenses.	The amendments include a new penalty clause, additional remedies for individual members and a wholly new category of offenses.
The congressional investigation was concerned with two main ends, the first, in aid of legislation, and the second of holding the executive branch of the government to a strict accountability.	The congressional investigation was concerned with two main ends: first, aiding legislation, and second, holding the executive branch of the government to a strict accountability.

As the last example illustrates, punctuation can be called upon to help in enumeration. The same consistency is required in listing a series of items, or in outlining:

    a. Due process

    b. Equal protection

    c. Whether entry without a warrant constituted an unreasonable search and seizure

    d. Did the officer have reasonable ground to believe a felony had been committed?

Here a and b consist of mere subject headings. C introduces a question with the word "whether," and d is a straight question. All should be put in the same form. If c and d are to conform to a and b, they should be changed to similar short titles, such as "c. Search and seizure, d. Arrest without a warrant." If the others are to conform to c, all should start with the word "whether." If they are to conform to d, all should be stated as questions.

The shift from the one form to another is sometimes made because the writer feels the catch line is sufficient for some of his items, but that a fuller statement is needed for one or more. But usually this can be had without changing the form. Thus c could be put into parallel construction with a and b by some such phrasing as "c. Entry without warrant as constituting unreasonable search," or "Search and seizure: entry without warrant." If a certain item does not lend itself to this treatment, the others may have to be conformed to it.

Parallel construction is effective not only to gain emphasis but also for other rhetorical purposes. We shall therefore say more about it in our final chapter.

Exercises

Correct the faulty parallelism in each of the following sentences:

Not only does the act violate the commerce clause but also the due process clause.

Because time is so short, the company will either submit a very simple plan or none at all.

The proposal neither complies with the terms of the contract nor with the statute.

The principal objections are that the federal legislation has pre-empted this field of regulation and because the state regulation is actually in conflict with the federal.

Before today, our judicial opinions have refrained from drawing invidious distinctions between those who believe in no religion and those who do believe.

If and when my son marries, should he choose to live with his wife on the premises, and if my daughter decides to discontinue living on the premises, then my son shall be obliged to make suitable provision for her maintenance and support elsewhere, so long as she shall remain unmarried.

Chapter 7

ORGANIZATION

Some aspects of your writing may improve after you are in practice. Your vocabulary may increase and you may develop tactful ways to say what you mean without unnecessary bluntness. But orderliness and logical arrangement you will either learn in college or not at all. A logical mind is almost invariably the product of rigorous training in school or college.

Master Your Subject

Just as water cannot rise above its source, so you cannot write more clearly than you think. "Thought and speech," said Cardinal Newman, "are inseparable from each other. Matter and expression are parts of one: style is a thinking out into language."

Ambiguity caused by muddled thinking can be avoided by learning to think straight and by taking time to think carefully. Painstaking care in thinking through both what you want to say and how to say it will help you avoid the blurry kind of writing that carelessness produces and give you greater clarity, conciseness and pungency.

To write clearly you must not only have gathered your material and arranged it in some sort of order; you must also have thought about it, perceived the relationship of one decision, rule or fact-situation to another, evaluated the importance or unimportance of one point over another, decided which one or two are primary, and worked out a logical plan of presentation. The novice, after doing his research, may be eager to get at his writing, without first digesting, organizing and thinking through the implications of his material. But time spent in thinking, before you even start to prepare an outline, is time well spent. It may be the most worth-while of all the time spent on the project. There is no more pathetic illusion than the trusting conviction that ideas will come, if we just start writing.

Psychologists have learned a good deal about how this sitting-and-thinking works. This is not the place for an explication of the psychological process of the structuring or recentering of thoughts; it will suffice for our purpose to put it in terms of the old cliché about failing to see the forest for the trees. The man who has just been collecting data for a legal paper is deep amidst the trees. The sitting-and-thinking process is one of backing away and trying to see the forest as a whole. To see an object whole, and see it clearly, one must have the right perspective, the right focus. Thinking over the principles and rules of the cases or other materials you have been absorbing is a way of getting them into proper focus, so that you can perceive how they group themselves, with some standing forth as dominant in the whole picture, and others retiring into the background of less important detail. Only when you yourself clearly see what is central or significant can you get your reader to focus on those points, instead of dispersing his attention over a mass of details in which nothing stands out. This is what Robert Louis Stevenson meant when he said, "If a man can group his ideas, he is a good writer."

A particularly bad and particularly common form of writing without seeing the subject in perspective is that which takes us through the facts of a series of cases without telling us what they are intended to prove or what the writer's own conclusion is. Case after case is briefed for us, and the court's holding summarized, but each case is left standing alone, without any thread of argument connecting it to the others. There is no thread because the writer has apparently not yet made up his own mind. He is really writing notes to himself, which eventually he will cogitate over and discuss. But this he should do before he writes the first word.

Another common product of writing without perspective is the uncritical exposition of a statute, as in a letter or opinion to a client, merely rephrasing the statutory language, sentence by sentence, much as an interpreter translates from one language into another. This is a shallow and unanalytic mental operation, which calls only for reading comprehension, and comprehension on a low and relaxed level, allowing the mind to be led wherever the written words lead. But the lawyer's function is not merely so to translate statutory jargon into layman's English. His task requires reflective thinking controlled by purpose, the purpose of giving the particular reader what he needs. To do this, he must first think about the general import of the statute, its major provisions and its scheme of control. Secondly, he must consider how these bear upon the client, his operations and his concerns. Then he must consider how to explain these to the client in language he can understand.

If a statute starts by providing that any person who violates any of its provisions shall be guilty of a felony and upon conviction be subject to certain penalties specifically spelled out, it is not purposive thinking for a lawyer trying to give a client the import of the act to start by spelling out the penalties he might encounter by violating it. The client's reaction to such an introduction is likely to be an alarmed or annoyed "Please! I'm not planning any violation. All I want to know is what I should do or not do to stay out of trouble." A man who knows what he is trying to do writes differently—right from the start—from one who does not, just as a man who knows where he is walking follows a different—a straighter and shorter path from that of a man feeling his way in the dark. The writer who knows where he is going will continually point up the relevance and significance of the data he presents, so that the reader always knows what stage of the development he has reached.

Writing is a Peep-Hole Art

The writer can present to his reader only one word or phrase at a time; the eye cannot take them in any faster. A painter presents his canvas whole, and the viewer can get his impression by standing back and seeing the whole at one time. But this is impossible with writing. The writer's art is more like that of the motion picture director, who must present one frame after another in rapid succession. Both must present their glimpses in such order that the audience can follow. The order in which the glimpses are presented is therefore vitally important.

One writer[1] has put the thought in another way:

Word must follow word in an orderly procession; and when the last word has filed into its place, the whole army should

1. Quoted in Robbins, An Approach to Composition Through Psychology 84–85 (1929).

be found drawn up so as to present exactly the formation from which it started. Suppose a regiment, massed in the form of a square, is ordered to pass through an opening too narrow to admit more than one man at a time, and to form upon the other side in the same square formation. As the men pass from the one place through the opening into another, so the words must pass from your mind by ear or eye into the mind of another; and as the men break off from the square, rank by rank, in a certain order, and fall in again in the same order, so must the words progress from your mind and rearrange themselves in a certain order. Then, when the process is complete, they will be found drawn up in the mind of another, in the same formation as that in which they are drawn up in your own mind.

Follow an Outline

Orderliness of presentation calls for a scheme of development, an outline.

The development must march in a straight line. Sentences and paragraphs must follow one another in a sensible and understandable way. Each sentence must be a step, each paragraph a point, closer to the conclusion. If sentences or paragraphs are inserted where they interrupt the line of development, or where they have no relevance to what precedes or follows, coherence is lost.

We are all optimistic enough to nurse the conviction that if we just start writing, the material will fall into place as we go. It won't. The material a lawyer has to work with is typically a confusing mass of refractory and contradictory data. If you start to write without having first reduced it to order, your writing will ramble; it will ramble just as badly and as obviously as would your speech if you undertook to talk extemporaneously on a subject without first organizing your ideas. But if you have thought through your material, so that principles and conclusions have taken shape in your mind, some sort of outline will also have suggested itself. Once you know what you want to say, the orderly way of saying it will not be hard to determine.

Time spent on an outline is time saved later. An outline is a kind of map, on which you can see the relation and the coordination of the parts of your material. An opinion of 1000 words or a brief of 5000 words is not easily looked at whole, to see whether the several points are placed in logical order and given proper emphasis, with the most important highlighted and the less important properly subordinated. Even if this could be done, making changes after the manuscript is written is awkward. Moving a point or a paragraph in the completed text is much more trouble than moving a sentence or clause in the outline.

If you try to write without an adequately detailed outline, you find yourself trying to do three things at once: with every detail that presents itself to your mind, you must decide (1) whether or not to include it, (2) if so, how and where to fit it in, and (3) how fully to develop it. Now, to ask your mind to make all these decisions in the course of the actual process of writing is unfair and almost sure to prove disappointing. If you have any warmth of interest in what you are writing, any strong conviction or emotion, you should be free to concentrate on the creative effort to put your conviction or your feeling on paper without at the same time having to think about the logical organization of the material. The stimulation of seeing your argument grow as you write may sweep organization out of your mind and destroy your perspective and your value judgment. It may fire you to expand a point far beyond its importance in your whole case. An outline holds you in line; it helps you keep in mind the relative importance of the immediate point and the proper tone to maintain in discussing it. It helps you keep a grip on your subject.

An outline may be made up of complete sentences or merely of key words or phrases. Complete sentences are sometimes necessary to help recall what one intended to say. A sub-heading labelled "procedure" or "due process" is so indefinite that even the writer may not remember what he meant. Even if it helps him recall the point in a general way, he may not recall some of the implications he then had in mind. Such vague and general topic-words and phrases are so hazy that the writer may not have had anything specific in mind when he wrote them down. An outline made up of such indefinite phrases is not very helpful. When a writer's ideas are hazy and he does not know precisely what he wants to say, writing is an unsatisfying chore. If he will prepare his outline in the form of declarative sentences, he will have to know what he wants to say before he can put it down, and once having put it down, he will have a reminder.

Headings and subheadings are common in legal writing. In briefs, not only is each of the major parts indicated by its appropriate heading, such as "Statement of the Issues," "Statement of Facts," or "Argument," but each point in the argument is given a heading. In other documents, such as legal memoranda, similar mechanical aids can be used. The run-in paragraph heading is helpful for break-down into smaller segments. In instruments such as contracts, some lawyers hesitate to use paragraph titles because they fear that a court may read a brief and inadequate title as part of the document. But any danger of this can be met with a simple recital to the effect that "Paragraph headings are inserted for reference only and form no part of this agreement."[2]

Say One Thing at a Time

For a simple subject, the outline may be very simple. It may consist merely of point one and point two. But many people fail even to have that much order in what they write. Having two things to say, they don't take them one at a time, but try to say both together.

Polanyi, the Hungarian mathematician, said, "The first rule of style is to have something to say. The second rule of style is to control yourself when, by chance, you have two things to say; say first one, then the other, not both at the same time."

Lawyers are not troubled by a dearth of things to say. But the second rule deserves careful attention; it is not as self-evident as it may seem. It means that when setting forth obligations or undertakings, as in contracts or conveyances, one sentence should whenever possible concern only one obligation or undertaking; when setting forth commands, permissions or prohibitions, as in a statute or regulation, one sentence should concern only one command, permission or prohibition; when mak-

2. Rothgerber, Simplified Semantics
    for Solicitors, 27 Ry.Mt.L.R. 306
    (1955).

ing allegations or denials of fact, as in a pleading, one sentence should deal with only one allegation or denial.

Here are examples of sentences that try to say two things at the same time:

> Unless all the Arkansas statutes on the subject (and the administrative regulations issued thereunder) are invalid, in which case a refusal by the state courts to restrain the suspension of Hays would eventually be reversed by the Supreme Court, which for the reasons expressed above would not be done, the state court was entirely within its powers in suspending Hays' state permit and his permission thereby to drive over state roads in the capacity of a contract carrier.

> In most cases, an officer of the law is justified in arresting a man without a warrant—and there is no evidence that any warrant had been obtained in this case—only when he has reason to believe that a crime is being committed in his presence.

The second of these sentences not only interrupts one thought with another, but does so at a point where the interrupted fragment apparently says something quite different from what the writer intends. An egregious example of that sort of blunder is the following:

> No other judge of this court has written so much and said so little, whether on criminal law, torts, or procedure, that is not still true and still important.

Sentence Structure and Organization

Lawyers are notorious for spawning tortuous and obscure sentences. Their sentences are often also long. One aid to clarity would be shorter sentences. But length is not itself a source of obfuscation. Good writers can turn out long sentences that are clear and easily readable. What obfuscates so much of legal writing is poor sentence structure and lack of organization.

Whether short or long, simple or complex, a sentence must be organized. It must be a closely knit unit of expression, not a mere string of loosely connected clauses. A poor writer who has just enough skill to know that a series of simple sentences will sound like a first-grade reader may try to avoid that effect by the easy device of connecting two or more simple declarative statements with a conjunction or relative ("and," "but," "which," "while").

Defendant had been drinking all evening and some time after midnight he undertook to drive home.	Defendant had been drinking all evening. Some time after midnight he undertook to drive home.

The absurd length to which such stringing of statements together with "ands" can be carried is illustrated by the following paragraph from a brief:

> We most respectfully submit it would be a travesty upon justice, a rape upon the fundamental principles of law and in violation of every decision that has been rendered by this Honorable Court, and an injustice that all the spices of Arabia could not cure, and would disgrace and bankrupt an honest citizen, an honest merchant and a blameless family and would not tend to enforce the law, but would cause hatred and disrespect to the law of our State and Nation and there would be a great injustice inflicted or could be inflicted upon a citizen of our state, and without extending this argument, which could be for many hours, but with an abiding confidence in the wisdom of this Court, we consign the future hopes, the tears of the loved ones and the laws of our nation to the bosom of this Court.

Although the court said that "this argument was eloquent and persuasive," it was not persuasive enough to persuade; the conviction was affirmed.[3]

The reader who must try to follow a long, rambling sentence cannot be sure until the end whether any of its assertions has been completed. The several statements may be so intermingled, with some more or less dependent on or modified by others, that he cannot sort them out and keep them all in mind. Had they been separated by periods instead of strung together with "ands," so that he could take them one at a time, he would have had no trouble.

Lack of privity between the promisor and the mortgagee was not overcome, as in the leading case, by an obligation of

3. Camp v. State, 66 Okl.Cr. 20, 89 P.2d 378 (1939).

the promisee to the mortgagee, so as to connect the mortgagee with the transaction so closely that it substituted for privity and, according to the court in the Vrooman case, the plaintiff was denied an action on two grounds: (1) no legal obligation from promisee to third party; and (2) no privity between the latter and the promisor.

Courts are not often guilty of sentences as bad as the foregoing, which comes from student work, but judicial opinions do sometimes contain sentences which, though grammatically correct, would be clearer if divided into shorter sentences. And sometimes they even lose themselves grammatically:

> The party who purchases property from utter strangers and receives it under unusual circumstances, and especially where all the facts of the case are passed upon by a jury, and the jury has come to the conclusion after hearing the facts and circumstances, that the defendant had knowledge that it was stolen property, and by so rendering their verdict it cannot be successfully maintained in an appellate court that defendant did not believe the property was stolen.[4]

How then does one construct well organized sentences? The first principle is to put the main idea in the main clause. When you find you have written a long sentence that you recognize is sprawling and awkward, ask yourself, what is the main idea it is intended to express? Then look at the sentence to identify its subject, its verb, and its predicate. These should state, in a simple sentence, the main idea. Look, for example, at this specimen, no worse than many others:

> The factor that was most influential in inducing the legislature to enact the bill was the fact that the governor had strongly endorsed it.

The subject of that sentence is "factor," the verb is "was," and the predicate is "fact." The "main idea" thus is: The factor was the fact.

That says nothing. You cannot construct a good sentence around a main clause that says nothing. What is the main

4. Camp v. State, 66 Okl.Cr. 20, 89 P.2d 378 (1939).

thing that this sentence tries to say? That depends upon context. Is the main point that the bill did finally pass? If so, the main clause might read, "The legislature finally passed the bill." Or is the main point that the governor's action was so important? Then it might be, "The strong support of the governor" (led to the enactment).

Putting the main point in the main clause means putting subordinate points in subordinate clauses.

> The customers watched in silence as the robbers scooped the money into a paper bag.

The main point in that sentence is surely not the inaction of the customers, but the act of the robbers. That should therefore make up the main clause:

> The robbers scooped the money into a paper bag as the customers watched in silence.

The injunction to put the main idea in the main clause and subordinate ideas in subordinate clauses has a corollary: give the context first, details later.[5] This means that in a statement of facts, as in a brief, the issue should be put before the facts.[6] A statement that starts by giving us items of information—things that happened, dates, statistics—without "setting the scene," calls on us to hold all this information in our memory until we are finally told what it is all about. Similarly, in framing questions presented, putting the question in context means starting with the broadest principle that the point concerns, then moving to the more specific.[7]

Compound and complex sentences have, broadly, two kinds of structure. They are either periodic or cumulative. A periodic sentence, of which this is an example, is one in which, by the interposing of subordinate clauses, phrases, modifiers, lists of items or other details between the subject and its essential predicate, completion of the main thought is suspended until the end.

5. "The first principle of organization in good legal writing is to provide contexts first, details later." Raymond, Legal Writing: An Obstruction to Justice, 30 Ala.L.Rev. 1, 12 (1978).

6. Post, p. 250.

7. Post, pp. 248–249.

A cumulative sentence completes the main thought early, and then adds details, such as subordinate clauses, phrases, or series of items, instead of injecting them between the subject and its predicate. That last sentence is a cumulative one. Its main thought is stated in the first nine words, and so is complete after the word "early." It has two other stopping or closing points: after the word "details," and after "items." The periodic sentence, on the other hand, has no stopping place short of the end.

Both forms of sentence structure are capable of producing clear and effective writing. The periodic sentence, as said in the chapter on Forcefulness,[8] is a useful device for emphasizing the point finally disclosed, or for building to a dramatic effect. It can also be used for humorous effect. Fielding so used it in *Tom Jones*:

> He would have ravished her, had she not, by a timely compliance, prevented him.

Periodic sentences must be used with discrimination and structured with care. Starting a statement and then holding off completing it calls on the reader to keep the start in mind while he also has to absorb a number of subordinate details until he is finally given the clue that completes the thought. The reader is waiting for that completion; until it comes, he is under what has been called grammatical tension.[9] Putting that strain on him is justified when it is done to emphasize an important idea by putting it at the end, or to sustain interest while you build to a climax. But if there is no climax, no reason to keep him in suspense, subjecting him to this strain is an imposition. One reason why so much of legal writing is hard to read is that it is largely made up of long sentences that have no closure point until at or near the end.

---

8. Ante, p. 130.

9. R.M. Eastman, Style 158 (1970). Helpful suggestions for structuring sentences, including the periodic, are provided in Raymond, Legal Writing: An Obstruction to Justice, 30 Ala.L.Rev. 1 (1978). See also L.E. Allen and C.R. Engholm, Normalized Legal Drafting and the Query Method, 29 J.Legal Ed. 380 (1978), in which the authors propound a detailed method of expressing ideas in which the syntax is simplified and standardized, so as to make legal materials easier to read and understand.

Criminal statutes, for example, typically have a simple main thought:

> A person who (commits such and such an act)
>
> Shall be punished (in such and such a way).

But more often than not, the prohibited act is so qualified that it takes many words to describe, with the result that we wind up with a provision that reads like this:

> A person who
>
> by means of any . . . or in any manner
> commits (such and such an act)
> in (this way or that)
>
> or who
>
> (does something else)
> with intent to (do this or that)
> and without the consent of (such and such a person or persons)
> while (such and such) is . . .
>
> or who aids, abets, or conspires with any person or persons to do any of the acts aforesaid,
> is guilty of . . .
> and punishable by . . ..

Such sentences, interposing a thicket of subordinate thoughts between the subject and the predicate, would be more easily comprehensible if they were broken into shorter ones. A first sentence, for example, could provide that a person who commits a named crime is guilty of a second degree felony and punishable in a certain way. A second sentence could then define the named crime.

The cumulative (often called "loose") sentence is easier to construct and easier to read. But it too must be organized. It should not consist merely of a string of clauses hooked together like a train of boxcars. One homely device that may help avoid churning out maundering sentences is to stop and think how you would express the thought in a simple conversation. We cannot literally "write as we talk," [10] but talking out our thoughts will often help produce a first draft that can then be refined and

---

10. Ante, pp. 77–79.

organized.[11] In such talking out, we would find that we use mostly cumulative sentences, expressing our main idea first and then tacking on subordinate thoughts. We put in more periods and other closure points, instead of injecting examples, exceptions and provisos between the subject and the predicate, as we are prone to do in formal legal writing. Such qualifications and examples can usually be left for a later sentence. Trying to get them all into the same sentence with the main proposition is one cause for the length and complexity of lawyers' language. Exceptions can sometimes be avoided by finding the precise category intended to be covered, instead of first naming a broader category and then making an exception. Thus, instead of saying, "All registered voters except those registered before 1978," say "All registered voters registered after December 31, 1977."

Exercise

Below is the concluding paragraph of a brief. The point it expresses is a good one on which to end, but its potential effectiveness is dissipated because the several clauses, strung together with "ands," have no focus and so no force. Rewrite it, using better organized sentences.

> All of the parties were familiar with all of the terms and conditions of the contract, and this being true, Metropolitan cannot now be heard to complain that the contract does not mean just exactly what it says, as hereinbefore indicated. This being true, there is no genuine issue as to any material facts and Herkenhoff was and is entitled to judgment as a matter of law and the lower court did not err in granting Herkenhoff a summary judgment.

Vary the Length of Sentences

Rudolf Flesch measures reading ease in sentence length (although he points out that it could even more exactly be measured in syllables). He ranges sentences from very easy (8 words in length) to very difficult (29 or more words). For three out

11. The technique of "talking out" difficult propositions is explained in Zoellner, Talk-Write: A Behavioral Pedagogy for Composition, 30 College English 3 (1969), cited in Raymond, Legal Writing: An Obstruction to Justice, 30 Ala.L.Rev. 1, 10 (1978).

of four American adults, sentences of an average length of 17 words are difficult enough.[12]

The readers of a lawyer's professional writings, such as briefs, are presumably of higher than average reading skill. On the other hand, the words are likely to be more difficult, so it is well to aim for an average sentence length of not much more than 20 words, the average for literary English.

The suggestion that long sentences are difficult, and that it aids clarity not to make sentences too long, must not be taken as a rule of thumb.[13] Nor does it mean that you should try to make all your sentences of nearly equal length. The contrary is true. A good sentence may be very long. Eighteenth century writers sometimes wrote sentences that ran over a page, yet were logically and clearly organized, so that the reader could follow the thought without undue effort. All that is necessary is that the sentence not be so complex that the reader gets confused.

More important than maintaining any average sentence length is getting variation in length. A style in which every sentence is of much the same length would be monotonous. You want a mixture of long and short sentences, a change of pace. Dr. Isaac Goldberg [14] put it well:

> Writing is symbolized speaking. In speaking, the relative length of our phrases is determined by their emotional or intellectual content and—more than we realize—by the normal flow of our breathing. We do not, in reading, like an uninterrupted succession of sentences containing two or three words each; we do not like an uninterrupted succession of sentences each containing ninety words. We instinctively ask for variation in sentence-length; we instinctively ask, indeed,

12. Flesch, The Art of Plain Talk 38 (1946).

13. Yardsticks that have been devised for measuring readability (reading ease and reading interest) take into account such factors as:
Average sentence length in words
Percentage of simple sentences
Percentage of strong verb forms
Portion of familiar words
Portion of abstract words
Percentage of personal references
Percentage of long words.
R. Gunning, The Technique of Clear Writing 32–33 (1952).

14. Goldberg, The Wonder of Words 354 (1957).

for variation in word-length, for variation in accent and pitch —in a word, for equilibrium, for harmonious, dynamic balance.

We dislike the succession of short sentences because they suggest asthmatic utterance; we dislike the succession of long ones because they suggest a different type of breathlessness, caused by talking without pause. Listening to music or singing that is consistently in the high registers induces a feeling of strain, and that feeling may begin in our throats, which unconsciously imitate, or have suggested to them, the vocalism required to produce such high tones. Such refinements of writing as rhythm, cadence, harmony of vowels and consonants, even choice of words, which constitute the aesthetics of rhetoric, of style, have a physical basis.

Strive for Continuity

Writing that moves along a logically direct path will have a natural coherence; its parts will fit together well. Nevertheless, it is worth knowing some of the devices that help to make one's writing flow smoothly from sentence to sentence and from paragraph to paragraph.

"A good transition," says one book on writing, "is like the statue of the god Janus: it looks before and after. It refers in some swift way to what has preceded and announces what is to follow." [15] There are at least four ways to do this:

1. Most commonly used are transitional or connective expressions. These take several forms:

    a. Those that enumerate or indicate order in time: "first," "next," "the second," "finally." Starting each statement with one of these words is effective when you want to enumerate points in order, but this is a rather mechanical device, and one so obviously available as to invite overuse. Inexperienced writers sometimes use cumbersome transitional phrases which impede rather than facilitate the progress of thought: "This leads us to our second point;" "Having proved our first point, we shall now . . . ." When you do use enumeration, you can make it somewhat less obvious by moving the connective words to a less prominent position

---

than the beginning of the sentence. You can subordinate them by such phrasing as, ". . . is the first (main, principal, primary) reason that . . .;" or ". . . is a second reason for . . . ."

b. Those that enumerate or indicate order in arrangement: "next," "secondly," "a further reason."

c. Those that add specifications to what has gone before: "especially," "in particular," "at least," "for example."

d. Those that indicate additions to what has gone before: "moreover," "in addition," "furthermore," "besides," "also," "indeed."

e. Those that indicate exceptions or negations to what has gone before: "but," "however," "nevertheless," "yet," "on the contrary."

f. Those that indicate cause or effect: "therefore," "thus," "accordingly," "as a result," "consequently."

Almost all these connectives are more gracefully used when put inside the sentence instead of at the beginning.

2. A word or phrase from the previous sentence or paragraph can be repeated or "echoed" in the new. Thus if the last sentence of the previous paragraph was about a "sense of personal security," the next paragraph may start, "This sense of security. . . ."

3. Instead of "echoing" a word or phrase verbatim, the new paragraph may start with a brief summarizing phrase referring to the subject just discussed. These last two devices are usually combined with the use of a demonstrative pronoun, such as "this" or "these."

> From this legislative history, it appears
>
> Applying these principles to the case,
>
> Against this background of judicial construction,

4. Parallel construction, which we have already said helps give emphasis and rhythm, also provides coherence. Repetition of the same sentence structure connects the two thoughts, and

so substitutes for connective words or phrases such as "and," "but" or "moreover."

The illegality of the scheme is shown by a reading of the court's decision in the Reston case. Moreover, it is absurd, as consideration of the consequences it would have for marital relations makes apparent.	That the scheme is illegal is shown by a reading of the court's decision in the Reston case. That it is absurd is apparent from the consequences it would have for marital relations.

All these devices quickly become obvious and monotonous, and so should be used sparingly. The best transitional expressions are those that do not seem artificial or strained, but arise naturally out of the development of ideas.

Lead the Reader by the Hand

Connectives and transitions not only make for coherence and smooth development; they provide signals that enable the reader to follow as you move from point to point. Unless you continually signal where you are going next, you may lose him.

> Making the decisions of the board final is constitutional. Kentucky has held that the courts may interfere where the property owner alleges that the board's decision deprives him of property without due process of law. Similarly, the Kansas court has held that judicial review cannot be denied. But in a great majority of jurisdictions, statutory provisions that the board's decisions shall not be subject to judicial review have been upheld.

Here, instead of enlarging on the point that the first sentence leads the reader to assume is going to be the subject of the paragraph (namely, that the proposition is constitutional) the writer without any warning signal switches directions on us and starts talking about the authorities *contra*. Reading the words, "Kentucky has held," we expect to be told that Kentucky has supported the proposition laid down. But as we get into the sentence, we find it doesn't seem to do so. We start over, thinking we have misread it, cannot find where we have, and are lost. Only when we get to the end of the paragraph do we see what the writer has done—thrown us off the track by slipping in the minority view when he seemed to be talking about the general rule. There is no objection to the way the writer developed his point. But he should have made clear to the reader the path he was following. He could have done this easily by introducing the second sentence with some such phrase as, "It is true that." This would have been a signal to the reader that what is to follow is an exception or limitation which the writer wants to get out of the way before going on with the main point.

Transition words can be used not only to signal such a shift in direction or concession to the other side, but also to introduce another item in a series (also, furthermore, similarly), or a later item (later, finally), or a conclusion (therefore, thus, accordingly) or a summary (to summarize, in short).

Continuity Through Punctuation

When two sentences have a logical connection, the writer may do one of three things: (1) he may write them as two separate sentences, separated by a period; (2) he may run them together, connecting them with "and" or some other connective; or (3) he may replace the connective with a semi-colon. It is this last possibility that is neglected. Some unskilled writers never use a semi-colon; their punctuation is limited to commas and periods. This gives a style that seems simple and vigorous for a short while, but it soon becomes monotonous.

The semi-colon is itself a kind of connective. Using it instead of a full stop tells the reader that there is a connection between the two statements. As Sir Ernest Gowers has said,[16] the full stop says to the reader, "Have you got that? Very well; now I'll tell you something else." A semi-colon says, "Got that? Now I'll add something else *that has something to do with what I just said.*"

16. Gowers, Plain Words 17 (1948).

The promisee does not owe a legal debt to the third party, but to all intents and purposes the third party is receiving a gratuity.	The promisee does not owe a legal debt to the third party; to all intents and purposes the third party is receiving a gratuity.
The quoted sentence was not the holding in the case, but was mere obiter dictum.	The quoted sentence was not the holding in the case; it was mere obiter dictum.

The colon is another mark whose usefulness is sometimes not fully appreciated. It is a mark of anticipation, suggesting a sequel: a list, a specification, an amplification or a quotation.

There is only one thing to do: resign.

This much is certain: we shall never surrender.

The parties finally agreed on a compromise: the union would abandon its wage demands in return for the granting of certain fringe benefits.

A time comes when men must make up their minds, and on the validity of retribution as a purpose of punishment, the time for equivocation is past: retribution is wrong.

The dash is a deliberate interruption of continuity, similar to a comma but more abrupt and emphatic. Legal writing should be couched in language carefully chosen; it therefore has little use for dashes, which give the impression of breaking off one thought to interject another. But sometimes an abrupt interruption or pause is effective: (1) to indicate a sharp turn of thought or to give a contrasting idea; (2) to interpolate a parenthetical or side comment or to give a striking detail, and to set it off in a more marked or emphatic way than by using commas or parentheses; or (3) to indicate a pause of suspense.

Made desperate by their depressed plight, the farmers of one district met a lawyer for the mortgagee bank on the courthouse steps and persuaded him—let us hope by fair means—not to proceed with the eviction.

He died in a concentration camp of an incurable blood infection—a Jewish grandmother.[17]

17.   Gross, 11 Shingle 79 (1948).

Interjections of any kind, whether set off with dashes, parentheses or commas, are likely to mar one's writing by impairing the smooth flow of thought and rhythm. Inserting a whole sentence within a sentence is particularly bad practice.

> Legal writing has been neglected (as have many other techniques and subjects) by many law schools as a vital part of legal education, though some schools have now gone quite far (Can one ever go too far?) to correct this situation.

Loss of continuity is not the only penalty for neglecting punctuation. Clarity may also be impaired. And even when the sense is perfectly clear, as Edgar Allan Poe said, "a sentence may be deprived of half of its force, its spirit, its point, by improper punctuation."

Organize Your Paragraphs

Paragraphing is a device to help the reader follow the plan of development that the writer has in mind. Each paragraph should be not merely a series of sentences, but an orderly series, with unity of purpose. It should have one point to make, and only one.

1. *Use Topic Sentences*

The first sentence should introduce or at least suggest this new point. An effective way to guard against including too many ideas in one paragraph is to write paragraphs that can be summarized in single sentences. A summary sentence is usually the best kind of sentence with which to start the paragraph.

In legal writing, this topic sentence can often be the statement of a legal proposition, with the rest of the paragraph devoted to its amplification, or to summaries of cases supporting it.

> Pension payments have been held to be "income" within the Internal Revenue Act definition. (Rest of the paragraph devoted to short summaries of cases so holding).

> The contention is unsound for several reasons. (Rest of the paragraph develops the reasons).

This is perhaps the most common way of organizing paragraphs in argumentative writing: the statement of a proposition in the first sentence, followed by its demonstration by evidence, examples or other data. Many of the paragraphs in appellate court opinions are so organized.

> Now, if any fundamental assumption underlies our system, it is that guilt is personal and not inheritable. Even if all of one's antecedents had been convicted of treason, the Constitution forbids its penalties to be visited upon him, for it provides that "no Attainder of Treason shall work Corruption of Blood, or Forfeiture except during the Life of the Person attained. Article 3, § 3, cl. 2 . . . .[18]

The topic sentence may be a question:

> The inquiry is, what are the privileges and immunities of citizens in the several states? . . . [19]

> The first step in our inquiry must be to answer the question: what is the source of power on which Congress must be assumed to have drawn? . . . [20]

The topic sentence may refer to an argument that the paragraph proposes to answer. Such a sentence may start, "The plaintiff contends," "The Union relies on observations made in Madden v. Bain," or "The court below held." Examples from judicial opinions follow:

> The act is sought to be sustained specifically upon the ground that it is reasonably calculated to promote the public health; and the determination we are called upon to make is whether the act has a real or substantial relation to that end. . . . [21]

> Aznavorian urges that the freedom of international travel is basically equivalent to the constitutional right to interstate travel, recognized by this Court for over a hundred years. . . . But this court has often pointed out the crucial dif-

18. Mr. Justice Jackson, dissenting, in Korematsu v. United States, 323 U.S. 214, 243 65 S.Ct. 193, 206, 89 L.Ed. 194, 213 (1944).

19. Washington, J., in Corfield v. Coryell, 4 Wash.C.C. 371 (1823).

20. Mr. Justice Frankfurter, in Perez v. Brownell, 356 U.S. 44, 57, 78 S.Ct. 568, 575, 2 L.Ed.2d 603, 613 (1958).

21. Mr. Justice Sutherland, in Liggett Co. v. Baldridge, 278 U.S. 105, 111, 49 S.Ct. 57, 58, 73 L.Ed. 204 (1928).

ference between the freedom to travel internationally and the right of interstate travel.[22]

The "topic sentence" need not always be the first sentence of the paragraph and indeed need not actually appear in the paragraph at all. It is the mark of an unskilled writer to make the structural details of his outline too apparent. To announce at the beginning of every paragraph the topic or point to be made is not only monotonous but awkward. The adroit writer does not leave the bones of the skeleton showing so nakedly. For example, the topic of a paragraph may be "the plaintiff's conduct constituted contributory negligence." The paragraph may actually start, "That the plaintiff was contributorily negligent clearly appears not only from the testimony of the impartial witnesses, but also from his own admissions." With such an introductory sentence, the reader knows what should follow, a summary of the testimony of the other witnesses and of the plaintiff showing contributory negligence.

In the leading case of McCulloch v. Maryland,[23] Chief Justice Marshall attacked the problem of finding that Congress had power to incorporate a bank by starting a paragraph boldly admitting that the power was not expressly given:

> Among the enumerated powers, we do not find that of establishing a bank or creating a corporation. But there is no phrase in the instrument which . . . excludes incidental or implied powers . . . .

In the following paragraph, the topic sentence might be worded somewhat as follows, "Although the constitutional guarantees of personal liberty are not always absolutes, government may not go so far as to compel public affirmations which violate religious conscience." But no such sentence actually appears. Instead, the idea is developed from the beginning to the end.

> Concededly the constitutional guaranties of personal liberty are not always absolutes. Government has a right to survive and powers conferred upon it are not necessarily set at

---

22. Mr. Justice Stewart in Califano v. Aznavorian, —— U.S. ——, ——, 99 S.Ct. 471, 474–5, 58 L.Ed.2d 435, 441 (1978).

23. 4 Wheat. 316, 404 (1819).

naught by the express prohibitions of the Bill of Rights. It may make war and raise armies. To that end it may compel citizens to give military service, Selective Draft Law Cases, 245 U.S. 366, 38 S.Ct. 159, and subject them to military training despite their religious objections. Hamilton v. Regents, 293 U.S. 245, 55 S.Ct. 197. It may suppress religious practices dangerous to morals, and presumably those also which are inimical to public safety, health and good order. Davis v. Beason, 133 U.S. 333, 10 S.Ct. 299. But it is a long step, and one which I am unable to take, to the position that government may, as a supposed educational measure and as a means of disciplining the young, compel public affirmations which violate their religious conscience. . . .[24]

Starting a new paragraph is the signal to the reader that one point in the development has ended and that the next one is beginning. Where you do not start a new paragraph, you imply that you are still talking about the same point. If your reader finds that you have moved on to a new point, without giving him the signal, he is confused.

In 1498, the Venetian Republic granted to Democrito Terracina a monopoly to print all books in Arabic, Moorish, Syrian, Armenian, Indian and Barbary for a period of twenty-five years. In 1518, the Holy Roman Emperor Maximilian gave John Shoeffer the exclusive right to print the works of Livy for a period of ten years.

In the Middle Ages another form of copyright protection was developed which we may call "institutional" protection.

.   .   .   .

The introductory words of the second paragraph imply that the writer is about to move on, in his historical development, to the Middle Ages. But that is where we were in the preceding paragraph. What he meant to say was, "Another form of copyright protection developed in the Middle Ages was what we may call 'institutional protection.'"

2. *Develop the Paragraph Topic*

Assuming that you have a good first sentence, which does properly introduce the new point, the next sentence should pro-

24. Mr. Justice Stone, dissenting, in Minersville School District v. Gobi-   tis, 310 U.S. 586, 602, 60 S.Ct. 1010, 84 L.Ed. 1375 (1940).

ceed to amplify or discuss that point. Do not betray the expectation you have created in the first sentence by switching to some other point. The easiest way to lose unity is to allow yourself to be distracted from your main thought by some side issue, with the result that a paragraph which started out purporting to discuss one thing wanders off into a minor or collateral point.

The following paragraph violates this rule, (as well as several others). We are not told at the outset what the main point is; in consequence, we must do some close reasoning to discover it:

> To the extent that any decision relies on the lack of competition between the parties or on the statement that the element of "passing off" was not present, it is submitted that the decision is incorrect. Neither should trivial differences in titles nor in the statement that the adversaries were equally entitled to the use of the title furnish the basis for a decision. The same can be said of the requirement that notice be posted to the effect that the work, blatantly advertised under a title that has elsewhere acquired a secondary meaning, is not that work at all.

This was later rewritten to read:

> Courts have allowed the continued use of competing titles of vaudeville acts on several grounds. In the Glazer case the court in refusing to enjoin stressed the difference in the titles, although that difference really seems insignificant ("Think-a-Drink Hoffman" and "Have-a-Drink Court Maurice"). Other grounds for similar decisions have been the lack of direct competition between the parties, the absence of the element of "passing off," and a feeling by the court that both parties were equally entitled to the use of the title. In one case, the court allowed the continued use of a similar title on condition that the defendant make public announcement that his was not the plaintiff's well-known production.
>
> None of these are satisfactory reasons for failing to enjoin the continued use of a title. The publicity value of the title is an important part of the originator's property right. The only question with which the court should concern itself is whether or not the defendant has converted this property right to his own use.

The revised version not only tells us in the first sentence what the paragraph covers, it also complies with another rule, already mentioned: when you have two things to say, say first one, then the other, not both together. Here, the writer wanted (1) to tell us the holdings of several cases; and (2) to argue that they were unsound. In his first draft, he tried to do both together. In the second, he did first one, then the other, devoting a separate paragraph to each.

An experienced writer may not make a conscious choice of method in paragraph development. The plan he follows, almost without specifically thinking about it, will depend on the nature of the point he is making. If he is laying down a legal proposition, he may, especially if it is an intricate one, want to develop it by giving illustratioms. Or he may want to support it with cases, which may provide illustrations as well as authority. The novice, however, may need to remind himself that some plan of development is called for, lest his paragraph become merely a string of loose and unorganized sentences that have no focus and make no point.

One book on "Communication" distinguishes five methods of paragraph development: (a) by comparison or contrast; (b) by analogy; (c) by example; (d) by evidence; and (e) by definition.[25] Each of these may be illustrated by examples taken from judicial opinions.

(a) *Development by Comparison or Contrast*

Development by comparison or contrast or by elimination of alternatives is illustrated by the following paragraph from Mr. Justice Black's dissenting opinion in Dennis v. United States, which begins: [26]

> At the outset I want to emphasize what the crime involved in this case is, and what it is not. These petitioners were not charged with an attempt to overthrow the Government. They were not charged with overt acts of any kind designed to overthrow the Government. They were not even charged with saying anything or writing anything designed to over-

25. Johnson, Schalekamp and Garri-
son, Communication—Handling
Ideas Effectively 138–143 (1956).

26. 341 U.S. 494, 579, 71 S.Ct. 857,
95 L.Ed. 1137 (1951).

throw the Government. The charge was that they agreed to assemble and to talk and publish certain ideas at a later date.

. . .

(b) *Development by Analogy*

This is really a special form of development by comparison. Sometimes in an argumentative paragraph the anlogy is merely a figure of speech.

> To propose to punish and reform people by the same opera-
> tion is exactly as if you were to take a man suffering from
> pneumonia, and attempt to combine punitive and curative
> treatment. Arguing that a man with pneumonia is a danger
> to the community, and that he need not catch it if he takes
> proper care of his health, you resolve that he shall have a se-
> vere lesson, both to punish him for his negligence and pulmo-
> nary weakness and to deter others from following his exam-
> ple. You therefore strip him naked, and in that condition
> stand him all night in the snow. But as you admit the duty
> of restoring him to health if possible, and discharging him
> with sound lungs, you engage a doctor to superintend the
> punishment and administer cough lozenges, made as unpleas-
> ant to the taste as possible so as not to pamper the culprit.[27]

(c) *Development by Example*

In legal writing a typical pattern might be the statement of a rule of law in the first sentence, followed by short factual statements from other cases.

> The price paid for property or services is only one of the
> terms in a bargain; the effect on the parties is similar
> whether the restriction on the power of the contract affects
> the price, or the goods or services sold. Apart from the cases
> involving the historic public-callings, immemorially subject to
> the closest regulation, this court has sustained regulations of
> the price in cases where the legislature fixed the charges
> which grain elevators, Brass v. North Dakota, 153 U.S. 391,
> 38 L.Ed. 757, 4 Inters.Com.Rep. 670, 14 S.Ct. 857; Budd v.
> New York, 143 U.S. 517, 36 L.Ed. 247, 4 Inters.Com.Rep. 45,
> 12 S.Ct. 468, and insurance companies might make, German
> Alliance Ins. Co. v. Lewis, supra; or required miners to be

27. G. Bernard Shaw, Preface to
Webb, English Prisons under Local
Government XIV (1922).

paid per ton of coal unscreened instead of screened, McLean v. Arkansas, supra; Rail & River Coal Co. v. Yaple, 236 U.S. 338, 59 L.Ed. 607, 35 S.Ct. 359; or required employers who paid their men in store orders to redeem them in cash, Knoxville Iron Co. v. Harbison, 183 U.S. 13, 46 L.Ed. 55, 22 S.Ct. 1; Dayton Coal & Iron Co. v. Barton, 183 U.S. 23, 46 L.Ed. 61, 22 S.Ct. 5; Keokee Consol. Coke Co. v. Taylor, 234 U.S. 224, 58 L.Ed. 1288, 34 S.Ct. 856; or fixed the fees chargeable by attorneys appearing for injured employees before workmen's compensation commissions, Yeiser v. Dysart, 267 U.S. 540, 69 L.Ed. 775, 45 S.Ct. 399; or fixed the rate of pay for overtime work, Bunting v. Oregon, 243 U.S. 426, 61 L.Ed. 830, 37 S.Ct. 435, Ann.Cas.1918A, 1043; or fixed the time within which the services of employees must be paid for, Erie R. Co. v. Williams, 233 U.S. 685, 58 L.Ed. 1155, 51 L.R.A.,N. S., 1097, 34 S.Ct. 761; or established maximum rents, Block v. Hirsh, 256 U.S. 135, 65 L.Ed. 865, 16 A.L.R. 165, 41 S.Ct. 458; Marcus Brown Holding Co. v. Feldman, 256 U.S. 170, 65 L.Ed. 877, 41 S.Ct. 465; or fixed the maximum rate of interest chargeable on loans, Griffith v. Connecticut, 218 U.S. 563, 54 L.Ed. 1151, 31 S.Ct. 132. It has sustained restrictions on the other element in the bargain where legislatures have established maximum hours of labor for men. Holden v. Hardy, 169 U.S. 366, 42 L.Ed. 780, 18 S.Ct. 383; or for women, Muller v. Oregon, 208 U.S. 412, 52 L.Ed. 551, 28 S.Ct. 324, 13 Ann.Cas. 957; Hawley v. Walker, 232 U.S. 718, 58 L.Ed. 813, 34 S.Ct. 479; Riley v. Massachusetts, 232 U.S. 671, 58 L. Ed. 788, 34 S.Ct. 469; Miller v. Wilson, 236 U.S. 373, 59 L. Ed. 628, L.R.A.1915F, 829, 35 S.Ct. 342; Bosley v. McLaughlin, 236 U.S. 385, 59 L.Ed. 632, 35 S.Ct. 345; or prohibited the payment of wages in advance, Patterson v. The Eudora, 190 U.S. 169, 47 L.Ed. 1002, 23 S.Ct. 821; Strathearn S. S. Co. v. Dillon, 252 U.S. 348, 64 L.Ed. 607, 40 S.Ct. 350; or required loaves of bread to be a certain size, Schmidinger v. Chicago, 226 U.S. 578, 57 L.Ed. 364, 33 S.Ct. 182, Ann.Cas.1914B, 284. In each of these cases the police power of the state was held broad enough to warrant an interference with free bargaining in cases where, despite the competition that ordinarily attends that freedom, serious evils persisted.[28]

---

28. Mr. Justice Stone, dissenting in Ribnik v. McBride, 277 U.S. 350, 374, 48 S.Ct. 545, 72 L.Ed. 913 (1928).

This example illustrates both the pattern and its overuse. Mr. Justice Stone here, as in some of his other opinions, piles example on example until we have rather more than enough.

When you have several examples, cases, or other items to present, consider the order in which they should be presented. At least four kinds of order are possible: (1) from the lesser to the greater, the order of climax; (2) from the general to the particular (deduction); (3) from the particular to the general (induction); (4) from the familiar to the unfamiliar.

(d) *Development by Evidence*

Primary elections are conducted by the party under state statutory authority. The county executive committee selects precinct election officials and the county, district or state executive committees, respectively, canvass the returns. These party committees or the state convention certify the party's candidates to the appropriate officers for inclusion on the official ballot for the general election. No name which has not been so certified may appear upon the ballot for the general election as a candidate of a political party. No other name may be printed on the ballot which has not been placed in nomination by qualified voters who must take oath that they did not participate in a primary for the selection of a candidate for the office for which the nomination is made.[29]

(e) *Development by Definition*

Of all the terms used in the Taking Clause, "just compensation" has the strictest meaning. The Fifth Amendment does not allow simply approximate compensation but requires "a full and perfect equivalent for the property taken."   .[30]

For Emphasis, Build to a Climax

Whatever the method of development it should, to get the best emphasis, put the most important ideas at the beginning and the end—the topic sentence at the beginning, and at the end the strongest of your series of examples, or the climax of your argument, or a strong summarizing sentence. This summarizing sen-

---

29. Mr. Justice Reed, in Smith v. Allwright, 321 U.S. 649, 663, 64 S. Ct. 757, 88 L.Ed. 987 (1944).

30. Mr. Justice Rehnquist, dissenting in Penn Central Transp. Co. v. New York City, 438 U.S. 104, 150, 98 S.Ct. 2646, 2673, 57 L.Ed.2d 631, 665 (1978).

tence is worth particular pains, to word it forcefully so as to drive home the point.

> If we cut through mere details of procedure, the operation and effect of the statute in substance is that public authorities may bring the owner or publisher of a newspaper or periodical before a judge upon a charge of conducting a business of publishing scandalous and defamatory matter—in particular that the matter consists of charges against public officers of official dereliction—and unless the owner or publisher is able and disposed to bring competent evidence to satisfy the judge that the charges are true and are published with good motives and for justifiable ends, his newspaper or periodical is suppressed and further publication is made punishable as a contempt. This is the essence of censorship.[31]

If a paragraph is so long as to make for tedious reading, even though it is logically a well-knit unit, consider breaking it up. You will usually find a place where a new paragraph can appropriately be started, even though you may have to recast the introductory words so as to show the dependence of the second paragraph on the first, or the relation to it.

Do not be afraid to have a one-sentence paragraph at intervals. A change of pace is as welcome in paragraphing as in sentence structure.

31. Chief Justice Hughes, in Near v. Minnesota, 283 U.S. 697, 713, 51 S. Ct. 625, 75 L.Ed. 1357 (1931).

Chapter 8

LETTERS

Writing letters is one of the best ways to learn to write. Drafting contracts and other agreements, deeds, pleadings, statutes and regulations may call for technical skill, but style is necessarily constrained. Such drafting bears a relationship to true writing comparable to that of mechanical drawing to free-hand. It is in writing letters, opinions, and briefs that the lawyer can develop a style of his own.

A letter is addressed to somebody. The writer can visualize the reader, and can visualize himself conversing with this reader. If he will remember that he is talking to this particular person, perhaps a friend or close acquaintance, he may restrain himself from using too absurdly pompous a style. Bearing in mind how ridiculous it would sound if said face to face, he will avoid starting with such a starchy formula as, "We are in receipt of," or "This is to acknowledge your letter of recent date, the contents of which have been duly noted."

The Opening

The first words of a letter do much to set the tone, so they deserve some attention. The stock phrase, "In reply to your letter of," is so obvious a way to begin that it has no personal touch. But because it is obvious, it is hard to get away from. Participial phrases of the same import are no less weak and hackneyed: "Replying to your letter," "Referring to your inquiry," "Confirming our telephone conversation." Variations that do depart a little from the formula include, "Thank you for your letter of," "I have your letter," and "This is in reply to your letter."

But why should we assume that every letter must follow the treadmill pattern of referring to the reader's letter and reminding him of its date? This is helpful if for any reason he may not immediately understand what letter you are answering, or if you are writing to a large organization where the mail clerk

164

who opens your letter will have trouble routing it unless you refer to some previous communication. But in the absence of some such valid reason, one need not start every letter in this routine way. Yet the files of every big law office (and every other kind of office) are stuffed with letters and copies of letters containing in the aggregate myriads of words whose only purpose was to assure the recipient that the letter which the writer was answering had been received and its contents noted—its date in particular. Think of the thousands of young women wasting the bloom of their youth in typing this useless verbiage —and being paid for it!

How then should a letter start? Here are four ways, all better than "In reply to."

1. Name the subject you are writing about: "The deposition of Officer Clancy, taken last Tuesday," "The information contained in your letter," "The statement that came with your letter."

2. Make a direct statement, without any preliminaries: "We have no objection to your," "Immediately after our telephone conversation of this morning," "The court has set our case down for hearing on December 5."

3. Ask a question or make a request: "Have you had time to," "How soon will you be able to," "Will it be possible for you to," "Will you please send me," "Please refer to," "Please let me have."

4. Focus on the reader: "You will be glad to know that," "You are quite right in thinking," "Your concern over .   .   . is understandable."

Pomposity versus Simplicity

The basic tenets we have laid down in previous chapters apply to letters no less than to other kinds of writing. Don't try to impress your client or other reader by using big words or pompous circumlocutions. Enough ridicule has been heaped on the "yours of the 5th inst. received" and "beg to advise" school of business-letter writing, so that no student is likely to need any warning against it. Competent businessmen do not write that way today, and certainly professional men should not. But certain stiff and formal business-letter expressions are still all too common. In addition to the clichés listed in the chapter on Forcefulness (pp. 121–122), here are others that crop up constantly:

Formal, Stuffy	Simple
Advise, inform, state	Tell, say
Attached please find	Attached is
Be good enough to advise me	Please tell me
Communicate	Write
Concerning, regarding, respecting	About
Contemplate	Plan, intend
Enclosed herewith is	Enclosed is
I am of the opinion	I think
I am (not) in a position to	I can (not)
I have endeavored to obtain the requested information	I have tried to find out what you want to know
I should appreciate your advising me	Please tell me
I would ask that you	Please
In compliance with your request	As you requested (asked)
In conclusion	In closing
It is my desire	I wish
Meets with our approval	We approve
Move for a continuance	Ask the court to postpone the case
Payment is due on July 1 and becomes delinquent on July 31	You may pay this at any time before August 1
Plaintiff alleges	Mr. Paine says
Please advise me as to	Please tell me
Please furnish me with information	Please tell me
Take advantage of this proposition	Accept this proposal (offer)
Transmit	Send
Under date of	On, dated
Will you be good enough to	Please

Some of these overstuffed phrases can be omitted entirely. This is especially true of introductory words that contribute nothing to the actual statement, such as, "I wish to inform you," or "wish to apologize." Start off by informing or apologizing and not by wishing to do so. Other useless warming-up words are:

I see from your letter

I should further point out, I may also add

It is my considered opinion

Permit me to say

Take this opportunity to

Your attention is called

Dear Sir:

At this time, the Conference program committee should like to express their sincere thanks to you for your participation in the conference. . . .

Why the emphasis on "at this time"? Speakers more than writers like to use this phrase (often blown up to "at this point in time"), sometimes as a pompous way to say "now", sometimes, as in the sentence above, without any meaning whatever. And why the subjunctive "should like to"? Even the most cautious lawyer need not hesitate to commit himself squarely to an unconditional "thank you." [1]

"Would hope" is another indecisive expression. "I would hope that the White House will cooperate," says one of our political leaders. Does he mean that he would hope if he could, but he can't? No, he means that he does. But "I would hope"—or, worse yet, "I would have hoped"—is not the way to say "I hope."

Some of these wheezy expressions are not only time- and paper-devouring verbosities, but are all too obviously evasive. "I am giving the matter my immediate attention" does not tell us precisely what the writer is doing about it, and we therefore suspect that he is doing nothing. If he is doing something, he should tell us what: "Tomorrow morning I shall file," "Prompt-

---

1. Even if the subjunctive is used, isn't "would like" preferable to "should like"? "Should" carries an undertone of obligation, derived from its Germanic origin, *sollen*, whereas "would" *(wollen)* implies desire.

ly on receiving your letter I sent a telegram," "I have arranged to take the deposition of . . .."

One way to make your letters sound more informal and personal is to use contractions: "can't," "won't," "isn't," "aren't." Contractions are out of place in a brief, but they are quite appropriate in a friendly letter.

Another way is to use personal pronouns, such as "you," "I," "we," and "us." Their use is a gesture of friendship, an effort to ease the flow of communication by throwing a connecting bridge across to the reader. The reader senses this desire to share, and tends to respond emotionally with an increased willingness to receive. Advertising writers know how important it is to make the reader or listener feel that he is being addressed personally. Popular magazine feature writers also know the usefulness of personal references. The abstract concepts that are so often the subject of legal discourse do not lend themselves to much use of such words, but at least in letter-writing, we can make good use of them. If you try, you will find that you can often change a coldly impersonal statement into a personal one; that you can talk about human beings instead of things and ideas.

A property owner has the right to sell	You have the right to sell
It is elementary that	We all know that
It will be observed from a reading of	You will see by reading

This device can also be used in more formal writing than letters—for example, in the argumentative part of a brief. You have perhaps noticed that "you" and "we" are used constantly throughout this book, as in this sentence.

Using the pronoun "you" is not only more human than is impersonal talk, but it is also more reader-centered. People are not only more interested in human beings than in things; they are also more interested in themselves than in other human beings. Focusing your language on your reader will help you to focus your attention on him, to consider how he feels and how your words will affect him.

Of course, merely using the word "you" is not always quite the same as centering attention on "you." A speaker may use the word "you" and still center his concern on himself, like the egocentric actor who, after a long monologue about his tribulations and his triumphs, broke off to say, "But let's not talk only about me. Let's talk about you. What did *you* think of my new play?"

When you do talk about things, the simple little pronoun "it" is useful to help take the stuffiness out of legalese—especially to avoid such legalisms as "therein," "thereof" and "thereto."

Thank you for your letter and for the information contained therein.	Thank you for your letter and for the information it contained.
In the first section thereof.	In its first section

Although students are more likely to be over-pompous in their letter writing than too informal, it is possible to lean too far backwards. Even a very informal letter, such as one written to a client who is also a friend, calls for a style that is somewhere between the formal and the conversational. If you dictate, your spoken style may be too colloquial and slangy for the written page. Read such letters carefully to see whether they do not need to have some expressions elevated.

In letters, both sentences and paragraphs should be shorter than in more formal writing. Sentences should not average more than two typewritten lines, and paragraphs not more than six lines. Even your longest paragraphs should not run more than about twelve lines. The first paragraph in particular should be short, preferably two to five lines long.

Don't try to put too much into one sentence. The carefully qualified phrasing that is often necessary in formal legal writing, such as a contract, a will or a statute, is not usually necessary in writing to a client. A statute must be so drafted as to provide the rule applicable under any of an indefinite number of circumstances that may arise at some time in the future. But the client is interested only in his particular circumstances. Do not in your effort to be painstakingly exact bother him with qualifications or exceptions that do not apply to him. This again is merely an illustration of our injunction to "Remember Your Reader."

Judgment is of course required in deciding what is relevant for your client and what is not. An exception that may come into operation in his case and may affect him should be mentioned, especially if he can do something about it. But even if exceptions need to be mentioned, they need not be tacked on to the main proposition, but may be dealt with in a separate sentence.

The Close

Certain trite closing phrases are used by some letter-writers with the same treadmill monotony as the introductory phrases already discussed. Among them are:

Hoping to hear from you at your earliest convenience

Hoping for the favor of an early reply

Thank you in advance for

Behind these ossified expressions no doubt lies a feeling that a letter should not end too abruptly and that courtesy calls for some closing amenity. But these stock phrases are much too mechanical to convey any sense of courtesy.

Three more effective and more felicitous ways of closing are:

1. A direct specific statement: "Promptly upon hearing from you we shall," "With this information, you will perhaps be able to," "I shall appreciate any information you can give me."

2. A courteous request or instruction: "Will you please notify us when," "Please mail the executed releases to," "If you agree, will you please give me your authority to," "May I have your answer at once?"

3. A question: "When would it be convenient for you to," "In the light of these developments, do you think we should revoke the offer?"

It is not good practice to merge the last line of the letter with the complimentary close. For example:

Thanking you for your prompt consideration, I am
Very truly yours,

This was the fashion two hundred years ago, but it is outmoded. Rewrite the following letter in plain English:

I am in receipt of your letter of the 16th inst., the contents of which have been duly noted.

In reply would say that at this time my client is not prepared to agree to accept less than the full amount of his claim.

For your information, suit in connection with said claim will be filed next Monday morning unless in the interim there has been received from you a definite proposition for the satisfactory disposition of this matter.

Thanking you in advance for giving this matter your immediate attention and trusting that the problem will be adjusted to our mutual satisfaction, I beg to remain,

Before any letter is allowed to go out, it should be read with a critical eye, not only for typographical errors but for style. Is it clear? Is the tone right—neither too colloquial nor too stiff? Are the sentences too complicated? Have you fallen into the easy error of using legal jargon or trite business-letter phrases that can be replaced with simpler words?

If, when you get into practice, you are so lucky as to have an intelligent and capable secretary (and if you are intelligent enough to recognize her capability), ask for her critical judgment—whether one word or another sounds better, whether the way you phrased a sentence is tactful, or is clear. She can give you valuable help. Certainly encourage her to feel free to correct obvious errors or to check with you any questions of grammar. The competent writer knows how easy it is to make grammatical slips that escape notice in dictating but are all too noticeable in print. Only the man who is unsure of himself feels impelled to pretend that he does not need help.

Letters to the Opposing Party: The Representation Letter

The first letter to the opposing party is usually to inform him that your client is making claim against him (or that the claim, which he already knows exists, has now been placed in your hands) and to make demand that the obligation be met. In some forms of legal proceedings, notice or demand is a prerequisite.

What sort of information should such a letter contain? Few generalizations are possible. The answer may depend on the nature of the case. One simple form follows:

Dear Sir:

We represent Mr. George Gordon, who has asked that we prosecute his claim against you for . . ..

I suggest that you transmit this letter to your attorney, in order that we may discuss it before we institute legal proceedings.

Would this form of letter suffice in writing to a businessman? Would it suffice in writing to a person who had injured your client in an automobile collision? In writing to the latter, might it be well to enlarge somewhat by (1) asking whether he is insured, and if so, asking for the name of his insurance company; (2) saying in effect that unless he responds to your letter promptly, you will (a) file suit, (b) institute proceedings with the Motor Vehicle Division to have his driver's license revoked, or (c) both of these?

Here is a letter to an insurance carrier:

Gentlemen:

Mr. Paul Plant, of this city, has asked us to represent him in prosecuting a claim against Mr. Dan Devlin, of Chappaqua, New York, who says he is insured by your company.

Mr. Plant sustained multiple injuries when the automobile he was driving was struck by a car driven by Mr. Devlin, at the intersection of 4th and Central Streets, in this city, on May 20, 1961.

You may wish to discuss the possibility of adjusting this claim without resort to litigation. If so, I should be glad to talk with you.

You will observe that this letter makes no demand for prompt action. It is addressed to an insurance agency that the writer knows is reasonably expeditious in adjusting claims. Suppose the company is one known to be slow in paying claims? Would you threaten to file suit unless a reply is received within a certain number of days? Would you try to achieve the same end more subtly by saying that you will withhold filing suit for a few days to give the recipient time to make a satisfactory adjustment?

Some lawyers do not write any such letter; they file suit first and then negotiate. This may be sound strategy when the amount of the claim is substantial and the company has a policy of limiting the amount for which adjusters may settle. Claims on which suit has been filed are taken out of the adjusters' hands and turned over to the company's attorneys, who probably have broader and perhaps unlimited discretion in making settlements.

The letter quoted above says almost nothing about the facts out of which the claim arose. Would reciting the facts (assuming they supported the claim) and arguing the justice of the demand have strengthened the letter? Should the writer anticipate and attempt to answer defenses that the other party will probably raise? Would it help to expound the law, to show that the claim is well founded? If your answer to these questions is "yes," just how do you think such amplification would help? The resolution of these questions depends on research into the substantive law and on judgment concerning the technique of negotiation and trial. These subjects are beyond the scope of this book. It must suffice here to point out that in letters, as elsewhere, effective writing requires careful planning and clear thinking about what you want to accomplish.

Other Letters to the Opposing Party

Letters written to the opposing party or his attorney call for careful planning. A first question is whether the letter should come from your client or from you. A personal appeal or a simple claim that can perhaps be settled without the intervention of a lawyer may better come from the client; a letter from a lawyer may frighten or otherwise stimulate the recipient into retaining counsel. But when you want to insulate your client against having to make any statement himself, or when the strength of your legal position is more likely to be appreciated by a lawyer than by a layman, or when for some other reason the intervention of a lawyer is desirable, necessary or inevitable, the letter should ordinarily be signed by counsel, and perhaps should also invite the recipient to consult counsel.

Even if you decide that the letter should come from your client, it had better be written by you, or at least read and edited by you before it is sent. A layman unconscious of the legal implications of his words may inadvertently say things that prove to be misleading or otherwise embarrassing.

If you have been told by the other party that a certain lawyer is representing him, courtesy and professional ethics dictate that you carry on any correspondence through the lawyer, and not by-pass him to communicate directly with the client.

If you write without careful planning and thinking, you may say things you will regret. If you write before you have adequately investigated the facts and explored the legal theories on which your case might rest, you may find later that some of your words undermine your position. If, in a contract case, your first letters assert that your client rescinded, or that there was a mutual rescission, you may have difficulty in reconciling this when you later want to assert a claim for damages for breach.

Evaluation of your case helps you to determine not only what to say, but the tone in which to say it. When you find you have a weak case, you may want to be more conciliatory in addressing the other side than if you have a strong one. Provoking an all-out fight is rarely wise; provoking a fight that you probably won't win is foolhardy.

Some basic desiderata we can lay down for any letter presenting a claim or a complaint against the other party: such a letter should be (1) courteous and even-tempered in tone; (2) precise in stating the grounds for complaint and what you are asking the recipient to do about it; and (3) explicit in making clear the good faith of the complaining party. Even if your client has in his own conduct of the dispute reached a point of anger or abuse, your letter on his behalf should be polite and evince good will. Never mail a letter that was written in anger. Giving vent to vituperation or sarcasm may, it is true, help work off one's feelings. If writing a letter giving someone "a piece of your mind" brings relief to the rest of it, why, do so—but don't mail it. If you will hold it for even one day, you will be glad you didn't send it.

In answering letters threatening suit, your aims will again dictate the tone of your letter. Since it is more often to the client's interest to take half a loaf and agree than to assume the burdens and the hazards of litigation, you should, whenever compromise is possible, adopt a tone that will facilitate rather than preclude settlement. Courtesy and an attitude of reasonableness are as important in answering as in presenting claims. Avoid opening with a negative: "I cannot," "I take issue," "The allegations in your letter of . . . are incorrect."

Some people seem to lack sensitivity to the tone their words give off. By tone we mean the connotation behind the words as distinguished from their literal denotation. Sometimes the connotation is very different from what the writer intended.

> It is unfortunate if, as you allege, the B44 Easton winch did not in your opinion perform satisfactorily the work which you expected it to do. Let me point out that my client, Easton Iron Works, was not told the use to which you expected to put this equipment and made no representation that it would be suitable for such work. It is therefore our contention that your assertions do not constitute a defense to our claim for the purchase price.

"It wa'n't so much as wot 'e said/As the narsty w'y 'e said it." Can you spot the words that give a "narsty" tone to this whole letter? Other words or phrases that lawyers as well as businessmen may find themselves using in their letter-writing but which carry unfriendly or even hostile overtones are:

Although you assert that
If this is the case
Let us have
We maintain, we contend
Your proposal is impractical

Just why is any one of these phrases likely to create resentment? Let us see if we can analyze the psychological reactions they arouse.

"Although you assert that." This implies that the assertion is wrong. An implication to your reader that he is in the wrong will only arouse resistance. Other phrases that tell him "You're wrong" are: "We cannot understand," "Your insinuation," "Your statement is not a fact."

"If this is the case." This indicates doubt whether his allegation is truthful. Never impugn your reader's good faith. Do not say, "You cannot really believe," "Do you actually mean," or "No one could conscientiously contend."

"Your proposal is impractical." Whether intentionally or not, this is insulting. So are other expressions that impugn a person's intelligence: "We question the wisdom of," "I wish to inform you," "We would have you know." Grossly insulting are phrases that imply even more bluntly that he is stupid: "This contention is too preposterous," "You evidently misunderstood," "You seem to be confused," "If you will reread my previous letter, you will see."

"Let us have." Your reader is sure to be offended if you seem to be ordering him around. Do not say, "You must," "We should like to have this done promptly," "You should execute that form at once, as we previously instructed."

"We maintain that." Unduly positive assertions may sound belligerent: "I take issue," "your neglect," "I do not intend to," "We do not see fit to." Even words that are usually inoffensive may give this impression when used in presenting an argument: "perfectly clear," "certainly," "obviously," "undoubtedly," "it stands to reason."

Subtly identifying oneself with the reader is one way to handle a situation requiring some tact: "I am sure you feel as I do about," "Perhaps we have not understood each other."

Softening terms, such as "perhaps" and "it would seem" are other ways of exercising tact.

Here is a letter to opposing counsel who has refused to allow inspection of exhibits in his possession:

Dear Mr. Cranall:

Thank you for your reply to my letter of July 3, in which I requested an opportunity to inspect and photograph the exhibits in your possession which were marked for identification during pre-trial depositions. We regret that the notice of the pre-trial conference finds you occupied with other matters. All of us, however, face the necessity of preparing for trial in this litigation.

As you remember, counsel agreed that exhibits retained by either side would be open for inspection by the other side. In order to prepare an index of the exhibits for the Court and to prepare our own files for an orderly and mutually beneficial pre-trial conference, we must ask that you grant us access to the exhibits in your possession. Since your associate, Mr. Bixler, is familiar with the case, we hope that in your absence he can take the few minutes necessary to open the exhibits to our inspection.

You suggest a meeting to discuss the setting of a trial date and Mr. Hardy's inspection of "advertising and possibly other documents which we [plaintiff] may wish to disclose to him." We await your suggestions concerning such inspection. We might point out that a few minutes of the time you plan to give to such a meeting can also be spent in turning over the aforementioned exhibits for our inspection.

We look forward to a reply to our letter of April 12, in which we asked whether you had possession of certain exhibits which are missing from the Court's files.

Very truly yours,

Answering Inquiries

In answering an inquiry or a statement you need not always begin by repeating it. If you start with such a phrase as, "In reply to your question whether," or "As concerns your suggestion that," you are likely to find yourself writing a long and awkward sentence, because you are trying both to restate the question or suggestion and to reply to it, all in one sentence. It may be simpler to make two sentences of it, one for the question, and one for the answer. Start the first, "You ask," or "You suggest." Then give your reply—without any introductory words such as "In reply."

> You ask whether you could effect any tax saving by incorporating. Probably not. The act provides . . ..
>
> You suggest that we stipulate the number of acres taken. I have no objection to this, provided . . ..

If the question or point you are answering can be referred to in few words, you may be able to refer to it and give your reply in one sentence. But you should still try to avoid the stilted and hackneyed "In reply to your question" introduction.

> The only answer I can give to your question of when your case will come to trial is that it will probably not be within the next month.

In answering questions that require some explaining, the best practice ordinarily is to give as direct and categorical an answer as you can right at the outset, and then give your supporting reasons or data. The ultimate answer is what the reader wants, so why try his patience? Moreover, if you tell him your conclusion first, he can follow your explanation more easily because he knows which way you are going. One of the few situations where it may be preferable to withhold the conclusion is where that conclusion is unfavorable. We shall say more about this in the next chapter, on Opinions.

When you have to explain to your client the other side's position or try to show him the fallacy of his own position, you may not want to present that other position more forcefully than you need. Words like rather, somewhat, and the "not un-" formulation will come to mind. It is a little easier to say to your client that his creditor "not unnaturally" wants his money; if you tell him that the fellow "naturally" wants his money, he is likely to ask bitterly, "Whose side are you on, anyway?" So it is easier to tell him that the other's position is "not unreasonable" than it is to tell him that it is "reasonable."

But here again: don't let the "not un-" form become a habit that you follow without good reason. Telling a grumbling client that the amount of your fee is "not unreasonable" sounds apologetic and unconvincing.

Letters of Refusal or Rejection

We often face the task of saying "no"—not only to the adverse party but also to clients and friends. You will normally want to do so courteously—because you don't want to hurt the person's feelings or because you want to keep his good will or at least not infuriate him into initiating litigation or taking some other step that you want to avoid. With careful wording, you can make your answer a good deal more palatable.[2]

2. It is not the function of this book to teach how to say no in words that seem to say yes, as in the note of the tactful editor to a would-be author: "I shall lose no time in reading your manuscript."

Lincoln had this tact. Importuned to write a recommendation for a certain book, he finally consented and wrote: "This is just the right kind of book for anyone who desires just this kind of book."

Politeness calls for promptness. If you have not been able to reply promptly, an explanation should be given showing that you have not neglected his complaint, have acted on it promptly and replied as quickly as you could.

Politeness also calls for avoiding an air of curtness. The blunt refusal can be softened by a circumlocution. "I will not" becomes "I am not in a position to," "cannot see my way to," or "am not prepared to."

These polite formulas for refusal are well-meant and not to be condemned. But you should be able to find better ways to carry out your good intentions than any of those quoted above. Saying that you are "not in a position to" may bring a flippant retort to the mind of a literal-minded reader. Saying you are not prepared tells him only that you have made no preparations for doing; it does not say you cannot or will not do. (Saying you "are prepared," as a way of giving an affirmative answer, is no better, and does not even have the excuse that you are trying to soften the blow; the best and most pleasing way to say yes is in the shortest and most direct words.)

The danger in these stock formulas is that overuse of them may rob your words of the ring of sincerity. Their function is to avoid a curt or unfeeling tone. But glibly tossing off the stereotype substitutes sounds just as unfeeling. The best solution is not to use any work-worn phrase, but to explain in your own words in some detail and with some expression of interest in the matter just why you must give an unfavorable answer.

Here is a letter of refusal written by an eminent New York lawyer:

Dear Mrs. Polodner:

After a careful consideration of the facts concerning your accident of September 22, 1959, and our subsequent investigation, I believe the probability of success in litigation is extremely remote, and I must regretfully advise you that I cannot undertake this matter.

Under the circumstances we think you would be well advised to make the best settlement possible with the representatives of the insurance carrier of the owner of the premises.

Our good wishes to you. Perhaps we may be of service to you at some future time.

Sincerely yours,

Emile Zola Berman

Using the subjunctive instead of the indicative is a meliorating device. "It would seem" and "I should think" sound even less dogmatic and less assertive than "It seems" or "I think." Bergen and Cornelia Evans say that expressions like "I would think" and "it would seem" "represent the most extreme caution. The thinking or seeming is first placed in the future and then made conditional or uncertain. It is a very modest way of speaking." [3] But "the most extreme caution" is sometimes exactly what is needed. And cautiousness is not synonymous with modesty.

A letter rejecting a claim or demand should try to be conciliatory. Ben Franklin's advice is worth remembering: when you must disagree with a person, try to start with some point on which you can agree with him, and so lead up to your point of disagreement. The more serious the disagreement and the more heat or bitterness that may be aroused, the more reason there is for trying hard to start on a pleasant note. An expression of willingness to do all that fairness demands or to meet all obligations that are legally owing shows good faith. The letter may also express concern or regret over the loss or disappointment that the party has experienced, and when possible and appropriate, should offer a constructive suggestion of some other remedy or source to look to or course of action to take. He will usually be grateful for such a friendly showing of interest.

Perhaps from the validity of using circumlocutions to avoid curtness in refusing requests or in giving other unfavorable answers has spread an impression that politeness calls for wordiness in any communication, even one conveying the most welcome news. There is a grain of truth in this. A brief and businesslike letter may be so short as to give the reader the impression that you consider yourself too important and busy a man to give leisurely attention to him and his problems, and that you do

3. A Dictionary of Contemporary American Usage 558 (1957).

not care to expend more time and words on him than you must. To avoid giving any such impression, you may want to add a few words that show a personal interest over and beyond the call of professional duty.

The owner of a local chain of five stores entered into a collective bargaining agreement with a labor union representing his 32 employees. The agreement called for a periodic cost-of-living adjustment in wage rates. The union has asked for such an adjustment and the owner has agreed to discuss this demand. He has now received a letter asking that before the time for the meeting he furnish the union with certain financial information. He does not want to give it. Compiling it would put him to some trouble and expense and he does not believe that the union is entitled to demand it. He consults his lawyer, who decides that the employer is not required to furnish the information. Here are two drafts for a letter to be sent to the union:

Dear Sir:

The information you ask for would require an undue amount of time and effort to compile and I do not see what relation it has to the subject of our meeting. If you will give me a more specific reason showing why it is essential to our agreement, I will supply it. However, without knowing what useful purpose it will serve, I will not take time to gather information which I feel to be irrelevant.

Yours truly,

Dear Sir:

Thank you for your prompt reply. I am glad that October 12 is satisfactory to you as the date for us to get together to discuss your proposal for wage renegotiation.

The information you requested, showing the number of hours' work per week for each employee and his total pay and rate of pay for the week before the contract went into effect, would require a considerable amount of time to compile. It probably could not be done in time for our meeting, as you request, or even for some time thereafter.

I do not think, however, that those figures will be needed for our discussions. None of this information would seem to be helpful either for purposes of wage negotiation or for administration of the contract. You can understand that we therefore do not want to assume the trouble and expense of compiling it. Nor, I assume, would you want to postpone the discussions until it could be compiled.

In the absence of a showing that this information is needed, I shall assume that we shall meet as agreed, on October 12th.

Yours truly,

Is the first letter "tougher" in fact, or only in tone? If only in tone, what useful purpose does such tone serve? Consider in this connection the point often emphasized that the relationship between the parties to a labor dispute, unlike that between parties to ordinary litigation, "is a necessarily continuing one and it is going to go on after the case itself is over." [4] The parties are going to have to go on living together, and anything that leads to bad feeling and bitterness is going to make living together more difficult.

Collection Letters

Many good customers have been lost to business firms by offensive collection letters. We have said earlier that planning is important in any writing. It is as important for writing collection letters as any other. Here, as elsewhere, the writer must ask, what am I trying to accomplish? "To get him to pay, of course!" is too simple an answer. It will frequently be fairly certain that your first letter will not accomplish this and so there may be other, more modest, objectives to aim for. Let us list some:

To get written acknowledgment of the debt. This may be important in cases where reasons exist for suspecting that the debtor will deny liability. When the amount may be disputed, it helps to get a written admission that the amount claimed is correct.

To obtain prompt payment from a debtor who is merely slow.

To persuade the debtor to visit the writer's office to discuss the matter.

To warn him that legal action will be taken unless he pays up.

---

4. Wirtz, Collective Bargaining: Lawyers' Role in Negotiations and Arbitrations, 34 A.B.A.J. 547 (1948).

To induce him to make a part payment on the account.

Not only your objective, but other considerations need to be taken into account. Do you want to suggest that he consult a lawyer—or do you want carefully to avoid doing so? Suppose, although he owes the money, some technical defense may be open to him, such as the statute of frauds or the statute of limitations. How "tough" should you be? Do you want to threaten suit? In your first letter? Your second? Remember that you need not try to do everything in one letter. It may be more effective to start with a mild and friendly reminder, withholding stronger language and threats for later.

If the creditor is a business firm with a well-run credit department, it will have sent the debtor a series of letters before turning the account over to you for collection. Before writing your first letter, you should review the file and read the letters that have been sent. Usually, there will have been a series of at least three or four letters before the account was turned over for legal action. Many firms have a carefully organized series of letters, starting with a mere reminder, followed by one or more stronger reminders, a "discussion" letter (asking, in effect, "Won't you tell us what the difficulty is?") and an ultimatum, expressed with some urgency, threatening action.

Some firms aim to make certain kinds of appeals in their various letters:

(1) The appeal to good will. The debtor's good intentions are not questioned; the letter assumes that he has overlooked or forgotten the bill, or that there is some reason for the delay.

(2) The appeal to pride. The letter refers to the debtor's good credit record, the standing and reputation of his firm, and implies that to maintain this good repute, he should pay up.

(3) The appeal to fair play. The purpose here is to make the customer feel that he is not treating his creditor fairly. Although sometimes used, this is not a very effective approach: people are not as concerned with their creditor's troubles as with their own. They are more impressed by suggestions that their own credit or reputation will suffer than by statements that "We need the money" or that "We have thousands of charge accounts and cannot afford" etc.

In reviewing the previous correspondence, you may want to check whether all these approaches have been exhausted. If not, you may want to make use of them. If they have already been tried, repeating them would presumably be futile.

Throughout his own correspondence with the debtor, the creditor probably has hoped not only to collect the money, but also to keep the customer's good will. Most customers who become delinquent do pay, eventually, and most business houses prefer to keep such customers than to lose them. Even when the account is turned over to a lawyer for collection, the creditor may hope that a letter from a lawyer will convince a slow-paying debtor that the time has come when he must pay up, and that he will do so and remain a customer. Whether there is any such hope left, or whether your client is "through" with him, is something you should find out. The tone of your letters, and the speed with which you proceed to start suit, may depend on what your client wants you to do: get the money merely, or also retain good will.

Compare the relative urgency or insistence conveyed by each of the following formulas:

Perhaps you have not intentionally neglected this obligation

We have had no response to our several letters

The company billed you for this item on June 1, and again on July 1. A reminder that the bill remained unpaid was sent you on July 15.

At your earliest convenience

Immediately, promptly

The stuffy pomposity that we have been inveighing against in the chapter on Simplicity and at the beginning of this chapter is encountered in collection letters as often as anywhere else. What could be done to take the windiness out of this one?

Dear Sir:

American Furniture Company has referred to us for our attention its claim as to your past due obligation to that company. Please be advised that unless a communication is received by either the undersigned or Mr. James Brobeck, credit manager of American Furniture Company, within ten days from date relating the manner in which you contemplate liquidating this delinquent obligation, we shall be constrained to inaugurate such proceedings as our client may deem appropriate to effect collection as to this item.

The example of advertising form letters may mislead students into trying to contrive far-fetched introductions or trick phrases to attract attention. These devices may have a place in advertising circulars, but they are in poor taste and fail to strike the right tone for the correspondence of a professional man.

Evaluate each of the following as an opening paragraph:

Jeffs & Trimble have been glad to extend credit to you over the years. But they too have obligations to meet. They cannot continue indefinitely to carry delinquent accounts such as yours and remain in business.

The Warner Appliance Co. has remained in business for many years largely because of its policy of courteousness and fair play.

I don't know whether you're a fisherman. If you are, you will agree it's a great sport.

I'm fishing this morning, but frankly it isn't such good sport. I'm fishing for some money that you owe to

No! Don't file this letter in the waste basket! This is not just another dunning letter! This is opportunity knocking!

Because during the past years you have shown that you have integrity and can shoulder responsibility, Mr. James Easy, credit manager for my client, Acme Builders, and I have agreed that you should be given an opportunity to make special arrangements for squaring your account.

I very much regret that you have not replied to my letter of Sept. 30. You leave me no alternative but to bring suit. Since that would entail some extremely unfortunate consequences for you, I am writing to give you this last opportunity to settle the matter out of court.

The debtor should be made to understand that your client means what he says. If the client's last letter threatened to turn the account over to an attorney unless it was paid by the first of the month, the debtor should get a letter from the attorney promptly after the first of the month. If you threaten to take legal action unless he pays or responds by a certain date, when that date arrives you will have to act. It is therefore a mistake to make a threat that you may not want to carry out. As Groucho Marx once put it, "Never take a position that you cannot back up—from."

When you do lay down an ultimatum ("Unless I hear from you by November 1, I shall have to institute legal proceedings"), it is good practice to enlarge on it somewhat. If too briefly worded, it may not sufficiently impress the recipient with the seriousness of his situation. A sentence pointing out the unpleasant consequences of a lawsuit may stir him to action.

Three home-owners on the outskirts of a city had obtained an agreement from the gas company to extend its mains to serve their houses. They paid the cost of the extension, but weeks passed, and the company did not get to this job. The owners wrote several letters, and finally wanted to put their case as strongly as possible to induce the company to act. They feared, however, that a letter that merely annoyed and did not scare would probably only cause more delay. They certainly did not want to resort to the expensive and slow remedy of bringing suit. The company was busy; the city was growing rapidly and it would probably be hard to prove that this job was being needlessly delayed. Their attorney wrote a letter reviewing the delays that had already occurred and closed with a paragraph carefully worded to be as strong as he could make it without arousing resentment:

> If you are still not able at this time to fulfill your contract, I urge, for your own protection, that you consult your legal department on the question whether the company is not rendering itself liable in damages for breach of contract.

The pipe was laid the next week—whether by coincidence or by reason of this letter we cannot know. But it is reasonable to guess that it would not have been laid if the letter had more bluntly threatened suit.

Exercise

Mr. John Wembley, owner of Wembley's Stationery Store, owes the Office Supply Company $274.50 on his account, now four months delinquent. Wembly has built his business himself, over the past six years. The credit manager of Office Supply believes that the delinquency in payment is due to Wembley's having over-extended himself. Four letters have been sent, the last threatening to turn the account over to "our attorney." None of these has brought any response and the account has now been given to you for collection. Your client tells you that he would be willing to accept as little as $50. on account, the balance to be paid over a six-months period. Write two letters to Wembley, the second to be sent two weeks after the first.

Form and Guide Letters

A lawyer will rarely if ever have occasion to send out printed form letters. He may, however, make good use of guide letters, a term used for standard forms of phrasing that can be copied as needed.

For some purposes, it is almost impossible not to devise a guide letter. A lawyer long in practice can hardly avoid evolving a form of wording for a representation letter in a common type of case, such as an automobile collision. Why not take time to do it well, once, and then use the same form of wording in other cases?

Even when some variation in wording is necessary to meet varying situations, different standard form paragraphs can be combined to meet specific needs.

Some law firms handling a large volume of plaintiffs' cases send out a form of letter to new clients which gives some general information about how the case will be handled. This saves answering individual questions that a person who has never before been a party to a lawsuit may want to ask. Here is such a letter:

Dear Mr. _____ :

You may like to know something about how the case that you have retained us to handle for you will be processed.

The first step will be an investigation, conducted by one of our investigators. When he has gathered all the relevant information and has submitted his report, we shall proceed to file suit.

A copy of the complaint will then have to be sent out to be served on the defendant or defendants. Sometimes they have moved away or are for some other reason hard to find. Until they are found and served, a case cannot proceed. But we place the papers in the hands of a process-server whose job it is to find the defendant.

After the defendant has been served, he generally has thirty days in which to file a written answer. Sometimes for one reason or another the time is extended. We do not, however, give our consent to unlimited extensions of time to any defendant. This is so that your case may be "at issue" as quickly as possible.

When the defendants have answered our complaint, the case is ready to go to trial. Unfortunately, the volume of litigation in our county is so great that the courts are now almost three years behind on their dockets. The judges are trying to cut down this delay, but without much success.

Some time after the case is filed, the defendants will probably want to have you examined by their doctor or doctors, and perhaps to take your deposition (that is, your answers to certain questions, in writing). We shall write to you at that time.

The defendant or his insurance company may offer to settle the case out of court. There is, however, no uniform practice about this. Some companies wait until the very day of trial; others are willing to negotiate earlier. If they think they can win the case, they may not be willing to settle at all. We shall inform you at once of any offer of settlement we receive.

If, for a period of time, you do not hear from us about your case, please do not think that we have forgotten it. We shall be waiting for the court to set a date for the trial. Before we go to trial, we shall ask you to come to our office to discuss it, together with any questions you may have.

If questions occur to you in the meantime, you will probably be able to find the answers to most of them by rereading this letter. I therefore suggest that you keep it so that you can refer to it when needed. If anything you need to know cannot be found in the letter, please write to us. You may find it hard to reach us by telephone; a lawyer, as you know, spends much of his time in court. But if you will write us to ask any specific questions, you will always receive a prompt reply.

Very truly yours,

Another type of case in which a guide letter (or even a form letter) can be used is workmen's compensation. Counsel representing either the claimant or the insurance carrier may want to use a standard form of letter addressed to the employer, requesting the information usually needed, concerning the claimant's rate of pay, the length of his absence from work following the accident, etc.

Form letters have been recommended for obtaining statements from witnesses: [5]

One of the best methods for obtaining statements from witnesses is to send out a form letter in which there are interrogatories for the witness to answer. Public utility companies use these form letters with great effectiveness. It is very difficult for any witness to refute any statements made in the answers to the interrogatories, because the answers are all in his own words and in his own handwriting, and are made in his home or office with no claim agent or investigator present to prompt him or suggest answers.

5. Roemer, Investigation and Preparation of an Automobile Case, 1953 U.Ill.L.F. 8, 14.

Chapter 9

EXAMINATIONS: OPINIONS

I. LAW SCHOOL AND BAR EXAMINATIONS

Law school examinations give students their first experience in legal writing. Those who learn to write examinations effectively will be able to use much the same process later in writing opinions, memoranda of law and briefs.

Bar examiners commonly inform examinees what kind of answers are wanted. Typically, they say examinees should aim to show their ability to analyze the facts presented and to discern the point or points of law on which resolution should turn. This calls for ability to distinguish material from immaterial facts, knowledge of the pertinent legal principles and ability to apply those principles to the facts and to think logically in reasoning one's way to a conclusion. Law school examinations are designed to test for essentially the same capabilities.

Think Before You Write

Before you put a single word on paper, think the problem through. Think until you have your answer clearly in mind. If your thoughts remain diffused and imprecise, no amount of effort to garb them in artful words will hide the deficiency of substance.

Time spent in thinking will not cost you time for writing. On the contrary, it will save time. You may not believe this, so it is worth emphasizing. Studies have shown that students write more, not less, when they have first spent 15 minutes out of an hour planning what they want to write than when they spend only five minutes in planning.[1] So take time to think. Do not

---

1. Brand and White, Legal Writing: The Strategy of Persuasion 60 (1976). This book is largely devoted to advice on how to write law examinations.

let the sight of others busily writing away infect you with the itch to start writing too, trusting that your thoughts will unroll as you write. It takes firmness to just sit there, thinking. But do it. Take plenty of time to (1) think through the fact situation, (2) identify the issues involved and the legal rule that governs each issue, (3) decide how the rule applies to the facts and (4) come to a conclusion. Once you know where you are going, you will get there more directly and so more quickly than if you ramble.

Use scratch paper to jot down your thoughts, and then organize them into some sort of outline. Even if the issues are few and uncomplicated, take time to write an outline. A simple one may be all that is needed, such as the following:

1.   Did D's act constitute a battery?

   A.   Was there intent to injure?

   B.   Was there consent to the touching?

2.   Did D commit false imprisonment?

Most questions will require more detailed analysis than that, but even for the simplest, consisting perhaps only of point one and point two, jotting it down in writing is useful. It will at least require you to consider which point is the more important and which therefore should come first. Even after you have thought through the problem and written the outline, it will be worth while to take a minute or two more going over the problem, to make sure that there is not something else that needs to be said. You may find that there is.

Even students (and lawyers) who know they should outline before they write may at times find their thoughts coming so rapidly and so smoothly that they decide they have the problem well in mind and do not need to complete an outline. All too often, they get so warmed up to their subject that they write on and on, until they have to stop and consider whether they haven't wandered off course.

First year law students tend to be overly concerned about finding the "right" answer. But both law school and bar examinations, especially the written, essay-type (we are not here concerned with objective-type questions), are typically designed to test for ability to reason even more than for knowledge of legal rules. The question may not even have a "right" answer. It may be designed to present a border-line situation on which a plausible argument can be made on either side. It may in effect ask whether a recognized principle of law should be extended to a novel situation. The purpose is to test whether you not only "know" the applicable law in the sense of being able to recall and state it, parrotlike, but whether you appreciate its rationale and the social purpose it is meant to serve, and whether you can evaluate how the facts presented comport with that purpose. Whichever way you decide to hold, you will be judged on how well you evaluate the considerations pro and con and how soundly and persuasively you support the conclusion you reach.

Reading a question, you may recognize the facts as resembling those of a leading case. "Ha, that's the Foley case," you say to yourself, happily because you well remember that case and the class discussion of it. So you quickly finish reading the question, eager to get down to answering a question you know you can handle well. But beware! Although the facts presented may indeed be much the same as those of the Foley case, the examiner may have changed or added a few details, in a way that presents a new issue or raises a doubt whether the result in the Foley case should follow here. Indeed, that some such change has been made is more than likely. As already said, the examination is designed to test your ability to reason, so the question is probably not merely asking whether you remember the Foley case; rather, it asks whether you can evaluate the distinction between the two sets of facts and reach a sound judgment on whether the Foley result should be extended to this somewhat different situation.

Not only a familiar case, but also a familiar rule of law may lead you astray. A question about an automobile collision, for example, may raise a question of last clear chance. Because you have that subject well in mind, you happily start off on a lengthly disquisition on the subject. Restrain yourself! Your task is to answer the question, which means coming to a reasoned conclusion concerning who is liable for what. You have not been asked to write an essay on last clear chance. You will need to discuss that subject in reasoning your way to your conclusion, but keep the discussion relevant to that end. Don't abandon your task to take off on a proud display of all you know about last clear chance. You may be able to show that you know a lot, but you will do so at the cost of displaying your inability to distinguish the relevant from the irrelevant.

The facts given may on a certain question seem incomplete or ambiguous. The purpose may be to test your ability to recognize that a sound conclusion will depend upon additional facts or upon what interpretation is given to the facts presented. Point out the lack or the ambiguity and say that your answer is based upon certain assumed facts, and how it would differ if the facts were otherwise.

Writing the Answer

Having thought the problem through and organized what you want to say, you are now ready to start writing. The best way to start is with a categorical answer. If the question is, "May plaintiff recover?" or "Should the motion be granted?" let your first sentence be, "Plaintiff may (may not) recover," or "The motion should (should not) be granted." That not only tells the reader right at the outset where you are headed, but restrains you from the impulse to start writing until you have firmly made up your mind.

Next, identify the issues and discuss them, one by one. That they should be discussed one at a time would seem obvious, but students having two points to discuss all too often slide from one to the other and back again, until the reader is unsure which point is being discussed at a given moment. One important rule of style, as already said,[2] is to control yourself when you happen to have two things to say; say first one, then the other, not both at the same time. You may properly identify several issues in one sentence: "Plaintiff has a cause of action against the other motorist and against the city." But you should then start a new paragraph, discussing the action against the motorist. Complete that discussion before you begin discussing the action against the city.

---

2. Ante, p. 140.

Do not waste time—yours and your reader's—restating the facts. The examiner has them well in mind. You need not inform him, for example, that "The defendant drove his car at a speed of 50 miles per hour on a city street within a 30 mile per hour speed zone." Refer to this fact as you make your argument: "Driving at 50 miles per hour through a 30-mile speed zone itself constituted negligence."

Your discussion should move in a straight line from beginning to conclusion, with no backing and filling—no insertions written in the margin, no new paragraph starting, "As I should have said earlier," or "A further thought on what I said in paragraph 1," no second thoughts that amend or even contradict what had been said before. Such additions or amendments show that the problem had not been adequately thought through to begin with. When you find that such changes are needed, instead of trying to patch things up, start over. Consider how the new thought should be integrated into the discussion, and rewrite your answer.

A common weakness of examination answers is failure to adequately support the conclusion. The writer states the rule and then the conclusion, as if the connection were self-evident. Sometimes it is, more or less. But even if it is, the steps by which the rule has been applied to the facts and the conclusion reached should be spelled out. This reasoning, as already said, is what the examiner is mainly interested in. So lay it out. One way to check whether you have done so is to ask yourself whether you have explained why. Why do you say the defendant is liable? Why does this conduct constitute an assault, or a contract?

Although a question may be one on which an argument could be made for one result or the other, take a definite stand and make as strong an argument for it as you can. This does not mean ignoring the unfavorable facts or arguments. On the contrary, it requires facing and meeting them. Explore all the considerations pro and con, but do not quit with such an "on the one hand and on the other" kind of analysis. Make a choice, and explain why that seems the better view.

Conclusion

A brief conclusion is a way of tying up your discussion neatly. This can be done in a sentence and needs no great time or effort.

Try to allow time to reread and edit your answers. Even the short time between writing your answer to the first question and the last will give you a fresh perspective. You may find passages that you now see are unclear or fail to say what you meant, or that are ungrammatical or poorly phrased. Tidying them up will improve the impression your paper makes.

II. OPINIONS

The primary—and usually the only—purpose of an opinion on a point of law is to advise the client concerning his rights, remedies or liabilities. May he take a tax deduction for a certain item of expense? Would he subject himself to liability if he pursued a certain contemplated course of action? Has he a valid claim against another?

But there may also be secondary purposes. The client may want to use the opinion to support his position in a negotiation or a dispute with an adversary party, such as a business rival, a labor union or a governmental agency. He may want to use it in dealing with his own board of directors or stockholders. He may want it for publicity purposes, as to explain his position in a statement to the press. In a large organization, an opinion from the legal department may be designed to guide or protect the administrative official who must make the decision. How the opinion is written may depend to some extent on the purpose for which it is intended.

One of the first questions to consider is whether you should give your client a written opinion at all. Suppose the question is whether a certain practice that a business client is following violates some regulatory provision, such as the blue-sky laws, the Securities Act, the Federal Trade Commission Act, the National Labor Relations Act, the Fair Labor Standards Act, or a fair-employment practices act. It may be your judgment that his practice violates the act or may be held to do so. If you tell him so frankly in a written opinion, you must consider the possibility that this document may subsequently be supoenaed in an investigation by the regulatory agency. This danger, if any, may have to be weighed against the desirability of having a written record of the fact that you warned him.

Outline

Although the internal organization of an opinion will depend somewhat on its purpose, the nature of the subject and the person to whom it is addressed, one general outline that will usually serve would include (1) a statement of the facts on which it is based, (2) the conclusion, giving the answer to the question put or saying what the client should or should not do, and (3) the explanation or documentation of the conclusion reached. In an evaluation of a personal injury case, the opinion will have to consider whether a jury question can be raised, and probably also the extent of injuries and special damages. Often a judgment will be called for on the feasibility of trying to settle the claim, and its value for settlement purposes.

Before writing an opinion on a question put by a client, it is well to discuss the subject with him. After a full explanation of his problem, you may decide that the question that needs answering is somewhat different from the one he originally put.

Reciting the Facts

The facts on which the opinion is based should be carefully narrated at or near its beginning. All too often, clients fail to give counsel all the relevant facts. If the court ultimately holds contrary to the opinion (the trial having revealed some damaging facts which the client had not disclosed), you are protected if your opinion shows that it was based on a statement of facts materially different from those proved. If your understanding of the facts is based on a conference with the client, it is well to refer to it: "On the following facts, which you related to me when we discussed the case in my office last Monday, May 10th . . . ."

No opinion should be written, of course, without adequate investigation. Getting all the relevant facts may not be easy. In law school, the facts of a case are usually presented in the distilled form found in an appellate opinion or in the even more condensed form of an examination question. In practice, "the facts" do not come to the lawyer so neatly packaged. Even when they are presumably all within the knowledge of the client, as in an automobile accident in which he was a party, it is still no simple matter for the lawyer to get a true picture. First of all, the client is not usually able to distinguish legally relevant from irrelevant facts; he will spend much time narrating trivial details without significance and fail to emphasize and perhaps even to mention things that may be crucial. Winnowing the few hard kernels of fact from the chaff may require going over his story several times. Secondly, his version of the facts is almost inevitably biased. It is colored by his interpretation and by memory-selection which leads him to overlook things, especially those unfavorable to his cause. Young lawyers often learn by hard experience that a case that seems clearly meritorious on the client's story may collapse at the trial because the other side has overwhelming proof that the facts were otherwise. Skillful and tactful discussion (not suspicious cross-examination) may help the client remember some of the unfavorable details that need to be taken into account. This fact-gathering is not the subject of this book. The point to be emphasized here is that it must be done in any case depending on facts before the lawyer is in a position to render an opinion.

Often the full facts cannot be obtained; exactly what happened may be one of the questions in the case. The opinion in such situation should make clear that it rests on certain assumptions and that the conclusions might be different if these assumptions should prove unfounded. For the protection of the lawyer himself as well as for his client, he should underscore his assumptions with such words as "Assuming that the facts stated above can be established" or "If we can prove that."

The detail with which facts are set forth will depend on whether they are disputed and whether a legal conclusion depends upon them. Irrelevant or incidental information should be omitted, but what is relevant and significant in a given case is a matter of judgment. Concrete data, even though not strictly necessary, may be helpful to clarify and illustrate abstract propositions.

The Conclusion

The nucleus of your opinion is the conclusion. It should be as definite and as clear as you can make it. It certainly should not be susceptible of different interpretations. If you can say without qualification that the answer to the question presented is "yes" or "no," that certain action is lawful or unlawful, do so. But the young lawyer should be aware that the hazards of judicial vagaries, prejudices and plain ignorance are such that he cannot be sure that even the most learned and logical opinion will be followed by the court. He should therefore be chary about offering confident assurance that his client "can't lose." The American Bar Association Canons of Ethics warn us that:

> The miscarriages to which justice is subject, by reason of surprises and disappointments in evidence and witnesses, and through mistakes of juries and errors of Courts, even though only occasional, admonish lawyers to beware of bold and confident assurances to clients, especially where the employment may depend upon such assurances.

In writing your opinion, should you give your conclusion first and then explain how you arrived at it, or should you trace your reasoning and lead up to the conclusion? The answer may depend on the nature of the case and the nature of the client. Perhaps the most important consideration is whether the conclusion is favorable or unfavorable. If it is favorable there is usually no reason for withholding the good news:

> The practice you have been following has been specifically approved by the Commission.

> Durkin Brothers' failure to fill your order of August 1st appears on the facts presented to constitute a breach of contract.

Since, as already said, the client is primarily interested in the conclusion and very little if at all in the legal reasoning, withholding the conclusion may only make him impatient. To find your ultimate answer, he may skip rapidly over the paragraphs in which you present all the arguments and difficulties. He may pay more attention to those difficulties if you tell him at the outset that your conclusion is so-and-so, subject to the conditions and qualifications that follow. He will also be more able to follow your arguments if he knows at the outset the direction in which they are pointed.

If your conclusion is unfavorable, and especially if you fear that your client may be disappointed or annoyed thereby, you may want to lead up to it, first explaining the situation in a way that will permit him to see the logic and inevitability of your conclusion and to accept it when you ultimately state it. He may accept it more readily if you not only tell him what the law says, but also explain in a sentence or two, the reason or policy behind it.

One bit of foresight a lawyer should exercise: the opinion you write today may be filed by your client and pulled out to solve another problem another day. In the meantime, of course, the statutes may have been amended and new decisions handed down, so that even if all the relevant facts of his new problem are the same as the old (which, of course, they may not be), the conclusion stated in your memorandum may be quite inappropriate for the new question. You cannot prevent clients' doing this any more than doctors can prevent patients from taking a swig of the old medicine prescribed at a different time for what may or may not have been a similar ailment. About all you can do is to include some hortatory words warning that your conclusion assumes certain specific facts, and might not hold if those facts were different; and that it is based on the current state of the law and the statutes and regulations currently in effect.

Never suggest that your client himself write a letter making a legal proposal. Draft such a letter for him, or at least be sure that you will have the chance to see and approve the wording before it is sent. Do not say, "I recommend that you try to have included in the contract a provision allowing you to repossess if payments become more than 30 days delinquent." Always follow such a general recommendation with a specific form of wording.

"I believe" is not an expression that should be used in an opinion. In the first place, it weakens the force of the opinion. Secondly, it is not the correct term for the meaning intended. An opinion should be based on logic and reason, not on faith. "I feel" is subject to the same objection; it carries the implication that your conclusion is a mere hunch or guess. Use the word "feel" only to refer to literal tactile sensing or to thinking that rests on internal groping or sensitivity. The word "guess," of course, should never be used in an opinion; as one writer has candidly said, "it carries professional candor much too far."[3] The best wording is, "in my opinion."

"I am inclined to think" is legitimate, when you want to give your tentative opinion, yet serve notice that you are still considering the subject and that your final conclusion may be otherwise. But like all vague phrases, this one may prove habit-forming. Don't be seduced into using it in situations where the reader has a right to have your considered conclusion, and not merely a hint of how you are leaning. The phrase will not serve to evade giving a straight answer, when a straight answer is called for. If you are unable or unready to give a straight answer, say so, explaining why. If you don't have a good excuse, you are, of course, in an embarrassing position. But that is because of your laziness or neglect, and you do not really avoid the blame you deserve by using words that purport to give an answer but really give none. Your reader will probably be no less annoyed by this double-talk than he would by a frank admission that you don't know or have not yet found out.

The Conclusion in Doubtful Cases

The important cases in a lawyer's practice are almost always those in which the outcome is uncertain, because the law, the facts, or both, are in doubt. Cases in which the answers are clear will usually be disposed of quickly; if your client is clearly wrong, you will tell him so and try to settle out of court; if you are clearly right the other side will be anxious to settle. The cases on which you will be spending most of your efforts are those in which there is enough support for each side to encourage it to stand its ground and litigate.

How do you write an opinion when either the law or the possible findings of fact are so dubious that you cannot predict the

3. Levitan, Dissertation on Writing
Legal Opinions, 1960 Wis.L.Rev. 22,
38.

outcome? The client has asked for and is paying for an opinion, and he is going to be disappointed if you tell him, in effect, "I don't know." On the other hand, you will be misleading him if you pretend to more certainty than the situation justifies.

Here the lawyer may need to be more cautious than in any other writing he does. He may try to find refuge in hedging or Delphic double-talk. But this is at least as likely to disappoint and perhaps annoy as an opinion that ultimately turns out to be an erroneous prediction of what the court would do. Another device is to outline the law on the subject and the facts that would have to be proved if the client is to bring himself within the rule, tacitly leaving it to the client to judge for himself whether he can do so. For example, if asked whether a certain trade practice or agreement would be held to "substantially lessen competition" in violation of the anti-trust laws, or whether profits realized on a sale of certain assets would constitute "capital gains" or "ordinary income" for federal income tax purposes, the lawyer might define the legal terms, illustrate them with examples and with cases, and conclude with some "iffy" sentence, in effect leaving it to the client to figure out whether his transaction is one or the other.

This kind of opinion may sound very learned but it can hardly satisfy a client who is faced with the necessity of making a decision. He cannot help see that he has not been given an answer to his question. Risky though it may be, the lawyer can only give the client his best judgment and hope that the courts will not ultimately disagree. Granting that he can only guess how the courts might hold, his is a more informed guess than the client's would be. He should, of course, make clear that it is a guess. If his conclusion depends upon certain facts, he should make clear, as already said, that it will hold only if these facts can be established.

If the outcome is in doubt because the law is uncertain, he may suggest steps to avoid an unfavorable outcome. Whenever possible, he should evaluate the chances for success and advise his client whether, in the light of the odds, he should stand firm and hope to win, or authorize the attorney to try to effect a settlement. If he can weigh the odds closely enough, he may even be able to suggest a specific basis for settlement.

The choice between different courses of action may involve considerations pro and con that the client will have to weigh for himself. Instead of recommending one solution, a lawyer may have to say to his client in effect: "You can do one of three things. If you do A you will run the following risks, or have to accept the following consequences; if you do B the risks or the consequences will be so and so and you will wind up in such and such a position; if you do C you will encounter the following difficulties. It is your money (or your business or your life) that is at stake and it is you, therefore, who must make the decision." But suppose the client doesn't want to accept the responsibility, and asks the lawyer to make the decision for him? Professor John S. Bradway has given what is probably the best advice:[4]

> If at this point the client insists that the lawyer make the decision, or demonstrates that he is in no position to decide for himself, he places the lawyer in a position where he cannot win. If the case comes out successfully, the client is likely to ascribe the results to the strength of the case itself. On the other hand, if the matter develops unsatisfactorily, the client tends to blame the lawyer for having made the fatal decision. Of course, there are times when a lawyer must assume this sort of responsibility. At least, he must tell the client that he is willing to work with him on solutions A, B, or C, but not on solutions X and Y. The lawyer should not shrink from making these decisions, but he should endeavor to protect himself from unreasonable attack.

Citing Authorities

If the client to whom you are writing is someone with legal training or experience in the specialized legal subject, such as the trust officer of a bank, you may be able to use technical terms and to discuss in some detail the reasoning by which you came to your conclusion. You may also want to cite the authorities and perhaps quote from them. Indeed, in some cases the best opinion for such a client is indistinguishable from a memorandum of law. If, on the other hand, the opinion is for a lay-

---

4. Bradway, How to Practice Law
Effectively, 16 (1958).

man who is interested only in the practical implications for himself, you will want to tailor your vocabulary and trim your discussion accordingly. Citation of cases will probably be of no interest to him; leave them out.

Trained as he is to back up all his statements concerning the law by citation of authority, the lawyer in laying down the law to his client may out of mere habit throw in citations to cases. But if he will think about what he is doing, he will see that it is rather silly to write, "The law forbids writing a post-dated check on an insufficient account. See Application of Windle, 179 Kan. 239, 294 P.2d 213." Does the writer really expect the client to hunt up and read the case? If not, why tell him to "see" it? Narrating the facts of a relevant case may help the client understand the point you are making, just as examples may help clarify any explanation. But the mere listing of citations is usually of no help to him.

Good reason for citing cases may exist even in writing for a layman, as when the opinion is to be shown to others, whom citation of authority may help to impress or even convince. But lawyers sometimes include citations for less valid reasons. Having done a lot of research on a question, they may be tempted to parade their newly-acquired learning. Or they may merely be writing notes to themselves. Having done the research and having found the cases, they want to keep a reference to them. But if you want to write a memorandum of law for yourself, do so in a separate paper. Don't try to write a memorandum to yourself and an opinion to your client at the same time.

When the question concerns a statute or regulation, the relevant provisions may need to be not only cited but quoted. In such situations, the words should be quoted as fully as may be necessary—but no more. The language of statutes and administrative regulations is likely to be annoyingly difficult for laymen to understand. If only one clause or phrase needs to be quoted, quote only the essential words, not the whole sentence or paragraph. For your client's purpose, you can probably word the nonessential parts better yourself. When you conclude that a section is irrelevent or of minor consequence and can be dismissed with brief mention, it is still helpful to clarity to identify it not merely by section number but by a few words describing its nature: "Sections 49–811(d), regulating tying agreements, has no bearing on our problem."

The Style for an Opinion

In writing an opinion, a lawyer is writing not as an advocate but as an authority laying down the law. He will typically be explaining fairly intricate technical points to a layman. The most important qualities of style for this form of writing are therefore clarity and simplicity. Here if anywhere you must strip your writing of unnecessarily legalistic and verbose wording and try to put your ideas in terms that are crystal-clear.

Don't let the opportunity to "lay down the law" to your client go to your head. Don't think you must adopt a style that seems suitable to a Law Giver handing down a pontifical pronunciamento. It is a mistake to write:

> I am of the opinion that there can be but little doubt that if Mr. Connor were to bring this transaction into litigation, plaintiff's case would predicate liability on your part on a theory of agency. In the event of such litigation, however, the probabilities are adverse to such a claim's succeeding. My reasons for this conclusion lie in those facts which tend to destroy the assumption that Mr. Sirkin acted in a representative capacity on your behalf and in the fact that the burden of proof would devolve upon plaintiff to establish the existence of such alleged agency.

The first sentence of this paragraph could be changed to read more simply as follows:

> If Mr. Connor should sue you, he would no doubt rest on the contention that Mr. Sirkin was acting as your agent when he authorized Connor to do the work.

Rewrite the rest of the paragraph in simple English that the average businessman client could comprehend without mental strain.

Mr. Robert Littler, a lawyer of San Francisco, illustrates our point concerning style in a useful short article entitled "Reader Rights in Legal Writing."[5] Working on an estate plan for a

5. 20 J. of State Bar of Cal. 51 (1950).

businessman, Mr. Littler wrote a memorandum in the course of which he undertook to explain to his client the law concerning the "marital deduction." He did so by paraphrasing the language of the regulations. The next morning his client was on the telephone.

"What the hell do you mean," he wanted to know, "sending me all this gobbledegook? Can't you lawyers ever write English?"

Littler believes that the reader, like the customer, is always right. If the reader cannot understand, it is the writer's fault. He apologized and promised to try again. He finally came up with this:

> The marital deduction means that you can will half your separate property to your wife free of tax if you do it in such form that they can stick her estate with a tax on what is left of it when she dies.

This, says Littler, is "not the sentence I would write for the Tax Court; but why should anyone suppose that what I would write for the Tax Court would also serve for the client?" For the client's purpose, the sentence served.

How well such a sentence will serve depends, however, on the particular client. A literate businessman who has merely asked to have the arcane jargon of the tax statutes translated into English, and who receives a reply worded in terms of whether "they can stick her estate with a tax," may get the impression that his lawyer is talking down to him.

You will probably never be in a position to do very much, if anything, to simplify the language of an insurance policy, a statute or a regulation. But as a lawyer you will have many occasions for interpreting such legal materials for your clients, and that will provide opportunity to make your own translation from legalese into simple English.

Rudolf Flesch quotes a paragraph from an insurance policy:[6]

> If total disability occurs during the grace period for payment of a premium, such premium shall not be waived, nor

6. Flesch, The Art of Readable Writing 152 (1949).

refunded if paid; provided that failure to pay such premium within the grace period therefor shall not of itself invalidate a claim hereunder for total disability commencing during such grace period if such premium with compound interest at the rate of 5 per cent. per annum is paid at the time due proof of the claim is furnished by the Company.

Why not, he asks, rewrite it like this?

You have a 31-day grace period to pay a premium after it is due. Suppose you become disabled during such a period before you have paid the premium. In such a case you can stop paying any *more* premiums, but you'll still have to pay the one that's already overdue. You have time to pay it (with 5 percent interest) when you furnish us proof that you're totally disabled.

That contracts should be written in this style, Flesch admits, is a radical suggestion, and it is probably pointless for us to consider whether it is a good one. But this is an excellent style to use when you are explaining a contract or other legal provision to a layman. Try it:

Exercise

Your client, Chuck Potter, owner of Potter's Drug Store, has had his attention called to the following section of the federal Food, Drug and Cosmetic Act:

Sec. 333. (a) Any person who violates a provision of section 331 of this title shall be imprisoned for not more than one year or fined not more than $1,000, or both.

(b) Notwithstanding the provisions of subsection (a) of this section, if any person commits such a violation after a conviction of him under this section has become final, or commits such a violation with intent to defraud or mislead, such person shall be imprisoned for not more than three years or fined not more than $10,000, or both.

(c) No person shall be subject to the penalties of subsection (a) of this section, (1) for having received in interstate commerce any article and delivered it or proffered delivery of it, if such delivery or proffer was made in good faith, unless he refuses to furnish on request of an officer or employee duly designated by the Secretary the name and address of the person from whom he purchased or received such article and copies of all documents, if any there be, pertaining to the delivery of the article to him; or (2) for having violated section 331(a) or (d) of this title, if he establishes a guaranty or undertaking signed by, and containing the name and address of, the person residing in the United States from whom he received in good faith the article, to the effect, in case of an alleged violation of section 331(a) of this title, that such article is not adulterated or misbranded, within the meaning of this chapter designating this chapter or to the effect, in case of an alleged violation of section 331(d) of this title, that such article is not an article which may not . . . be introduced into interstate commerce; or (3) for having violated section 331(a) of this title, where the violation exists because the article is adulterated by reason of containing a color additive not from a batch certified in accordance with regulations promulgated by the Secretary under this chapter, if such person establishes a guaranty or undertaking signed by, and containing the name and address of, the manufacturer of the color additive, to the effect that such color additive was from a batch certified in accordance with the applicable regulations promulgated by the Secretary under this chapter . . . .

Potter wants to know what liabilities this might expose him to and what if anything he can do to protect himself.

Section 331 of the act prohibits, among other acts: (a) the introduction or delivery into interstate commerce of any food, drug, device or cosmetic that is adulterated or misbranded; (c) the receipt in interstate commerce of any such adulterated or misbranded articles; or (d) the introduction in such commerce of any "new drug" (as defined in the act) without first having filed application with the Secretary, showing its components, investigations that have been made to show whether it is safe for use, etc.

The Style for an Opinion to a Client Who is Also a Friend

The client to whom an opinion is addressed may be a friend. The lawyer need not use a stiffly formal tone in writing to a man with whom he was playing golf the day before. He may—and should—use an informal style that reflects their personal relationship, such as the following three opening and three closing paragraphs illustrate:

Dear Stu:

It isn't difficult to put the finger on what is wrong with your ingenious plan, but finding a better one is a littler harder.

Dear Bill:

Plenty of other taxpayers have found themselves in the same bind that you are in, if that is any consolation.

Dear Phil:

What you want to do seems eminently sensible. The only question is whether Uncle Sam will let you do it without sticking you with a walloping big tax.

There are other ways to reach the same end, but they all encounter the same pitfalls. When you make up your mind which road to travel, let me know and we'll get at it.

You could perhaps keep a few more strings on the operation and still be in the clear. But I don't think it is prudent to see how close to the line one can skate. The plan I have outlined plays it safe.

All these ramifications of the problem, even if they do not clarify your liability on the notes, will at least make clear why I didn't give a direct answer to your question at Brenda's cocktail party. I said I'd prefer to write you a letter, because I knew that no opinion I could give you then would suffice—except to spoil the party.

An example of an opinion in such an informal style, written by an able practitioner, appears later in this chapter.

Our ideals of clarity and simplicity sometimes collide with more mundane but nonetheless important considerations. Suppose you have been asked for an opinion on whether a certain business practice which your client has followed is legal—for example, whether giving certain discounts for quantity purchases contravenes the Robinson–Patman Act. Finding the answer took a number of hours of research. You found a number of cases discussing various price-discrimination practices, but after careful study, you conclude that your client is completely in the clear. The practices that have been held to violate the act are all distinguishable, and in three cases the specific practice he has been following has squarely been held to be permissible. The clearest and simplest way to answer his inquiry would be in a short letter saying, in effect, "I am happy to tell you that your system of quantity discounts is not illegal."[7]

The client will probably be more pleased with such an answer than any other you could write. But how will he feel when you send him a bill for $100 for your services? Such a charge, "just for writing a short letter," may strike him as outrageous. You cannot expect him to appreciate the work that went into writing that short letter. Unqualified assertions do not require many words, but an enormous amount of work may be necessary before one can say, "Every court that has passed upon this contention has upheld it," or "This question has never been passed upon by the Supreme Court."

The lawyer who has given a lot of time to a question may understandably want to let the client know it. The way to do it that most often occurs to lawyers is to show a client how many cases he has read by not only citing them all but by reviewing their facts and quoting a paragraph from each. This may convince the client that his attorney has worked hard but not necessarily that he has worked well.

The point can be made with a lighter touch: "A search of the reported cases since the beginning of the century reveals," "A careful rereading of the numerous cases that have passed on the question leads to the conclusion."

The impression that the lawyer's opinion is the product of painstaking work can also be conveyed by its physical form. Instead of being given in a mere letter, it can be typed on legal-sized paper, double-spaced, with blue backing and other accessories of formal dress.

7. Although clear and simple, such an answer may be more positive than counsel thinks he should be. He may prefer to say, more objectively, that the legality of the practice has been passed upon by three (named) appellate courts and that each has upheld it, perhaps adding a carefully worded conclusion of his own that a similar decision might reasonably be expected if the client's practice should be subjected to litigation.

Examples of Opinion Letters

The opinions of the attorney general of every state offer a readily available collection of formal opinions that may profitably be read as models.

That an opinion even on a matter of substantial monetary importance can sometimes be brief is illustrated by the following opinion written in the offices of a leading New York law firm (names of parties have been changed):

The Eastland Trust Company of New York,
000 Fifth Avenue,
New York 99, New York

Attention: Mr. Harvey Redpath

Re: Loans to Appalachian Associates, Inc. and
Subsidiary and Affiliated Corporations

Dear Sirs:

In connection with the loans to be made by you secured by Aircraft Chattel Mortgages on 2 Douglas DC 6B's, 2 Douglas DC 3's, 1 Convair 240, 2 Grumman 621 A's, 1 Beachcraft D18 and 1 Lockheed Ventura and by Guarantees, General Loan and Collateral Agreements and Collateral Deposit Agreements of Appalachian Associates, Inc., its subsidiaries and affiliates, we have examined the Aircraft Chattel Mortgage instruments and such corporate records and other papers as we have considered relevant. We have also reviewed the title examination prepared by Messrs. Cox, Emlin & Cox with regard to the 2 Douglas DC 6B's, the Convair 240, and the 2 Douglas DC 3's. In expressing our opinion regarding the validity and priority of the Aircraft Chattel Mortgages on these aircraft we are relying on the title examination of Messrs. Cox, Emlin & Cox, which examination we believe to be reliable. We have not examined the titles of the other aircraft for which you have received Aircraft Chattel Mortgages and express no opinion as to the priority of your lien on those aircraft.

On the basis of such examination, it is our opinion that the Aircraft Chattel Mortgages on the 2 Douglas DC 6B's, the 2 Douglas DC 3's and the Convair 240 will be, when properly recorded and filed, valid liens upon said aircraft securing payment of up to $750,000 subject only to prior mortgages now held by you, and that the Guarantees, General Loan and Collateral Agreements and Collateral Deposit Agreements of

Appalachian Associates, Inc., its subsidiaries and affiliates were validly executed and delivered.

Very truly yours,

Here is an opinion from a leading Arizona attorney written in his capacity as general counsel for an insurance company:

Mr. A. Carl Caton, President
Coronado Life Insurance Company
P. O. Box 98765
Phoenix, Arizona

Dear Carl:

The Committee on Rules of Professional Conduct of the State Bar of Arizona has issued an opinion clarifying Canon 27, of the Canons of Ethics of the American Bar Association. The opinion, which is binding on all Arizona lawyers, has a bearing on the use of my name, and the name of the firm, in connection with Coronado Life Insurance Company. The opinion embraces three different aspects of the matter:

1. It is improper for any periodical publication or advertising of Coronado Life, either in the masthead of the publication or otherwise, to make any reference to me or to this office as general counsel or counsel for the company.

2. In any material issued which lists the names of all members of the board of directors of Coronado Life, my name may be included, and if other members of the board of directors are identified as respects their other business connection, I may be similarly identified by a simple indication that I am a member of the firm of, or a partner in (or by merely a reference without qualification to) Lewis Roca Scoville Beauchamp & Linton. It is better practice, however, not to state that I am an attorney or that the firm is a law firm.

3. In any annual report which may be issued to stockholders, as well as in any securities prospectus, it is permissible to use the name of the firm as general counsel. If such an annual report to stockholders contains a listing of the board of directors, then the comments under paragraph 2 also apply.

So that we may be sure to be safe, I should naturally like to see a copy of any material of this nature before it is actually issued.

Yours very sincerely,
Paul M. Roca

When the client is a personal friend, the style, as already said, may be quite informal. Fortune magazine some years ago published a series of "Informal Letters from a Tax Lawyer," written by Mr. Merle H. Miller, of the firm of Ross McCord Ice & Miller, Indianapolis, Indiana, which were excellent examples of such a style. Here is one of Mr. Miller's letters:[8]

Dear George:

Who ever thought that the old warehouse we used to play in would someday sell for $60,000! You must have done quite a job of revamping, which, I assume, accounts for your present cost basis of $20,000. From my recollection of the place, if you haven't fully depreciated it you have been using the wrong depreciation rate.

That $40,000 profit will not be taxed as ordinary income but will be treated as a capital gain, giving you the option of including one-half of it in your ordinary income, or of paying a maximum tax of 25 per cent on the entire profit, whichever results in the lesser tax. Section 117(j) [§ 1231] of the Internal Revenue Code gives this favorable treatment to gains from the sale of real estate, or property used in the business which is subject to depreciation if held more than six months. Your warehouse qualifies since you have been using it somewhat in your business and anyone can look at it and know it is subject to depreciation.

But knowing your aversion to taxes even at bargain rates, I have cast about for other methods of disposing of the property at less tax cost. The proposition you are now considering calls for a down payment of 50 per cent of the sale price with the remainder payable in installments over a period of five years. Even though you get only half the sale price this year you will have to pay a tax on the entire gain, notwithstanding your cash-basis method of reporting income.

But if the total payments received the first year do not exceed 30 per cent of the sale price you can spread the tax payments so as to pay the tax only on each year's installment. In this case, if you were to limit the payments during the first year to not more than $18,000 you would pay a

8. Reprinted from Fortune magazine for April, 1949, p. 54. Mr. Miller's references to section numbers of the Internal Revenue Code have been supplemented by adding in brackets the present section numbers.

tax this year only on the gain represented by the $18,000 and you would pay a tax in subsequent years on the amounts then received. The gain on each installment payment would be that proportion which the total gain would bear to the selling price or the ratio of $40,000 gain to $60,000 sale price. So you would report two-thirds of the original down payment of $18,000 as capital gain for the year of sale, and two-thirds of each subsequent payment in the year in which received. The size of the payments in subsequent years makes no difference, but it is necessary to keep the payments during the first year below 30 per cent of the entire selling price so as to qualify for this special treatment under Section 44 [§ 453] of the Internal Revenue Code.

I am sure it will not take you long to see the advantage of paying a tax this year on only $12,000 gain instead of the entire $40,000 gain, come what may in later years. And unless your income combined with Grace's is so high this year that you would elect the flat 25 per cent rate, you should land in lower surtax brackets by spreading the gain over several years. But this, too, is subject to the condition that you do not have the misfortune of having your income increase in those subsequent years.

In reporting on the installment basis, you also run the risk that the rates might be increased, or the law might be changed so that the gain on the sale of this type of property would not be taxed as a capital gain. The installments received in subsequent years are reported under the laws then in effect and the nature of the income is dependent upon the laws then in effect. Thus if the law were changed so that the gain on the sale of this type of property were not a capital gain, then the subsequent installments would be taxed as ordinary income. That danger does not seem imminent for property that has been held so long, but even so you may sleep better by paying the entire tax this year and not worrying about what Congress might do later.

I was interested to learn that you are contemplating buying additional ground adjoining your main plant at a cost of $50,000. Have you considered the possibility of trading the warehouse for that land? The owner of the land could sell the warehouse later on, but so long as he kept it neither of you would have to pay any tax on the transaction. If he later sold it, he would pay a tax on that gain, if any, the same as if he were to sell the land to you for cash. So he could be no worse off and you would be much better off. Each would carry over the cost or other basis of your present property to the new property, and the government would wait to collect its tax until you sold the new property.

Under Section 112 [§ 1031] of the Internal Revenue Code it is possible to trade like property held for use in the trade or business (except for securities and stock in trade) without incurring any tax whatever. The properties in this case exchanged would be regarded as being of like kind since they are real estate even though they are different types of real estate. This rule applies even though cash is given by one of the parties, in which event the party receiving the cash pays a tax on it to the extent that it represents gain. If the owner of the land gave you $10,000, say, as the difference between the value of his land and your warehouse, then you would report only the $10,000 as a capital gain.

You have, then, three possibilities:

1. Sell the warehouse for $60,000 as you suggest, with a $30,000 down payment, and pay the entire capital gains tax on the $40,000 profit this year. You would then pay no tax on the subsequent installments.

2. Sell the warehouse for $60,000, taking not more than $18,000 as total payment this year and pay the tax as the installments are received. This would involve payment of less tax this year, but you would risk having the law changed so that you would be taxed at increased rates or the gain represented by subsequent installments might be taxed as ordinary income instead of capital gain.

3. Try to trade the warehouse for the land you want to acquire. This would be a tax-free trade unless you received cash, in which event you would pay a tax only on the gain represented by the cash received.

Whichever way the deal goes, let us look over any proposition before you accept it in order to make certain that the real-estate taxes are to be paid by the party who can deduct them for federal income-tax purposes. Such taxes are deductible only by the party who is liable for them regardless of what the contract says, and if the other party assumes the payment of the taxes, then no one gets the deduction.

Sincerely yours,
Merle H. Miller

Saying "No"

Clients, like the rest of us, resent being told that they cannot do what they want to do. When the law seems to forbid, the lawyer may face a problem of tact and of ethics in finding an answer that will satisfy the client and yet not advise him to do something of doubtful legality. When a corporate client wants to make a certain expenditure, but research shows that it would be illegal, no conscientious lawyer would advise making it in the hope that no stockholder, creditor or other interested person will litigate it. But other cases may not be so clear-cut.

Even if your client is intelligent enough not to hold it against you personally when you tell him the law says "no", he will think a good deal more highly of you if he finds you ingenious enough to discover a way around his difficulties—if you can tell him that although the law forbids his doing exactly what he has in mind, you can suggest a course of action that will achieve essentially the same result. This may not always be easy. There may be no way open, but a suggestion that goes even part-way to this end is more palatable than a flat "no."

Before offering suggestions about business or technical occupational practices, however, it is prudent to learn something about the business. A suggestion that may sound workable to the outsider may, to someone familiar with the operation, be obviously impractical for some reason the outsider did not know about. Such a naive suggestion is more likely to annoy than to mollify a client. Ideas for ways around the difficulty are better explored in oral conversations with the client, where they can be advanced very tentatively, instead of being presented for the first time in the written opinion.

But one must sometimes say "no" clearly and perhaps emphatically. Below is an opinion written by the Chicago firm of Stevenson, Rifkind & Wirtz to a labor union. The officers of the union wanted to proceed with disciplinary action against certain members. Counsel believed that such action would violate a court injunction that had been issued, and said so in the following opinion (Names and dates have been changed and part of the opinion has been omitted because of space limitations):

Mr. Carl F. Howard,
Legal Department,
United Stopnut Workers of America,
3790 E. Chicago Ave.,
Chicago, Ill.

Dear Mr. Howard:

Re: Pitts v. Dolan

You have asked our opinion regarding the legal propriety of USWA's filing charges now against one or more of the plaintiffs in the above entitled case, in view of the temporary injunction entered by the Court. . . .

. . .

On March 20, 1961, United States District Judge Paul B. Jonas issued a preliminary injunction, in which he made the following "finding of fact":

"4. Plaintiff JAMES A. PITTS has been notified that charges leading to expulsion from USWA will be brought against him for commencing this action and other plaintiffs are subject to similar charges and a municipality of hearings and expulsion proceedings."

. . .

The Judge then entered an order, providing that "Defendant MATTHEW DOLAN, his agents and all persons acting in concert with him," are restrained from (in part):

"(d) Initiating, authorizing or supporting the prosecution of disciplinary action against the plaintiffs brought in whole or in part because of the institution of this action;

"(e) Initiating, permitting, authorizing or supporting the prosecution of disciplinary action against any member of USWA because of joining or supporting the plaintiffs in the maintenance of this action."

Article V, Section 2(b) of the Constitution and By-Laws of the United Stopnut Workers of America provides as follows:

"(b) Such charges to be heard must be filed within 60 days after the accuser becomes aware of the alleged offense, but in no case more than one year after the alleged offense."

Therefore, another specific question is presented: Whether the 60-day limitation provided in Article V, Section 2(b) requires that charges against Pitts must be filed prior to May 6.

It is our considered opinion that it would be improper to file such charges in the face of the injunction issued by the Court. Although we recognize that there is a serious question whether USWA is "acting in concert" with defendant Matthew Dolan (and we will press this question in Court), we nevertheless conclude that it would be exceedingly dangerous to proceed with the filing of charges at the present time. This would very likely be the subject of a contempt action brought by the plaintiffs and would impair our chances of success in our effort to persuade the Court to dissolve the injunction.

With respect to the application of Article V, Section 2(b), we are of the opinion that the 60-day period in which charges are to be filed is necessarily extended by the pendency of the injunction, and are of the further opinion that charges may be filed at such later time when and if the injunction has been dissolved.

Hearings will be conducted this week in the United States District Court and before a Special Master appointed by the Court, concerning the injunction. Until these hearings are terminated and a judicial determination reached, we conclude 1) that no disciplinary charges should be brought against the plaintiffs, 2)· that this course of action will not prejudice rights to bring disciplinary charges at a later time.

Very truly yours,
STEVENSON, RIFKIND & WIRTZ

When you must say "no," try nevertheless to be reassuring. Even if you cannot suggest an alternative course of action that might in some measure accomplish the desired end, maintain an air of unperturbed good spirits. Our clients come to us not only for advice, but also for solace and support. Finding themselves embroiled in a legal wrangle is for most of them a worrisome and even frightening experience. They will be grateful if our response gives them a sense that their problem is in strong and competent hands.

Evaluation Letters

Counsel for insurance companies are regularly called upon to write letters giving their opinion on whether the insured seems to be liable, and if so, their evaluation of the claim for purposes of settlement. Here is such a letter, together with a supplementary letter listing additional data needed, somewhat condensed (and with names changed) from an actual letter written by a New York City law firm:

Industrial Indemnity Company
7218 John Street
New York 88, New York

Attention: Mr. Joseph Hertzler

Gentlemen:

Re: Peter Quinn v. Metropolitan Edison

Claimant's decedent, a 61 year old white male steamfitter, was employed by Elmore & Co., the heating sub-contractor engaged in the construction of a new addition to the Metropolitan Edison Generating plant No. 3.

On September 13, 1960, at 2:10 p. m., decedent was assisting in the installation of a 28-foot steel steampipe while stationed on a steel mesh grating, in which 2 openings of approximately 5′ each separated by a steel mesh walk some few feet in width were maintained in order to facilitate the reception of this steam pipe and its companion piping. This area was surrounded by wooden barriers which seem to have been in conformity with the requirements of Industrial Code Rule No. 23, and were installed by William J. Herd Corporation. The steel gratings were installed by Roos Iron Works. The steel pipe itself was at that time being lowered by a guy derrick leased to Metropolitan Edison by American Bridge, and operated by Gross Transfer Company. Decedent was reportedly guiding the pipe at that level, his back to the second hole, when he either stepped backwards or fell backwards into the second hole, falling from the 72′ platform to the 16′ platform, and sustaining injuries that resulted in his death.

It is reasonable to assume that decedent, as a steamfitter, earned approximately $7,500.00 a year which will in all probability be claimed as a pecuniary loss to decedent's dependents. The funeral bill may be estimated at $1,000.00. The decedent was 61 years of age at the time of his death, with a life expectancy of approximately 14 years, which gives a probably monetary loss to his dependents of approximately $100,000.00.

An owner of a building under construction is under no duty to protect employees of his independent contractors against the negligence of their employers or other contractors on the job, nor is such owner under a duty to inspect machinery or tools furnished by sub-contractors. Nor in the better view was any duty owed decedent to furnish him a safe place to work. Should claimant be able to prove, however, that your assured retained control over the course of construction, then he may be able to predicate liability either on the theory advanced above or on a violation of Section 240. That section imposes a duty only where the owner has assumed direct control over the course of the work to be performed. On the current status of your investigation, it is extremely difficult at this time to evaluate these possibilities.

It is also possible for the claimant to establish a prima facie case of liability by the introduction of proofs of an "assurance of safety" under the doctrine expounded in Broderick v. Cauldwell-Wingate Co., 305 N.Y. 882, 114 N.E.2d 216. At this time we do not have sufficient information to evaluate this issue.

A violation of Section 241 of the Labor Law and its companion, Industrial Code Rule No. 23, imposes an absolute nondelegable duty upon the owner of the building under construction. Although having an opening in a floor violates this statute, in this instance it appears that the required safeguard (a wooden barrier) was provided. In addition, the opening was necessitated by the very nature of the work to be performed, in that the steel pipe was to be inserted in one of the two openings, and the presence of the decedent was necessary to facilitate the installation of the pipe. A defense to this theory may be predicated upon the proposition that an employee cannot recover for injuries sustained while engaged in doing an act to eliminate the hazard which caused the injury. Kowalsky v. Conreco Co., 264 N.Y. 125, 190 N.E. 206.

The defense therefore may have a good position for contesting liability grounded on an alleged violation of Section 241, Labor Law.

The ambit of Section 241 has been so broadened by the Court of Appeals, however, that liability may depend on whether the failure of the contractors, as well as of your assured, to plank over the second opening behind the decedent on the 72nd foot level constituted a violation of that section.

Since a violation of Section 241 imposes upon an owner an absolute non-delegable duty which precludes the possibility of contribution or indemnification by reason of a cross-complaint, or third-party action, it is suggested that we be immediately notified upon receipt of summons and complaint so that we may be able to advise claimant's attorney of the possibility of bringing in the various sub-contractors as additional party-defendants in the main action. We may thus acquire partners who would have an exposure as joint tort feasors in this action.

The analysis set forth above is, of course, contingent upon the development of appropriate proofs. Many avenues of investigation remain to be pursued, and we must of necessity hold in abeyance a more detailed evaluation of the claim pending receipt of additional information. I am enclosing suggested items of supplemental investigation, which may establish for the defense a position for contesting liability.

Respectfully submitted,

Industrial Indemnity Company
7218 John Street
New York 88, New York

Attention: Mr. Joseph Hertzler

Gentlemen:

Re: Peter Quinn v. Metropolitan Edison

A thorough review and analysis of your file in the above entitled matter indicates the necessity of further supplemental investigation. I am therefore enumerating below several items to be pursued.

1. Obtain a copy of the police report.

2. Since this is a construction accident, an investigation was probably made by the Division of Industrial Safety of the Department of Labor. An effort should be made to obtain a copy of any investigation report and any statements taken.

3. Since this is a case of accidental death, an autopsy probably was performed. A copy of the autopsy report should be obtained.

4. Copies of all contracts between your assured and decedent's employer, as well as the other sub-contractors, should be obtained. Your file indicates that among the pertinent sub-contractors are American Bridge Company, Gross Transfer Company, Elmore & Co., William J. Herd Corporation and Roos Iron Works.

5. A determination should be had whether or not Metropolitan Edison has conditions or specifications pertaining to this particular construction job. If these exist, a copy should also be obtained.

6. Plans and specifications for the construction at this point should be obtained.

7. Our past experience indicates that Metropolitan Edison makes its own investigation into the circumstances of an occurrence of this sort. Suitable inquiries should be made of Mr. Spiro concerning this possibility.

8. A statement of decedent's earnings should be obtained from his employer at this early date in order to avoid the possibility of changes later on.

9. On every construction job done for Metropolitan Edison that company assigns an inspector to follow the progress of the work and to see that the job is being performed pursuant to contract and specifications. Such person or persons should be contacted immediately and negative signed statement obtained, as well as information pertaining to their activities on the day of the accident and the day before. It is imperative, if possible, to remove them from the scene of the occurrence so as to obviate the possibili-

ty of a future claim of an assurance of safety by these persons.

10. A more detailed investigation should be made of the operation of the guy derrick leased to Metropolitan Edison by American Bridge and operated by Gross Transfer Company for installing the steampipe. An attempt should be made to get signed statements from the men who operated the crane, to the effect that Metropolitan Edison retained no control over its use or operation. This statement should include confirmation of the fact that the system of voice and hand signals used in its operation was in accordance with the custom and usage in that particular trade and that it operated smoothly.

11. A list of all persons employed in the general area of this construction work should be obtained. A negative signed statement should be secured to the effect that none of the Metropolitan Edison employees or inspectors assumed any operative control over the progress of the work. Special effort should be made to obtain this kind of statement from decedent's co-workers.

Upon completion of this investigation, we shall of course reevaluate the matter and send you a supplemental report.

If I may be of any further assistance to you in this matter, especially as to the nature of the statements desired, please let me know.

Very truly yours,

Some of the phraseology in the supplementary letter is noticeably less lucid than the rest. What is a "negative signed statement" as the term is used in paragraphs 9 and 11? What is meant by the statement, in paragraph 9, that "It is imperative, if possible, to remove" witnesses from the scene of an occurrence long since past? Was the writer trying to be clear? If not, why not?[9]

---

9. This book deals with legal writing. But Legal Ethics is also an important subject, not to be neglected. A lawyer "should avoid any suggestion calculated to induce any witness to suppress evidence or deviate from the truth." Code of Trial Conduct, adopted by the American College of Trial Lawyers, 32 Miss.L.J. 65 (1960).

A Checklist of Questions

After writing an opinion, it may be well to read it critically with the following questions in mind:

1. Should it be sent? Would its purpose be better accomplished by a telephone call, or a personal conference?

2. Does it tell the client what he wants to know? What he needs to know to dispose of his problem in an enlightened way?

3. Is the level of discussion appropriate for the client? Is the style too abstruse, too theoretical? Does it need more examples or illustrative cases? Is there too much citation of cases?

4. Is the opinion too discursive? Does it discuss exceptions, limitations and collateral points not relevant to the client's specific problem?

5. Is the conclusion too cautious, qualified, inconclusive? Or is it unjustifiably positive?

Chapter 10

MEMORANDA

In this chapter we shall discuss three kinds of memoranda: trial briefs, intra-office memoranda of law, and memoranda to be submitted to the trial court.

I. TRIAL BRIEFS

Notwithstanding its name, a trial brief is materially different from an appellate brief. It is really a form of memorandum, organizing all of counsel's preparation of a case for trial. One book dealing with the subject[1] says it should contain:

1. A résumé of the facts in narrative form and, where possible, in chronological order.

2. Quotations, abstracts or digests of the Constitution, statutes, regulations, orders, etc., involved.

3. Abstract or digest of the pleadings with reference to the paragraph numbers of the original pleadings.

4. Information for probable and possible questions in examining the jurymen.

5. List of witnesses, both in the order in which you expect to call them, and alphabetically.

6. List of exhibits keyed to the names of the witnesses through whom they will be offered in evidence.

7. Abstract or digest of the expected testimony of each witness in narrative form and, where possible, in chronological order.

8. Separate facts which you expect to prove, naming the witnesses and exhibits in support thereof.

1. Pittoni, Brief Writing and Argumentation 3 (3d ed. 1967). See also Re, Brief Writing and Oral Argument 29 (4th ed. 1974); Joiner, The Trial Brief—The Lawyer's Battle Plan and Ammunition, 1 Practical Lawyer (Oct. 1955) 53, reprinted in Rossman, Advocacy and the King's English 45 (1960).

9. Separate facts which your opponent may try to prove, naming the witnesses and exhibits in opposition thereto.

10. Evidence, facts and other material for cross-examination of anticipated opponent's witnesses.

11. Brief on the law, including authorities supporting your contentions and those refuting anticipated contentions of your opponent.

12. Expected requests to charge or instruct the jury.

With these data before him, a lawyer can analyze his case in the light of the applicable law, evaluate its strengths and weaknesses, and decide whether he should try to settle it out of court. An adequate trial brief will also serve as a checklist during trial, to prevent overlooking anything important and to prepare for foreseeable questions at the trial. It will also be a source of self-assurance and an alleviator of nervousness. Nothing gives more confidence than a feeling of being prepared.

Sound practice calls for the preparation of a trial brief in almost every case. It need not in every case cover all the twelve topics listed above. A simple automobile collision case being conducted by counsel specializing in such cases may require only the briefest summary of the facts and the names of the witnesses with a short abstract of what each will testify. Counsel may have the controlling statutes and decisions at his finger-tips. But when the facts are complicated, it will usually be necessary to lay them out in orderly form, with references to the names of the witnesses and the exhibits needed for establishing each fact. The applicable law will need to be stated, with citations to the authorities. Because the trial brief is a working paper for the writer's own use (or for the use of an associate), style is a minor consideration.

II. MEMORANDA OF LAW

The first test of a young lawyer's professional competence may be his ability to write a clear and useful memorandum of law. If he enters practice in a large office, his first assignment is likely to be to draft a memorandum for a senior member. If the novice performs this task well, he will be given wider responsibilities. A leading Philadelphia lawyer who has written on effective writing in law practice says that whenever one of the young associates in his firm submits a memorandum that shows not only a grasp of the facts and a sound analysis of the law but also an ability to express himself succinctly and convincingly, he is promptly assigned the further task of compressing it into an opinion letter or converting it into a brief. From this, it is only a short step to direct contact with the client and to appearance in court, with final responsibility of conducting the trial or presenting the argument. The lawyer who practices alone also has occasion to write memoranda of law, not only as part of the trial brief for litigation but also on questions arising in performing counseling and client care-taking functions.

Some lawyers do not prepare memoranda even for the trial of cases involving difficult legal issues. They may say that they do not have time, or that the monetary amount at stake in many of their cases does not justify the expenditure of time. But this is usually a mistake, if not mere rationalization. An adequate memorandum will almost always save rather than add time. Sound legal research, committed to writing in a well-organized memorandum, is fundamental to competent handling of every step in the case, whether it is the rendering of an opinion, the negotiation of a settlement, the drafting of pleadings, or the preparation for and strategy of trial. It will also serve as the raw material for a trial brief and, eventually, an appellate brief.

Scope

A busy senior lawyer may ask a junior to prepare a memorandum without saying exactly what he wants. Given only vague direction, the junior may produce a vague, unfocused memorandum that his superior finds unsatisfactory. That's his own fault, to be sure, but the hapless junior is hardly in a position to tell him so. The junior is the one who must take the initiative in getting the assignment straight. The primary thing he needs to know is what purpose the memorandum is to serve. Sometimes this is evident; sometimes he will be told. But sometimes it is not evident and his senior doesn't think to tell him. It is up to him to find out. Does the senior want it to (1) decide whether to take a case; (2) provide information for a client in an opinion letter; (3) draft a pleading or other document; or (4) gather data for a trial or an appellate brief? The purpose of the document determines how it should be written, how extensive the research should be, and how long and how technical it should be. As in all writing, one cannot do a good job without knowing what one is trying to accomplish.

As work on the memorandum progresses, further conferences with the senior may be necessary. Research may turn up questions not anticipated. Especially if the assignment was in broad terms, the presumption should be that the memorandum is to cover all issues. Thus it should discuss not only the basic issue of liability or guilt, but also, if litigation is foreseen, such questions as capacity to sue, statute of limitations, burden of proof, and availability of witnesses. Questions of procedure or strategy may need to be considered: Should a certain motion be filed? Should a client be advised to take steps to avoid risk of future liability? Some questions may seem marginal, yet would require extensive research. Should they be covered? Time may be a factor. Should certain action be taken promptly, such as seeking an injunction? If so, should such a pressing issue be dealt with first, leaving others for a later, separate, memorandum? If the relationship between senior and junior is good, it should be easy to get answers to such questions simply by asking. Getting answers as you go may avoid finding when you submit your memorandum that it is too short, or too long, or for whatever reason not what your superior wanted. But use some judgment. Don't waste his time with questions you should be able to answer for yourself.

Form

Since an office memorandum is written only for one's own use or for the use of some other members of the firm, its form will depend on the wishes and convenience of the persons concerned. In a large office, a standard form may have been developed. Typically, this will include (1) a heading or title, (2) the name of the person to whom it is addressed or by whom it was requested, (3) the name of the writer, (4) the date, (5) the question presented, (6) a brief answer or conclusion, (7) the statement of facts, (8) discussion, and (9) conclusion. The heading or title should use key phrases that will facilitate filing and indexing. The files of memoranda written for past cases are part of an established law firm's most valuable assets. Duplication of effort is saved if a question arising in a current case has already been the subject of a memorandum which can readily be found.

If the memorandum pertains to a specific case, it should set out the name of the case, the court in which it is pending, its docket number and other relevant data concerning it.

The outline of organization suggested above may need to be varied depending on the nature of the question. If it concerns a case, for example, the statement of facts may be placed before the question or questions presented. In other instances also, it may be difficult to frame the question in any meaningful way without first reciting the facts. But sometimes the facts can be followed more comprehendingly if the question is stated first. A memorandum on a simple point may consist of (1) a statement of the factual situation concerning which a question has been raised, (2) citation or quotation of the applicable statute, and, perhaps, (3) reference to the case or cases raising similar facts, and their decision, and (4) a conclusion that the same conclusion governs the instant case.

Formulating the question or questions presented requires analyzing the problem so as to see clearly what the issues are. In seeking answers, defining the question is the first big challenge. You will not be able to phrase the issues until you have clearly identified them in your own mind. But striving to phrase them precisely and clearly, you will find, helps to sharpen your thinking about them.

The conclusion may be withheld until the end. Ordinarily, however, it is helpful to have a categorical or brief statement of the conclusion immediately following the questions, so that, for example, the busy senior for whom the memorandum is prepared can see the answer at once if he wishes, without first reading through the entire memorandum. If the question can be answered with a simple "yes" or "no," that's the best way to answer it. If it cannot, it should be answered as concisely as possible.

The Statement of Facts

The statement of facts should be succinct but full. Do not decide that it can be abbreviated because the person for whom you are preparing the memorandum already knows the facts. Stating them shows the basis for your conclusion. Also, your memorandum may ultimately be read by others, or be put in the files for possible use in later cases.

Learning what the facts are may not be easy, especially if the memorandum is being prepared at an early stage, when there has been no decision, no record, and no findings. You may have only the client's story, which you know, perhaps from sad experience, may not embody the whole truth. Investigations may be under way, but it may not be feasible to wait for them to be completed; legal questions may have to be answered now. Your memorandum should say that further inquiries are being made or are required, and that your analysis and conclusions are based on assumed facts.

Irrelevancies should of course not be included, but when a memorandum is being prepared at an early stage, it may not be possible to foresee what facts will be relevant. Reviewing your statement after you have formulated the issues will help you see what facts do not play a role. If an item may or may not be relevant, resolve the doubt in favor of including it. Let your superior decide whether it can be disregarded. It can always be deleted in the later writing of the opinion or brief. Your object should be to show that in reaching your conclusion, you have taken into account everything you have been told about the problem.

Always state the facts in the past tense. This applies to statements of court decisions and rulings. But legal rules should be stated in the present tense: "The court applied the rule that the burden of proof is on the plaintiff."

After you have assessed the facts, organize your presentation so as to tell the story in a way the reader can easily follow. The best way, ordinarily, is to present the facts in chronological order.

The Discussion

The "discussion" presents the authorities on which the conclusion rests. The research and analysis required is, of course, similar to that on which any lawyer's opinion or brief must rest. The important distinction between the memorandum and the brief is that the purpose of the memorandum is not to convince but to explore. Its style, therefore, is not argumentative, but expository and descriptive. If its subject is a question presented without reference to any case, its style should be as impartial as that of a judicial opinion. Even when it deals with questions presented by a case in which the firm represents one of the parties, the purpose of the memorandum is to explore and evaluate candidly the strength and weakness of the client's case. It should therefore be as much concerned with the weaknesses of the case as with the favorable aspects, and should devote at least as much attention to precedents and other authorities against the client's position as to those that are for him. The cases and authorities contra should, of course, be carefully analyzed to see if they can be distinguished or otherwise minimized, but this too should be done with complete willingness to face the situation realistically.

Students and young lawyers often fail to give adequate attention to the opponent's case, not only in preparing memoranda but even in writing briefs. They focus their energy and enthusiasm on developing their side of the issue, and neglect the counterarguments. Try to put yourself in the position of your opposite number. Ask yourself: if I were he, how would I answer the analysis or argument just made? How would I rebut or distinguish the cases cited? What countervailing arguments could I offer? Minimizing or covering up what may prove to be fatal weaknesses is the worst thing you can do. It is your responsibility to point out where the dangers lie, where the decisive battles are going to be fought.

This does not mean you should write from a neutral point of view. In law school, cases are discussed from such a neutral, judicious standpoint, and students writing law review notes and other papers are usually free to weigh the considerations pro and con and come to any conclusion their reasoning may lead to.

But now you are an advocate, representing one side in a dispute. And although you want to evaluate your case candidly and with full recognition of its weak points, your objective is to uncover all the arguments that can be made for it.

The best way to start your discussion usually is to state the controlling rule or principle, or to quote the controlling statute, and then show that it applies to your case. Although in writing briefs it is best to focus on the relatively few precedents constituting one's strongest authorities, in a memorandum of law every case in point on major issues should be cited. For each, state the nature of the case, the relevant facts, and the holding. A short quotation from the opinion may also be helpful if particularly well phrased, or if the specific wording seems significant. Thus if you are citing a case for a position that may be disputed, you may want to quote its specific language to support your position. Although more use may be made of quotations in a memorandum than in a brief, one should still be on guard against falling into the easy habit of having the typist copy lengthy quotations from opinions and statutes. And one certainly should not be so undiscriminating as to quote mere dicta, no matter how fine they sound in their broad sweep.

Remember the Holmes aphorism, that "general propositions do not decide concrete cases." Do not cite cases for merely general propositions. Give the concrete context; that is, give enough of the facts and the issue or the procedural point on which the decision rested so that the case will appear in its true setting. Say explicitly what the court did, whether it affirmed or reversed, granted a motion or dismissed.

Some law firms want every important case referred to in the memorandum abstracted on a separate sheet, giving the facts, the specific point or points decided, and any quotations from the opinion that seem apt.

For other than major propositions, full presentation of all the cases is not needed. For a rule that is generally accepted, one or two recent cases or even a recognized secondary authority will suffice. If limitations of time or diminishing returns caused research efforts to be curtailed, the memorandum should report that certain subsidiary issues were not researched or certain sources not examined.

The cases cited should be arranged in the order that most logically builds to the conclusion. A novice will sometimes conscientiously gather and brief a number of cases, but fail to organize them so as to lead to his conclusion, or perhaps even to show how they are relevant to the issue. If the cases take conflicting positions and the memorandum adopts one, it should explain why. A liberal use of headings and subheadings will help your reader to follow as you move from point to point.

Conclusion and Recommendations

Although putting your conclusion first, and then giving your reasons, is a good way to write a memorandum, it is not a good way to think your way to a conclusion. Yet some lawyers do work that way. Some hunch, or a desire to give a client the answer he wants, leads them to jump to the conclusion first, and then scrabble around for arguments to support it. Arguments dredged up this way are likely to sound weak and unconvincing. What is worse, they may be convincing to your superior and to the client, only to be brushed aside by the court. Never let wishful thinking distort your analysis and your judgment.

Often, a memorandum will call not only for a conclusion derived from a reasoned judgment of the impact of the law on the relevant facts, but also a recommendation of action to be taken or strategy to be pursued. In a case raising the question of whether a trust created by a wealthy man, since deceased, should be construed to include adopted grandchildren among the beneficiaries, a memorandum written in the offices of a leading New York law firm concluded after several pages of discussion:

> Thus, the correct approach to ensure the admissibility of extrinsic evidence in the Pierrepont [2] trust case would apparently be to designate it as evidence of an actual intent to include adopted children on the part of Mr. Pierrepont at the time he signed the trust instrument. The court would probably allow the evidence to be admitted on these grounds; and even if it was later held that the evidence did not disclose an actual intention on the part of the donor to include adopted children and that canons of construction would thus have to be applied as an aid in ascertaining his intention, the evidence would at least have been gotten before the court.

2. The name is fictitious.

As already said in other connections, the big cases in a law-yer's career are always those whose outcome is difficult to pre-dict, because the facts or the law or both are unclear. It is pre-cisely in these cases that the young lawyer can demonstrate his competence by so shrewdly judging the weight of the facts, prin-ciples and policies that will influence the court as to enable him to make a reliable prediction of what the outcome will be. Al-though he should evaluate the strengths and weaknesses of his case realistically, when he does reach a conclusion he should present it as clearly and convincingly as he can. If analysis of the cases shows that the law is unclear on the point, he may le-gitimately say that the conclusion represents his best judgment in the circumstances.

A Checklist of Questions

After writing a draft of a memorandum, one might well read it and ask oneself the following questions:

1. How does the question arise? At what stage of the pro-ceedings does the case stand? What is the next step contem-plated? Is the purpose of the memorandum to help the sen-ior member (a) decide whether the firm should accept the case; (b) write an opinion letter; (c) draft pleadings or motion pa-pers; or (d) prepare for trial?

2. Did I put myself in the place of the man for whom I was writing? Does the memorandum give him the information he wanted? Can he now take the required next step without ask-ing further questions or doing further research?

3. Does the question stated in the memorandum correctly fo-cus on the essential issue?

4. Are the assumed facts true? Should the facts be more fully investigated?

5. Do the legal authorities cited adequately support the con-clusions reached? Are the facts of the cases cited given in suffi-cient detail to show their relevance?

Example of Memorandum of Law

Limitations of space do not permit reproducing any extensive memoranda. Here, however, is a relatively short one, written in the offices of a large law firm (names have been changed):

> To: Mr. Essary
>
> From: Mr. Youngblood
>
> Re: Delta Corp. Compensation of Directors
>
> I. QUESTION PRESENTED: Can Delta's Board of Directors validly adopt a by-law providing for compensation of non-management directors, or must the adoption of such a by-law be left to the shareholders?
>
> II. CONCLUSIONS: The Board of Directors cannot validly adopt such a by-law if the presence of any director to be benefited thereby is necessary for a quorum at the meeting at which it is adopted, or if the vote of any such director is necessary for passage of the by-law. Assuming that such directors absented themselves from the meeting, leaving a quorum, such a by-law· probably could be validly adopted by the remaining directors. It is recommended, however, that the proposed by-law be submitted to the shareholders, preferably as part of a general revision of the by-laws.
>
> III. DISCUSSION: It is the law of Delaware and the general rule throughout the country that directors "have no right to compensation for services rendered within the scope of their duties as directors, unless it is authorized by the charter, by-laws, or the stockholders of the company." Lofland v. Cahall, 13 Del.Ch. 384, 389, 118 A. 1, 3 (Sup.Ct.1922). Delta's by-laws contain no authorization for the payment of compensation to directors. However, Article Tenth of the Corporation's Certificate of Incorporation gives the Board of Directors power to "make, alter, amend and repeal" the by-laws. It could be argued that the stockholders gave the directors power to enact any by-law they might think to be in the best interest of the Corporation, including one providing for their own compensation. The only authority found that is directly in point, however, is to the contrary. Note, Participation by Corporate Director in Vote or Meeting Fixing Compensation for His Own Services, 175 A.L.R. 577, 581 (1948):
>
> > "The fact that directors are given general power to enact bylaws does not give them the authority to enact a bylaw con-

ferring on themselves the authority to fix salaries and, under the authority thus conferred, to proceed afterward to vote themselves salaries. . . ."

Accord, Holcomb v. Forsyth, 216 Ala. 486, 113 So. 516 (1927); Martin v. Santa Cruz Water Storage Co., 4 Ariz. 171, 36 P. 36 (1894); McConnell v. Combination Min. & Mill. Co., 30 Mont. 239, 76 P. 194 (1904), aff'd on rehearing 31 Mont. 563, 79 P. 248 (1905); see Carter v. Louisville Ry., 238 Ky. 42, 36 S.W.2d 836 (1931).

If, however, a majority of the directors were "disinterested" in the benefits of the by-law, they could adopt it in the absence of the minority. The proposal is to provide for the compensation not of all the directors, but only of non-management directors not serving as counsel to the Corporation. There are six such directors, leaving seven who could pass the by-law.

The adoption by disinterested directors of a by-law benefiting other directors would be in accord with Article Twelfth of the Corporation's Certificate of Incorporation, which reads in part as follows:

"In the absence of fraud, no contract or other transaction of the Corporation shall be affected or invalidated in any way by the fact that any of the directors of the Corporation are . . . parties to such contract or transaction, provided that such interest shall be fully disclosed or otherwise known to the Board of Directors at the meeting of said Board at which such contract or transaction is authorized or confirmed and provided further that at the meeting of the Board of Directors authorizing or confirming such contract or transaction there shall be present a quorum of directors not so interested or connected and such contract or transaction shall be approved by a majority of such quorum, which majority shall consist of directors not so interested or connected. . . ."

Such a procedure was approved in the only case found in which it was specifically discussed. Carter v. Louisville Ry., 238 Ky. 42, 36 S.W.2d 836 (1931).

The danger of this course of action lies in the fact that each member of the Board depends upon the others to vote him his compensation, as director, counsel, officer or consultant. It could thus be argued that none is truly "disinterested." According to Ballantine, Corporations 190 (Rev. ed. 1946):

". . . It has generally been held that where various directors are interested in the common object of procuring a salary or a salary increase for each of them as officers, the device of passing several resolutions for each instead of one joint resolution for all will not be effective. The mutual back-scratching or reciprocal voting invalidates the action as to each."

The safest course would be to submit the entire matter of compensation to the stockholders. Even if the courts would eventually uphold a by-law adopted by the directors, action by the stockholders would go far toward forestalling an attack on the motives and integrity of the Board. This thinking accords with that of Washington and Rothschild, Compensating the Corporate Executive 337–38 (Rev. ed. 1951):

". . . we find many statements in the cases to the effect that directors have no power to grant each other compensation for their services as directors, unless there is some provision in the charter, statutes or by-laws or a resolution of a disinterested board permitting them to do so. In other words, the directors can compensate a member of the board for his services as an officer or employee; they should leave to the stockholders the question of compensating directors for their services as such. Accordingly, the safest course would be for the directors to leave the entire matter to the stockholders, by having the complete plan placed in an amendment to the by-laws. Proper, too, would be a resolution of the directors themselves adopting the plan of compensation, but making it effective only upon a vote of approval by the stockholders."

Asking the stockholders to pass upon the proposal as part of a general revision of the by-laws would avoid exaggerating its importance. Such a revision would also enable us to correct minor errors that have crept into the by-laws.

III. MEMORANDA OF LAW FOR THE COURT

A "memorandum of law for the court" is really a kind of brief. When, in the trial of a case, an intricate or controversial question of law arises, the judge may ask counsel to submit written memoranda on the point, or counsel may offer to do so on his own initiative. A careful lawyer can often foresee that a certain question may arise and will arm himself with such a memorandum and offer it at the proper time.

A memorandum prepared for this purpose will, of course, differ in style from the office memorandum and resemble instead an appellate brief. Its purpose is not merely to explore but to convince the court. It differs from the brief, however, in that it seeks not affirmance or reversal, but some specific act or ruling by the judge: granting or refusing a motion, admitting evidence, giving an instruction, or dismissing a suit. Also, unlike a brief, it is usually limited to one specific point of law.

Some judges have urged lawyers to submit such memoranda in all cases. A judge sitting in a trial term must often decide questions of law on the spur of the moment, without the thoughtful consideration that an appellate tribunal can give to its decisions. It is expecting too much to assume that he knows all the law.

In an important trial, the memorandum of law submitted to the court may be as extensive as an appellate brief. But even though counsel may be discussing complex points of law, he should never forget that it is a trial court he is addressing. His point headings, for example, should be framed in terms of what the trial court should do, especially the instructions it should give the jury:

> The jury should be instructed that if it finds that at the time of the impact defendant's vehicle was not illuminated with one or more red lights visible for a distance of 300 feet to its rear under normal atmospheric conditions, defendant is guilty of negligence as a matter of law.
>
> Plaintiff is entitled to recover in full for all his loss of earnings as well as the fair and reasonable value of all hospital and medical expenses, notwithstanding any benefits he receives from the government as a serviceman.
>
> This court should take judicial notice that this collision occurred more than a half hour after sunset and more than a half hour before sunrise.
>
> The only issue for the jury's determination is whether the defendant's negligence, proximately caused, concurred in or contributed to the injury.

Memoranda must be tailored to the needs and wants of the individual judge (or, increasingly, the law clerk) who will consider it. In the federal District Court for the Southern District of New York, the trial judge may have as many as 200 motions before him on one day. In state courts in the metropolitan areas the situation is much the same. Perhaps only five or ten minutes will be allowed for oral presentation. The judge may not have had an opportunity to read the memorandum before the hearing, and he will probably make a ruling immediately. The memorandum must therefore be short, serving only to direct the judge's attention to the controlling points and authorities. Here is a memorandum opposing a motion, written by Berman and Frost of New York (the caption, naming the parties, has been omitted):

> MEMORANDUM OF LAW SUBMITTED IN OPPOSITION TO PLAINTIFFS' MOTION FOR AN ORDER DIRECTING THE FURTHER EXAMINATION OF DEFENDANT AND THE PRODUCTION OF CERTAIN EQUIPMENT IN CONNECTION THEREWITH.

> ### STATEMENT OF FACTS.

> Briefly, plaintiff seeks to recover for personal injuries suffered when his right eye was struck by a stone ejected by a power lawn mower purchased from defendant. The action is predicated on a breach of express and implied warranties of fitness for use and on seventeen items of negligence encompassing the design, manufacture, etc., of the lawn mower.

> Plaintiffs filed a note of issue and statement of readiness on September 25th, 1957, in which it is stated:

>> "b. The plaintiff has completed all such proceedings except an examination before trial of the defendant and plaintiff does not intend to conduct these proceedings".

> Defendant has produced the lawn mower for plaintiffs' discovery and inspection and has been examined as to the purchase and return by plaintiff of the lawn mower.

> Plaintiff now seeks an order for further, additional and continued examination of defendant.

POINT I

PLAINTIFFS' MOTION IS UNTIMELY.

Having filed said statement of readiness plaintiffs have given up their right to examine defendant at this time.

Special Rule Respecting Calendar Practice Of The New York County Supreme Court Rules

> Brozin v. Lapkin
> Suskin v. Howmore Realty Corp.
> New York Law Journal—March 4, 1958,
> Special Term, Part I Supreme Court,
> New York County, Matthew M. Levy, J.

POINT II

PLAINTIFFS HAVE NO RIGHT TO EXAMINE AN AGENT OR EMPLOYEE OF DEFENDANT CONCERNING THE MECHANICAL DESIGN, CONSTRUCTION AND OPERATION OF THE LAWN MOWER.

There is no connection shown between the person sought to be examined and the manner, direction, supervision or use of the lawn mower. Plaintiffs therefore, can examine such person only as a witness and not an adverse party.

> Goepp v. American Overseas Airlines Inc.,
> 72 N.Y.S.2d 862

POINT III

IN EXAMINING DEFENDANT AS TO DESIGN, MANUFACTURE AND OPERATION OF THE LAWN MOWER, PLAINTIFFS ARE SEEKING "OPINION EVIDENCE" AND ARE NOT EN- TITLED TO SAME.

> Vaughn v. City of New York
> 132 N.Y.S.2d 919

POINT IV

THE FACTS RELATING TO THE CARE, STOR- AGE, OPERATION AND OTHER DISPOSI- TION OF THE LAWN MOWER FROM ITS DATE OF RETURN BY PLAINTIFF TO DE-

FENDANT, BEAR NO RELATION TO MAT–
TERS WITH RESPECT TO WHICH PLAINTIFF
HAS THE BURDEN OF PROOF UPON THE
TRIAL.

Re: Levine
112 N.Y.S.2d 713

CONCLUSION

DEFENDANT RESPECTFULLY REQUESTS
THAT PLAINTIFFS' MOTION INSOFAR AS
SAME RELATES TO THE MATTERS DIS–
CUSSED HEREIN, BE DENIED.

Memoranda of Law During Trial

In the hectic practice of big city trial attorneys, questions of law frequently arise during the trial. The lawyer trying the case will send a message to his office that he needs a memorandum on the point, to be submitted at two o'clock that afternoon. He may want to submit it to the court, or he may want merely to refer to it in making oral argument. Here is such a memorandum, prepared for a prominent New York trial attorney:

ATTEMPTED DENIAL OF OWNERSHIP BY A
REGISTERED OWNER TO AVOID LIABILITY
UNDER SECTION 59 OF THE VEHICLE AND
TRAFFIC LAW.

The landmark decision in this field is Shuba v. Greendonner, 271 N.Y. 189, 2 N.E.2d 536 (1936). A Connecticut resident permitted his minor son to register the son's automobile in the father's name because the son was too young to register it himself. The son admittedly paid all expenses of the automobile, but insurance was carried in the father's name. Collision in New York State, and the father attempted to deny ownership. The Court said at page 194:

"To permit the respondent (owner) to relieve himself of liability by proving that he was not in fact the owner of the automobile and thereby establish his illegal and fraudulent act in procuring its registration in his own name would be against public policy and would encourage fraudulent and illegal deceptions on the state in procuring the registration of automobiles in the names of persons who were not the owners thereof, directly in violation of the statute."

In Allen v. Ennis, 253 App.Div. 769, 300 N.Y.S.2d 1323 (3d Dept.1937), a commission employee of the defendant automobile dealer in demonstrating a car negligently caused the death of the passenger (plaintiff's intestate). The car was licensed in the name of the corporation-defendant, but the corporation argued that the automobile was actually owned by the salesman-defendant. The Court said (769):

> "There was convincing testimony that the corporate defendant carried on a plan for the *apparent* sale to its agents of the cars used by them for demonstration, and for the registration of these cars in its own name, and they were in fact operated under its license and with its number plates thereon, until sold by the agents. Upon these facts the corporate defendant was not in a position to deny its ownership."

See also Sease v. Central Greyhound Lines Inc., 281 App. Div. 192, 118 N.Y.S.2d 433 (1952).

Soos v. Soos, 4 Misc.2d 727, 162 N.Y.S.2d 373 (County Ct. Niagara County, 1956). Judgment for the plaintiff in City Court was reversed because the plaintiff was not the registered owner of the automobile, but had caused it to be registered in the name of his mother, who was the wife of the defendant. Plaintiff sued for property damage. The Court said that it is immaterial that the plaintiff had paid the repair bills for the car.

> "Section 11 of the Vehicle and Traffic Law requires vehicles to be registered in the name of the owner. Shuba v. Greendonner holds in effect that such distinctions as those between legal ownership and equitable ownership cannot, under this statute, be recognized, at least in collision cases. Accordingly, a defendant in whose name an automobile was registered, was barred from escaping liability by claiming that in fact he was not the owner. Since one may not escape liability by such an assertion, it seems reasonable that likewise he may not impose liability. The public policy embodied in the statute would be equally offended in either case."

Since the memorandum of law for the court is really a brief, both in substance and in form, the material in the next two chapters, on Briefs, is relevant here.

Chapter 11

BRIEFS: QUESTIONS AND STATEMENT OF FACTS

A century and more ago, when life was more leisurely and oratory more esteemed, lawyers were allowed to take all the time they required or thought they required to argue cases orally. Today most appellate courts limit oral argument to an hour, or even a half-hour. Lawyers can do little more in this time than present the facts, define the issues and argue them in general terms designed primarily to show the essential justice of counsel's case. Penetrating analysis of the legal principles and of the precedents must be left to the brief.

The brief offers your last chance to affect the outcome of the case. Oral argument may come after the brief is submitted, but appellate opinions are typically written weeks or even months after argument. By that time, the effect of even the most brilliant oral argument has largely faded. The judge in his chambers drafting the opinion has before him only your brief to speak for you.

What one writer said about how pressed for time the justices of the United States Supreme Court are is true in greater or less degree of every appellate court: "For the law student and practitioner there is the obvious moral that written arguments filed with the Court are not documents like law review essays which the author is entitled to expect each of his readers to peruse carefully and reflectively from beginning to end. Perhaps the writer of an opinion reads a brief this way. But for the other members of the Court these documents necessarily serve a different function than the communication simply of a connected line of thought. They are documents from which busy men have to extract the gist in a hurry. Petitions for writ of certiorari and statements as to jurisdiction on appeal need to bring home concisely and with utmost clarity the nub of the reasons why the case has a just claim upon the limited time and attention of the Court. Briefs on the merits need not only tell their story to one who takes the time to read all the way through them, but to be so organized that they can be used, like a book of reference, for quick illumination on any particular point of concern." [1]

You therefore owe it to your judicial reader, and so indirectly to yourself, to write your brief as tersely as you can. Don't let the practice of dictating orally to a stenographer or a machine get you into the habit of droning on interminably. Printing costs money.[2] The writer who has to push his own pen is much more likely to learn not to throw in useless words than is the man who just talks.

The essential components of the brief are determined by the rules of the particular court. These vary, but the following are always required:

    (1) A jurisdictional statement.

    (2) Questions presented.

    (3) Statement of the facts.

    (4) The argument (usually consisting of points of law discussed under separate headings).

    (5) The conclusion.

Rules often also require a subject index and a table of cases. But these raise no questions of writing style. In almost all the federal Courts of Appeal and in a number of state courts, there are limits on the lengths of briefs. Constitutional, statutory or self-imposed limits on the court's power to review questions of fact or legal issues are not uncommon. These restrictions are not the subject of this book, but they must be borne in mind before one can write or even plan a brief.

1. Henry M. Hart, Jr., The Time Chart of the Justices, 73 Harv.L. Rev. 84, 94 (1959).

2. Inquiries of 1,773 lawyers in upstate New York "indicated that in 45% of the civil cases in which an appeal was deemed desirable but not taken, printing costs barred the taking of the appeal; whereas all costs together barred 49% of such civil appeals. Printing costs alone, likewise, barred appeals in a quarter of the criminal cases where an appeal was deemed desirable but not taken." Willcox, Karlen and Roemer, Justice Lost—By What Appellate Papers Cost, 43 J.Am. Jud.Soc'y 6 (1959).

I. THE JURISDICTIONAL STATEMENT

The jurisdictional statement, sometimes called a "preliminary statement," "statement of the case," or merely "statement," should briefly point out the nature and history of the case and how it comes before the appellate court. It will usually identify the parties, the general nature of the action (that it is, for example, a personal injury suit, divorce action or will contest), the court from which the appeal is being taken, the disposition in that court, including the date of the entry of judgment or other relevant rulings or orders, and the rulings below that are being appealed. It should also include any other information that the appellate court needs in order to see at the outset how the case comes before it and to assure itself that the controversy is one over which it has jurisdiction, that the time for taking an appeal has not expired and that all necessary procedural steps have been taken.

The following are representative examples:

> The defendant appeals from a judgment of $10,000 in favor of the plaintiff, entered on May 29, 1961, after trial before judge John Smith and a jury, and from an order of said judge denying a motion to set aside the verdict.

> This is an election contest filed in the Superior Court of Maricopa County, which entered an order dismissing the contest and entering judgment for the contestee on June 5, 1961. Appeal is taken to this Court under A.R.S. sec. 12–2101B.

> This is an appeal from an order of the Santa Fe County District Court, dismissing appellants' petition for a declaratory judgment pursuant to 44–6–1 et seq., NMSA 1978 Comp. The ground for dismissal was narrowly defined in the Order; the Trial Court found "that this action is a suit against the State and that the State has not consented to be sued."

> Thereafter, this appeal was perfected in due course, the basis of the appeal being limited to the single contention: "That while the suit is against the State, it is one requiring a purely ministerial act in which no discretion is involved, and that therefore the State's consent is not a prerequisite to suit" (Tr. 9).

Appellant was charged in the police court of the City of Springfield with driving while intoxicated, reckless driving, carrying a deadly weapon, disorderly conduct by resisting an officer and escaping custody. On trial in the police court, he was found not guilty of reckless driving and carrying a deadly weapon, and guilty of driving while intoxicated, resisting an officer and escaping custody. Upon appeal to the District Court (Honorable David E. Carmody presiding) Appellant was found not guilty of resisting an officer and escaping custody, and guilty of driving while intoxicated upon which conviction he was sentenced, and from which he appeals.

Sometimes, as when the issue on appeal involves a complicated pleading question, the preliminary statement of the case will need to be longer than any of these examples. But the brief-writer should guard against pointless review of all the steps in the trial —the date of filing the complaint, the motion for permission to file an amended complaint, the filing of the amended complaint, etc.—when nothing depends on these steps. He should also not allow himself to spout a flow of useless words such as congest the following example:

On September 22, 1978, the State filed its complaint against the defendant, Michael Mentes, in the office of the District Court Clerk, in Clovis, Curry County, charging that Michael Mentes, while armed with a dangerous weapon to-wit, a gun, feloniously robbed Lloyd Roberts (Tr. 1). It further appears that on October 6, 1978, the defendant appeared before the District Court of Clovis, Curry County, for the purpose of arraignment, and entered a plea of Not Guilty, whereupon the Court set the defendant's trial for Tuesday, November 21, 1978 at 9 o'clock a. m. (Tr. 3). The defendant was then tried before a duly empaneled jury on the 21st day of November, 1978, and a verdict of Guilty in manner and form as charged in the Information was returned by the jury (Tr. 15).

On December 22, 1978, a Motion for Appeal was filed in the District Court of Curry County, and on the same day the District Judge, E. T. Hardy, signed an Order Allowing Appeal (Tr. 16, 18). It further appears that on January 8,

1979, a Praecipe for Record was filed in the District Court of Curry County (Tr. 19). The transcript was then filed in the Supreme Court within the time provided by law.

Everything said in these two paragraphs could be better said in one sentence:

> Defendant appeals from a conviction entered by District Judge E. T. Hardy of the District Court of Curry County on a jury verdict, returned on November 21, 1978, finding defendant guilty of robbery with a gun.

Appellee will not usually have reason to question appellant's statement of the case. If minor errors appear, appellee can mention them briefly:

> Except for several minor and apparently unimportant inaccuracies as to dates, the appellant's statement of the case is satisfactory. The complaint is alleged to have been filed on January 9, 1979. The correct date was January 19, 1979 (Tr. 1). The answer is alleged to have been filed on February 26, 1978; the actual date was February 26, 1979 (Tr. 3).

II. THE QUESTIONS PRESENTED

The "questions presented" (the exact wording of the heading varies with the several jurisdictions [3]) tells the court the question or questions raised. Not only novices but some experienced lawyers fail to appreciate the importance of a competent statement of the issues and the drafting skill that it requires. A well-formulated statement allows the court to see at a glance what the issues are and enables it to focus on those issues in following the argument. Some eminent trial lawyers consider the formulation of the issues the most important task in brief-writing and the thinking that goes into it as the most vital part of their preparation. Yet appellate judges say that a shockingly large number of briefs require undue labor to discover what the points at issue really are.

3. In Arkansas, New Mexico and the Court of Appeals for the Tenth Circuit, it is called "The Points Relied on for Reversal"; in Illinois, "Nature of the Case."

Competent craftsmanship in formulating a statement of the issues will go a long way toward getting your arguments across. It will direct attention to those questions that counsel considers determinative. Just as a general who is able to choose the site for a battle starts with an important advantage of position, so the lawyer who can frame his questions so as to focus on the vital points of attack starts with the advantage of having carefully selected his battleground.

The questions presented must of course, be limited to those raised at the trial. A party may not on appeal advance new contentions. For example, a party who at the trial relied on the contention that he had established a valid water right by prior use of water will not be allowed on appeal to argue for the first time that the State Engineer lacked power to limit the acreage that a landowner may irrigate.

Make Your Questions Specific

The questions presented must be specific. They must not be so general as to be meaningless:

> The question is whether there was sufficient evidence to go to the jury.
>
> The question on this appeal is whether the trial court was correct in ruling that the complaint did not state a cause of action.
>
> The order of the Board should be reversed because it is not consistent with the evidence and testimony in the record.

In every appellate case the ultimate question is whether the judgment of the court below should be affirmed or reversed, whether it was supported by the evidence or whether the lower court committed prejudicial error. Stating the issues in such general terms, therefore, tells the court essentially nothing about the particular questions in the case. A fairly concise but adequate question might read:

> Whether oil transported by appellants from New York or elsewhere outside of Texas to their warerooms or warehouses

in Texas, there held for sales in Texas in original packages of transportation, and subsequently sold and delivered in Texas in such original packages, may be made the basis of an occupation tax upon appellants, when the state tax applies to all wholesale dealers in oil engaged in making sales and delivery in Texas.[4]

How to Frame a Question Incorporating Numerous Facts

When the issue arises on the specific facts, a number of factual elements must usually be included, and this may make for an involved and perhaps confused sentence. A good general rule is to start with the broadest principle that the point concerns, and thence move to the less significant ones. Compare the two wordings below:

Where at the time of a man's death he is living separate and apart from his wife and is not contributing to her support, whether she is entitled to compensation as his widow under the Workmen's Compensation Act?	Whether under the Workmen's Compensation Act a woman is entitled to compensation as a widow when at the time of her husband's death she was living separate and apart from him and was not being supported by him?

Why is the one on the right clearer? Because it starts by telling us the general field in which the question lies ("under the Workmen's Compensation Act"). The left-hand statement gives us details first; but we cannot relate these details to any legal principle, because none is mentioned until the end. If you wanted to describe a scene, you would first tell us where we are (in the forest, in a rowboat, on the desert) before depicting details. Similarly, you should orient the reader generally before narrowing your focus on the specific point.

4. From the court's statement of the question in Sonneborn Bros. v. Cureton, 262 U.S. 506, 43 S.Ct. 643, 67 L.Ed. 1095 (1923). See also the discussion of "Point Headings," in the next chapter, p. 191 et seq. What is said there is relevant here, because the point heading may be merely the question recast into assertive form.

To see how this rule is applied, let us look at another statement, also containing several elements:

> Whether a tax on a sale of goods in the "original package" effected by delivery to the purchaser upon arrival at destination in the taxing state after an interstate journey, when the extra-state seller has shipped them into the taxing state for sale there, is forbidden by the commerce clause.

The relative importance of the various elements in this statement can best be made graphic by arranging them in an outline. Obviously, the broad category in which the question fits is the effect of the commerce clause to restrict state power. Starting with that concept, we may construct our outline as follows:

  I. This question concerns the effect of the commerce clause

      A. As a restriction on state power

          1. Of taxation

             a. Of sales

                (1) By the state of the buyer

                    (a) Of goods in the "original package"

                        (i) Imposed upon arrival at destination

                            (aa) When shipped into the taxing state for sale there.

If we now simply follow this outline, we shall have little difficulty in putting the several elements into proper order, somewhat as follows:

> Whether the commerce clause forbids imposition of a state sales tax by the state of the buyer upon a sale to the buyer of goods in the "original package," imposed upon arrival at destination after an interstate journey, when the extra-state seller has shipped them into the taxing state for sale there.

It will not be necessary actually to write out an outline in most cases; it will suffice for the writer to remember to arrange the elements in the way suggested—from the general to the specific.

Do Not Refer to Facts Not Yet Given

In jurisdictions requiring that the Statement of Facts follow rather than precede the statement of the issues, the questions should not refer to facts not yet related:

> Whether plaintiff sustained the burden of showing that his reliance upon the apparent authority of defendant's sales representative to contract for the purchase of the office equipment was justified without making inquiry of an officer of the defendant corporation.

Such a question, put before the facts are given, is incomprehensible. When the issue can only only be framed in terms of the facts, a very short statement of facts may be necessary to introduce the question. For example, in Lambert v. California,[5] brief of amicus curiae for appellant stated the questions as follows:

> A Los Angeles municipal ordinance makes it a crime punishable by imprisonment for a "convicted person" to be or remain in the city for more than five days without registering with the Chief of Police and supplying detailed information to him. On appeal from a conviction for failure to register, the questions presented are:
>
> 1. Does conviction under the ordinance in the absence of wrongful intent violate due process of law?
>
> 2. Does the ordinance constitute an unwarranted invasion of the right of privacy, right to liberty, and privileges and immunities of a citizen of the United States in that it (a) purports to make unlawful a morally innocent and passive status and (b) is not reasonably restricted to the evil with which it purports to deal?

Even when reciting the facts is not essential, and the issue can be compressed into one sentence, counsel may prefer to present it in a series of shorter sentences which give the essential facts and then state the question. In the left-hand column below, a fairly complex issue is put into one sentence; in the column on

---

5. Lambert v. California, 355 U.S. 225, 78 S.Ct. 240, 2 L.Ed.2d 228 (1957).

the right, this is broken into a series of sentences giving somewhat fuller facts before putting the question:

Whether appellee's employees are engaged in the "production of goods for commerce" within the meaning of the Fair Labor Standards Act when 95% of their work consists of moving steel from certain steel companies to the plants of auto manufacturers, or from place to place within the steel plants for the purpose of further processing of such steel in the course of its manufacture prior to sale and shipment.

Appellee is a corporation operating heavy equipment for the moving of steel and other heavy articles. Some of its employees transport steel from certain steel companies to the plants of automobile manufacturers. Others move steel from place to place within the steel plants for the purpose of further processing of such steel in the course of its manufacture prior to sale and shipment. These operations comprise 95% of the work of these employees. The question is whether such employees are engaged in the "production of goods for commerce" within the meaning of the Fair Labor Standards Act.

Be Concise

We have devoted a chapter to extolling the virtue of conciseness. In wording issues, conciseness is particularly important, because often more difficult to attain than elsewhere. It is not easy to frame an issue in a reasonably short sentence. Some word-wasting habits, however, should not be difficult to eliminate. One is the habit of stuffing sentences with stock legal phrases that serve no purpose, especially in introductory clauses: "Whether it was reversible error for the trial court to hold that a contract . . ." Such a sentence can be pruned by simply deleting needless words: "Whether a contract . . ."

In one case, there were two appellants.   Each submitted a brief, arguing the same point.   One worded it this way:

> The judgment of the district court setting aside the order of the state Corporation Commission dated October 3, 1957 denying the application of Alfredo Gonzales, transferor and Bekins Van and Storage Company, Inc., transferee, of a portion of certificate of public convenience and necessity No. 739, should be reversed for the reason that said order of the Commission is in all respects reasonable and lawful, having been entered pursuant to the Commission's power to approve or disapprove a proposed transfer as the public interest may require, and upon a finding that said transfer would not be in the public interest.

The other put it as follows:

> The state Corporation Commission's order denying permission to transfer the certificate of convenience and necessity was lawful, reasonable and supported by substantial evidence. The district court therefore erred in setting it aside.

Does the first say anything not said in the second?

A strictly legal issue can usually be more succinctly worded than one depending on the facts:

> Whether a taxpayer must pay the full amount of an income tax deficiency before he may challenge its correctness by a suit for refund under 28 U.S.C.A. § 1346(a)(1).[6]

> May Texas promote its policy of freedom for economic enterprise by utilizing the criminal law against various forms of combination and monopoly, but exclude from criminal punishment corresponding activities of agriculture?[7]

> Whether evidence obtained as a result of wiretapping by state law-enforcement officers, without participation by federal authorities, is admissible in a federal court.[8]

6. Flora v. United States, 357 U.S. 63, 78 S.Ct. 1079, 2 L.Ed.2d 1165 (1958).

7. Tigner v. Texas, 310 U.S. 141, 60 S.Ct. 879, 84 L.Ed. 1124 (1940).

8. Benanti v. United States, 355 U. S. 96, 78 S.Ct. 155, 2 L.Ed.2d 126 (1957).   For other examples, see Appleman, Approved Appellate Briefs, § 5.17 et seq. (1958).

Strive for a Favorable Wording

Although the essential qualities in framing the issues are accuracy, fairness and clarity, if you can achieve these qualities you may aim for a bonus in the form of a wording that will be most favorable to your side.   This is not to be done by using argumentative or biased words, or by distorting the question into something other than a correct presentation; it must be done by emphasizing those data that should lead to the answer you want. The formula is simple, but its application is not.   The facts must be selected, yet they must present a fair picture; they cannot assume as true what is actually hotly disputed.   They must include all the essential facts on which the answer will have to depend.   A question that is rigged with disputed assertions will be demolished by your opponent.

"The essential technique," says Mr. Frederick B. Wiener in his valuable book, *Briefing and Arguing Federal Appeals,* "is so to load the question with the facts of the particular case or with the relevant quotations from the statute involved, *fairly stated,* that you can almost win the case on the mere statement of the question it presents." [9]   He gives examples, including the following:

> Whether a lost grant of a fee simple may be presumed when there has been only spasmodic possession at long intervals, where the original grant and the first mesne conveyance in a complete chain of title disclose the defect in the claimed title and show that only a five-year lease was granted by the sovereign, and where no record of a grant from the sovereign appears although the law required records of such grants to be kept.

"There's your chain of title," says Wiener, "—and your case —in a nutshell."

In Mitchell v. Oregon Frozen Foods Company,[10] the brief for the petitioner, Secretary of Labor James P. Mitchell, stated the Questions Presented as follows:

> 1.   Whether a frozen foods processor who freezes vegetables and packs them in bulk containers during the harvesting

---

9.   Wiener,   Briefing   and   Arguing   Federal Appeals, 73, 77 (1967).

10.   Mitchell v. Oregon Frozen Foods Co., 361 U.S. 231, 80 S.Ct. 365, 4 L. Ed.2d 267 (1960).

season, stores them until after the season has ended and thereafter repackages them in consumer packages, is engaged in the "first processing of . . . fresh fruits or vegetables" during the post-seasonal storing and repackaging so as to be exempt under § 7(c) of the Fair Labor Standards Act from the overtime requirements of the Act.

2. Whether a frozen foods processor who mixes vegetables previously frozen by it with vegetables purchased, already frozen and packed in bulk, from others is entitled to the exemption under § 7(c) while engaged in preparing and packaging the mixed vegetables.

3. Whether the repackaging or mixing operations qualify for an additional exemption under a determination made by the Administrator under § 7(b)(3) of the Act.

The respondent company preferred to put them somewhat differently:

Respondents are satisfied with appellant's statement of the second and third "Questions Presented" but differ with the language in the first question, particularly: "stores them until after the season has ended and thereafter packages them." Actually part of the bulk stored vegetables are "repackaged" during the harvest season (R. 154) and as such is first processing.

We would like that thought expressed in the question and suggest the following:

Whether a continuation of repackaging, after harvest season, of previously frozen and bulk packaged vegetables continues to be a part of "first processing of . . . fresh fruit and vegetables" under Section 7(c) of the Fair Labor Standards Act so as to exempt the processor from the overtime requirements of the Act.

Or as otherwise, but less succinctly stated:

Whether a frozen food processor who freezes vegetables and packs part of them in consumer-packages and the balance in bulk containers a portion of which is repacked in consumer's packages during harvest season, as time permits and the balance following the harvest season, whether the latter continues to be "first processing of . . . fresh fruits and vegetables" so as to be exempt under Section 7(c) of the Fair Labor Standards Act from the overtime requirements of the Act.

In accordance with the principles discussed in the chapter on Clarity, the wording can sometimes be made stronger for one side or the other by merely changing the word-order. Which of these two ways of wording the issue would be preferable for the Government's brief?

Whether the defendant's right against unreasonable search and seizure, as provided in the Fourth Amendment to the Constitution, was violated when the United States, through its agents, obtained evidence from the house of the defendant incident to an arrest for probable cause, without a search warrant?

Whether a criminal defendant's constitutional protection against unreasonable search and seizure was violated when federal officers obtained evidence from the house of the defendant without a search warrant but incident to a lawful arrest upon probable cause to believe defendant had committed a felony?

Strength can sometimes be added by simply adding a few emphatic words. Which of the following is stronger for the defendant, and why?

Are federal agents justified in arresting, without a warrant, an occupant of a dwelling that they suspect houses contraband?

May federal agents, having no warrant for either arrest or search, enter a house and arrest an occupant merely because they have reason to suspect that the house contains contraband?

Courts in writing opinions not infrequently frame the question in a way that foreshadows the conclusion they have decided upon.

Illinois law provides that "Writs of error in all criminal cases are writs of right and shall be issued of course." The question presented here is whether Illinois may, consistent with the Due Process and Equal Protection Clauses of the Fourteenth Amendment, administer this statute so as to deny adequate appellate review to the poor while granting such review to all others.

When the question is put this way, we can foresee what the answer is going to be.[11]

Don't Overstrain

Law students, earnestly trying to word questions in a way that suggests the desired answer, sometimes go too far. They set up a straw man they can easily knock down. Unfortunately, this leaves their opponent's actual contention untouched.

> It is error for a trial court to refuse to make a finding of fact requested by a party to the suit which is abundantly supported by uncontradicted testimony and particularly by the testimony of principal witnesses of the opposing party, against whom the finding would operate.

The opposing party is not likely to dispute this proposition. What he probably will dispute is that the facts assumed in the proposition are true.

> Under the Labor-Management Relations Act, Section 10, does the court have the power to set aside findings of the Board which are not supported by substantial evidence on the record considered as a whole?

Section 10 specifically provides that the court does have this power. Counsel framing his issue in this way has succeeded in posing a question that will have to be answered his way, but does it state a real issue in the case? Almost certainly, the other side will point out that this is not the issue. Raising such a false issue can only do one harm. It will probably not mislead the court; opposing counsel will see to that. Nothing can be as destructive to your case as a misstatement or a false issue that your opponent can publicly rip to shreds. If he can show that your statement of the issues is incorrect, the court may conclude that it cannot rely on what you say, and that it had better turn to your opponent to learn what the case is really all about.

In a federal case in which the Postmaster General had held D. H. Lawrence's novel, "Lady Chatterley's Lover," obscene and

11. Griffin v. Illinois, 351 U.S. 12, 76 S.Ct. 585, 100 L.Ed. 891 (1956).

therefore unmailable, the government attempted to frame the question in these absolute terms:

> Was the dominant theme of the book, considered in the light of the opinion evidence, so innocent that reasonable minds could no longer differ over which inference was the proper one to be adopted?

The Government added ("with considerable understatement," as the Court of Appeals commented), "To state the problem thus is to actually resolve it." But the court refused to let the case be resolved so easily.[12]

Do Not Raise Too Many Issues

In any long trial, many issues and many rulings on evidence may arise in which error could be argued. Trial counsel may still be feeling strongly about issues that bulked large at the trial and may want to argue them, but calm thought may make clear that they are no longer relevant on appeal. Raising a great number of issues only diverts the court's attention from the most important ones. One able lawyer has said categorically that the points to be argued should not exceed four. Another has estimated that "75% of all cases could be reduced to a single question and the chances for reversal would be improved." [13]

In one case, after taking more than three pages of the opinion merely to summarize the many allegations of appellant's complaint (which, notwithstanding its sweeping scope, had been dismissed for failure to state a claim on which relief could be granted), the upper court felt moved to say:

> We think it would scarcely be possible for any statute, ordinance or transaction to be burdened with as many legal infirmities and shortcomings as the large number said to inhere in the transactions here challenged. Some, though by no means all, of the claimed defects and infirmities pointed out, merit consideration and decision by us. All such will be tak-

12. Grove Press v. Christenberry, 276 F.2d 433 (1960).

13. Paxton Blair, Appellate Briefs and Advocacy, 18 Fordham L.Rev. 30, 39 (1949); Appleman, Successful Appellate Techniques 591 (1953).

en up and resolved and the others will be disregarded as not meriting discussion.[14]

Restricting yourself to four or fewer issues calls for what Mr. John W. Davis, late Solicitor General of the United States, called the "courage of exclusion." In a case of historic importance, concerning the power of the President to seize the steel industry in time of peace,[15] Mr. Davis was able to reduce the issues presented to the United States Supreme Court to three. If you will ask yourself whether the upper court is really likely to consider a given point crucial, you will often be able to conclude that it will not. Including it will only dissipate the emphasis that you want to focus on your main points, in the brief, in oral argument and in the judges' conference.

Do not make the mistake, so often seen, of restating what is essentially only one point under two headings. In one brief, counsel listed two points:

> 1. Evidence inadvertently discovered while pursuing a reasonable course of lawful arrest is not evidence obtained by illegal search and seizure in violation of the rights secured by the Fourth Amendment.
>
> 2. Evidence revealed by search incident to lawful arrest of appellee was properly seized, and is admissible in proceedings against appellee, and such search and seizure is not a denial of rights secured by the Fourth Amendment.

Counsel then proceeded in his argument to say, "The Points Relied On are so inter-related that Appellant believes a unified discussion will better serve the interests of clarity than will separate arguments on each point." At that point, if not sooner, counsel should have asked himself whether he did not really have only one point instead of two.

14. Gomez v. City of Las Vegas, 61 N.M. 27, 293 P.2d 984, 987 (1956). See also Judge Voelker's observation in Taylor v. Milton, 353 Mich. 421, 92 N.W.2d 57, 59 (1958): " . . . defendant alleges 52 separate grounds of error, most of which are irksomely repetitious. While this scatter-gun approach may possess a certain primitive effectiveness when a man seeks to persuade another to marry his daughter, it scarcely persuades this Court." The appeal might have been dismissed, "had we felt disposed or had the appellee made a timely motion to that end."

15. Youngstown Sheet & Tube Co. v. Sawyer, 343 U.S. 579, 72 S.Ct. 863, 96 L.Ed. 1153 (1952).

Appellee's Wording of Questions

The appellee is in the position of the defender of a position. He does not have to attack; he is in possession of a judgment, and his is a holding operation. In framing the questions, his aim is not to arouse the upper court's interest, but rather the opposite. His theme will normally be that the appellant has had his hearing in the court below, that that court passed on all the issues and made its decision and there is nothing in it that requires the upper court to intervene. Appellee may therefore want to put the question calmly and in a deprecating way:

> Whether there is evidence in the record to support the judgment.

> Whether the trial court abused its discretion in denying defendant's motion for a new trial on the ground of newly discovered evidence.

But appellee will have to use some judgment in adopting this approach. If his formulation leaves the issue unclear, he will merely lead the court to turn to his opponent's brief to learn what the specific issues are.

Counsel representing appellees sometimes assume that they should not or at least need not start work until they receive appellant's brief. This practice is more often the result of dilatoriness than of deliberate strategy. Nine-tenths of the work on appellee's brief can be done without seeing appellant's. Counsel knows what the issues are going to be and what he will have to do to meet them. True, he may occasionally be surprised to find that the other side has raised a novel and unexpected argument, but this does not happen often. If he prepares a draft of his brief, he will rarely have to do more later than add a few sentences answering a particular assertion or argument.

III.   THE STATEMENT OF FACTS

In stating the facts, "the advocate has his first, best and most precious access to the court's attention."[16] Just as the effectiveness of a scene in a dramatic play may depend on how it is

16. Llewellyn, Commercial Transactions 20 (1946).

presented, so the effectiveness of the story behind the case may depend on how the lawyer as producer and director, presents his story. An eminent lawyer who early in his career served as law clerk to Mr. Justice Stone says, "The statement of the facts is the heart of the brief and draws most heavily upon the skill of advocacy." [17] Some cases, such as personal injury suits, may rest almost wholly on the facts.

Young lawyers—and some older ones, too—may underestimate the importance of the statement of facts. The legal points and the argument thereon, they may believe, are the substance of the brief, with the statement of facts serving merely as stage setting. This is a mistaken notion. Except in cases that went off on a purely legal question, as on a motion to dismiss, the facts are usually of prime importance. True, the ultimate purpose of your brief is to persuade, but to persuade you must first inform; the most eloquent argument will be ineffective if addressed to a reader who does not understand the context. Some experts therefore advise preparing the statement of facts before writing any other part of the brief. The process will usually turn out to be circular: one must have a fairly clear idea of what the legal issues are going to be before starting to write the brief, but painstaking summary of the facts may show which issues are crucial and which arguments most promising.

The main qualities to be sought in writing the statement of facts are six: it should be accurate, objective in style, clear, concise, interesting—and it should present your side of the story in a favorable light.

Be Accurate

The statement of facts must be scrupulously accurate. Opposing counsel will be quick to point out any misstatements, distortions or omissions, with the result that the court will lose confidence in your reliability. Take the word of the Chief Justice of the Supreme Judicial Court of Massachusetts: "Nothing will forfeit the confidence of the court more effectively than the misstatement of the record or the statement of a fact off the record." [18]

17. Westwood, Brief Writing, 21 Am.Bar Assn.J. 121 (1935).

18. Wilkins, The Argument of an Appeal, 33 Cornell L.Q. 40, 42

Above all, do not omit reference to unfavorable evidence. Here again, you may be sure that it will be pointed out by your opponent and that he will make it sound more unfavorable than you would. Telling it your way can only help you. Where the facts are in dispute, make clear what is conceded or established and what is in conflict. If, for example, liability hinges on whether defendant stopped his vehicle at a stop sign before driving into the intersection, you mislead the court if you baldly assert that he stopped, when the evidence was in conflict and the issue is whether the inference drawn from the conflicting testimony was permissible.

The statement of facts must be constructed from the record. Even in a case of moderate length, that is a formidable task. But it is one which, like the problem of finding the law, is beyond the scope of this book.[19]

Every assertion should be supported by a reference to the page or pages in the record or transcript where the supporting testimony can be found. Even if the rules do not require this, the judge may want to turn to the record to see exactly what the witness said. If he reads passages of appreciable length without seeing any reference to the record he may wonder whether they are supported or not. The practice of the particular court determines whether the reference is indicated by "TR" for transcript, "R" for record, or page-number alone.

Use Objective Language

The statement of the facts must be objective in wording and in tone. It must never be argumentative. You will have plenty

---

(1947). Another justice of the Massachusetts Supreme Judicial Court has similarly said: "In the statement of the case some counsel are tempted to distort the facts a little their own way or omit troublesome facts. I think there is nothing more irritating to a judge than to have counsel purport to state a case and then state it untruly. It is very bad psychologically, because omitted facts stand out conspicuously when the counsel on the other side call attention to them or the court discovers that they exist. They are much more conspicuous than they would have been if they had been stated properly in the first place." Lummus, How Lawyers Should Argue Cases on Appeal, 26 J.Am.Jud.Soc'y 151 (1943).

19. Helpful suggestions are offered in Wiener, Briefing and Arguing Federal Appeals 129–134 (1967).

of scope for arguing the facts later in the brief; the statement is not the place for it.   The brief writer is sometimes so fired with the justice of his cause that he throws in argumentative or derogatory words.   When this temptation overcomes you be sure to strike them out on rereading.   Avoid expressions such as:

> The evidence is convincing and uncontradicted that . . ..
>
> It is obvious that the Board's decision was based upon an assumption . . ..
>
> A defendant who refuses to take the witness stand, as this defendant did, to explain . . ..
>
> Payment was denied, however, because of the arbitrary and discriminatory refusal of the treasurer to recognize . . ..

Tell Your Story in a Clear and Orderly Way

Context first, details later.   This principle, discussed in Chapter 7, on Organization, requires that the ultimate or crucial fact come first.   A statement that starts by giving us details—preliminary information, dates, statistics—without first "setting the scene," requires us to hold all these bits of information in our memory until we are told what they are all about.   Suppose a brief starts by telling us that:

Rufus Hart on March 2 rented a Ford sedan from Acme Car Rental, Inc., in Trenton, N.J.;

The rental agreement called for a fee of $18 per day, plus a charge for mileage;

Hart rented the car to drive from Trenton to New York City to attend a convention of the Association of Credit Managers;

The convention lasted two days, March 3 and 4.

Hart drove to New York on the afternoon of March 2, arriving there at 6:30 P.M.

He left New York at 4:45 P.M. on March 4, to drive back to Trenton.

At this point, the reader still has no inkling of what the case is all about.   Did Hart have an accident and injure someone? Is he or the rental company being sued for such injury?   Was Hart injured or killed?   Or did he abscond with the car?   Until the writer reveals the context by telling us the crucial fact, we cannot judge the importance or even the relevance of the several items of information given us.

Although chronological order is most natural and usually best, counsel may want to depart from it in a given case when he wants to emphasize certain facts. In a criminal case counsel may want at the outset to call attention to facts throwing doubt on defendant's guilt. In a personal injury suit, appellant may want to emphasize the grievousness of his injuries.

The most unimaginative and ineffective way to present facts is to go through the record summarizing the testimony of each witness in the order in which they appeared. At the trial, it was necessary, of course, to put on one witness at a time and usually to have him testify to all the facts of which he had knowledge. But there is no reason why the story must be told to the upper court in that way. The story itself should be outlined and the testimony of all the witnesses on a given event should be marshalled in narrating that event.

Even worse than summarizing the testimony of one witness after another is quoting such testimony at length. Quotations slow the movement of your writing. You can usually summarize the testimony more briefly in your own words. If a quotation seems helpful, it should be kept brief. If the first and last sentences of a witness' statement are worth quoting, it is not necessary also to quote the intervening sentences; they can be omitted or summarized in your own words.

When the facts are many or complicated and the statement therefore long, it should be subdivided into topics, with run-in paragraph headings for the several subdivisions. Solid pages of text look formidable, and the judge or other reader wades into such a solid body of type without joy. The going would be made a lot easier, if, after relating the essential facts in a few paragraphs, counsel said something such as the following:

> For the conveneience of the Court, we divide the narration of the proceedings chronologically into events leading up to the 1957 decree and events leading up to the dissolution of that decree in 1960.

When there is much testimony on a given point, one authority recommends arranging the statement in somewhat the following order: (a) matters admitted by pleadings, stipulations, or in argument of counsel; (b) those admitted by a party in his testimony—especially upon the trial, but also at an inquest, in a deposition, or in an impeaching statement; (c) those established by disinterested and unimpeached witnesses; (d) physical facts; (e) controverted matters.[20] Identifying controverted matters alerts the reader to look for the points of conflict.

You will make it easier for your reader to follow the story if you will always use the same appellation for the same party. Do not call a party "Appellant" in one sentence and "Smith" or "Defendant" in another. If court rules permit, it may be helpful to designate the parties as "plaintiff" and "defendant," rather than "appellant" and "appellee". This enables the court more easily to identify the parties with the issues. It may be still more helpful to refer to "Plaintiff Ames," "the Defendant railroad," or "the Complainant union," or to "Defendant-Appellant" and "Plaintiff-Appellee." Some able lawyes like to refer to their client by name, but to let the opposing party remain impersonal: "the Appellent," or "the Defendant." If you refer to the opposing party by name, it may be prudent to refer to him as "Mr. Smith" rather than as "Smith," in order to avoid any appearance of rudeness.

Facts should of course be narrated in the past tense: "The Court held," rather than "The Court holds." Propositions of law (unless since abrogated) should be put in the present tense:

> The Board found that the discharge was discriminatory and held that the Act makes [not made] such a discharge an unfair labor practice.

> The court said that to be a real party in interest the litigant must [not had to] be the owner of the right sought to be enforced.

If the legal proposition is not correct today it should be put in the past tense:

> Under the original Wagner Act, this was not an unfair labor practice, but under the Taft-Hartley amendment it is.

20. Appleman, Approved Appellate Briefs, § 5.23 (1958).

Be Brief

The statement should be as brief as you can make it without omitting salient points. Nothing material should be left out, but the story should not be encumbered with details that will not affect the outcome. Some conscientious students (and some of their elders), having painstakingly combed the records for all the facts, then arrange them in careful order and give us all of them exactly as they happened. The error in this method is the same as underlies the thinking of the tedious bore who tells us a good deal more about his subject than we care to know.

Only those general facts need be stated that the court must have if it is to understand what the case is about. Additional facts, relevant only to certain of the several issues presented, may be left for presentation in connection with the specific question to which they are relevant. Following this practice serves two purposes: (1) it enables the reader to learn the essential facts at the outset without encumbering him with unnecessary details; (2) it gives him the additional facts when they are needed and saves his having to remember or go back to review them.

Bearing in mind that the appellate court will review only questions of law, and only those questions of law raised by assignments of error, the brief writer must present his facts so as to tie them to the rulings complained of. Some facts that seemed important at the trial may have lost their importance when evaluated as a basis for appeal.

It may be too strict to say that nothing irrelevant should be included. A legally irrelevant detail may add color that will help effect the impression you are trying to make. Whether to include or omit any given detail should be judged by the end in view: will it help present the correct picture? If it contributes nothing to that end, leave it out. In a suit for injuries sustained when the defendant, a policeman, threw the plaintiff out of a bar, the jury awarded the plaintiff $7,000 compensatory and punitive damages. On appeal, the brief for the policeman-appellant described the specific act in the following words:

> After the Appellee re-entered the bar, the testimony is in
> conflict on whether the Appellant immediately evicted Appel-

lee from the bar by pushing him out the door (tr. 129 and
147) or whether the Appellant took the Appellee's arm and
walked him out of the door (tr. 170). Witnesses for the Appellee, Mead, testified that after the Appellant pushed Mead
out the door Appellee complained that the Appellant,
O'Connor, had hurt or broken his leg (tr. 129 and 147).

But appellee protected his verdict by giving the court a more
graphic account:

> Defendant grabbed plaintiff by his left side and right
> shoulder, and threw him out the door with a twirling motion,
> with such force as to rip the seams of his jacket under the
> arms and cause him to land four feet away from the doorway
> on the asphalt, missing the step. (R. 53) Plaintiff landed
> on his left foot in a twisting motion, making a half-circle as
> a result of the twisting motion with which he was thrown.
> (R. 52) Lying on the ground with the bone of his left leg
> protruding through the skin, plaintiff called out to defendant
> that he had broken his leg. (R. 54) The latter replied, "I
> don't believe you're hurt. Other people have pulled that on
> me before." (R. 54) Plaintiff, incidentally, was a man
> weighing only 145 pounds. (R. 49)

Even if you decide to include a given detail, weigh its relative
importance, and make sure you do not give it more space than it
deserves. The importance you attribute to an item is indicated
by the amount of space you give it. Unimportant items should
be subordinated by being given less space than important ones.

One way to subordinate minor items is to sketch them in light
and rapid diction. Sentence structure affects the rapidity of
your style. Short sentences make for fast-moving style. They
are therefore more effective than long ones in narrating facts,
especially minor facts. Sentences can be made shorter by cutting out words. The restrictive relative "that" generally gives a
lighter and more rapid effect than the coordinate relative
"which." Participial phrases also help: "each having" is faster
than "each of which has." Using a semi-colon instead of a full
stop or a connecting "and" speeds the reader up; it moves him
swiftly over several steps to a conclusion. Long sentences,
slowed by pauses, lend an air of deliberate solemnity which is
more appropriate to the discussion of complicated legal problems
than to narration. Alexander Pope told us more than two hun-

dred years ago that the words should move slowly "when Ajax strives some rock's vast weight to throw", but that they should quicken when swift Camilla "flies o'er the unbending grass or skims along the main."

The rapidity of one's style is also governed to some extent by punctuation. Heavy punctuation slows the tempo of the sentence. The emphasis on speed in modern life has made for a trend toward what is called "open punctuation," the use of a minimum of marks. "Close punctuation" uses many marks. Especially after an introductory phrase the comma can often be omitted; in this sentence, for example, omission of a comma after "phrase" does not impair clarity. When you want to give your style snap and speed use open punctuation. For complex ideas, which it is important that the reader comprehend clearly, and which, therefore, you want him to take slowly, close punctuation may be preferable.

Make It Interesting

Objectivity in wording does not require dullness. For dramatic interest, plunge immediately into the heart of your case. Instead of starting with routine procedural steps, start with a simple narrative of the incident that led to the litigation. From that start, follow your story in a direct path. Do not allow the story-line to become obscured by lengthy discussions of minor or irrelevant side issues.

Action and excitement are suggested by words that are sharp and short. Terse, choppy rhythm in narrating facts, especially dramatic facts, conveys emotion as well as movement. Edmund Pearson wrote a book entitled *Studies in Murder*, in which he narrated a number of interesting cases. In one, entitled "The Hunting Knife," the story begins with a calm, somewhat involuted rhythm, until we come to the point where the old father opens the door to his daughter's bedroom, and sees her body lying on the floor. Observe the rhythm of the paragraph that then follows: [21]

> Mr. Page felt his daughter's hand, and found it cold. He tried to listen to her heart-beat; he spoke to her, but she was

21. Pearson, Studies in Murder 231,
237 (1926).

dead. He saw blood on the floor, and looking at her throat saw a jagged wound in the neck   After a short time, he went downstairs and looked about the main living-room. He noticed that the fire in the open fireplace had gone out; had been put out, apparently, by the removal of the two logs so that they lay besides the andirons .   . ..

Compare with this the following paragraph,[22] relating facts of a killing by a husband of a wife who had been having an affair with her employer:

In January 1953 she ran away to San Francisco. Her husband looked for her frantically and he finally located her and persuaded her to come back. He drove to Albuquerque to meet her at the train but she wasn't aboard; the other man had reached her first, and had induced her to leave the train at Gallup and to drive with him to Albuquerque. White stayed in Albuquerque for two days, meeting all trains. Then he gave up and returned to Santa Fe. Soon she telephoned him, saying she was at the Zia Lodge on East Central Avenue in Albuquerque. White bought a revolver, borrowed a car from a friend, and drove to Albuquerque. He talked with his wife; he testified later that she abused him and used foul language. Finally he got up and bent over to kiss her good-bye. She responded, he said, by spitting in his face, whereupon he shot her five times.

Assuming that the prosecution is more likely than the defendant to want to arouse an emotional reaction to the facts of a crime, which of the forms of sentence structure represented in the two paragraphs quoted above is more appropriate for a brief for the prosecution, and which for the defense?

Present the Facts in a Light Favorable to Your Side

Judges, like ordinary mortals, can be made to feel the righteousness of a cause. They are not impersonal hacks grinding out a slot-machine justice. The precedents usually leave some room for discretion, and a good statement of the facts may impel the court to feel that the equities are on your side. And

22. From Weihofen, Crime, Law and Psychiatry, Second Annual Research Lecture, University of New Mexico, reprinted in 4 Kan.L.Rev. 377 (1956), discussing State v. White, 58 N.M. 324, 270 P.2d 727 (1954).

when a judge's heart is on one side, his mind is usually ingenious enough to construe the law that way too.

Although the words used must be objective, the able brief-writer will try to present his facts in a way most favorable to his client's cause. But the facts must seem to argue for themselves. Counsel must not appear to be arguing them. In a brief for appellant, arguing that the judgment of the court below is erroneous, it may help to quote a phrase or sentence from the lower court's opinion or ruling where it seems glaringly wrong. Conversely, counsel representing appellee may want to quote wording from the court below that seems particularly apt or well-put. The higher court usually has no power to weigh conflicting testimony. Appellee therefore may wish to emphasize findings of fact made by the court below. If the judge (or master or referee) below has made findings of fact which accurately present the situation, it is effective to adopt and quote relevant passages. This lends an air of authority to your statement. Damaging admissions and vulnerable statements made by the opposing party may also be worth quoting.

In stating facts as in other writing, the indicative mood is more forceful than the subjunctive. "The court held that this stated a cause of action" is stronger than "this would state a cause of action."

When the testimony is conflicting, one cannot, as already said, simply give one's own side of the story and ignore evidence to the contrary. But one can do a number of things to minimize the unfavorable data:

1. Put the favorable facts first and bury (but do not omit!) the unfavorable. Sometimes it is more effective to tell the opponent's story first, and then one's own. In relating facts as in presenting argument, the closing side has an advantage.

2. Take the spotlight away from the unfavorable facts by giving them relatively little space, that is, describing them briefly (which usually means broadly), while emphasizing the favorable ones by giving them space enough to be described in detail.

3. Choose favorable words. We have synonyms for most words, some of which have more positive connotations than others.

4. Call attention to evidence, if any exists, showing that the unfavorable testimony was biased, or was contradicted by the testimony of others, or is not to be believed because the witness elsewhere in his testimony showed himself to be unreliable or untrustworthy.

In the early morning hours of a summer day, after a festive evening spent in visiting a number of bars, one Violet Mitchell fell into a hole outside the last establishment visited and broke her ankle. She sued the bar owner, whose principal defense was that she had stumbled into the hole because she was too drunk to watch where she was going.

The jury having found for the plaintiff and awarded her $2,000 damages, defendant appealed. Here is a paragraph from a brief for defendant written by a novice, summarizing the evidence concerning her condition:

> The bartender at the Glen Rio Bar testified that although he sold Mrs. Mitchell liquor, she was getting "pretty close" to the point where she was too drunk to be sold liquor, and that that was the reason he closed up the bar. (Tr–152). Mrs. Mitchell testified that she was drinking but that she was not intoxicated at the time of the accident. (Tr–67). A state policeman who warned Mrs. Mitchell to behave herself or be put in jail (Tr–163) testified that in regard to intoxication, "She was pretty well along, her speech was impaired quite a bit." (Tr–166). But Richard Brown, a member of Mrs. Mitchell's party, would only testify that she "had been drinking" and not that she was intoxicated. (Tr–108). Frances Speed, a member of another party at the bar, testified she could tell from Mrs. Mitchell's behavior that she "had had something to drink" (Tr–121), but this woman wasn't paying attention to Mrs. Mitchell, she said. (Tr–121).

This obviously does not present the picture in the most effective way for the defense. Let us see if we can specify what the writer did and what he failed to do that colored the final product. First of all, he fails to apply a general rule (discussed in the chapter on Forcefulness) that the end is the most emphatic position, whether in a sentence or in a paragraph. This rule calls for building our evidence to a climax. As written the para-

graph closes on a weak note. It should be reorganized somewhat as follows:

> Mrs. Mitchell admitted that she had been drinking, but she
> denied that she was intoxicated at the time of the accident.
> A member of her party, Richard Brown, also testified that
> she "had been drinking"; he refused to say that she was
> drunk. Frances Speed, another patron of the bar, testified
> that although she was not paying attention to Mrs. Mitchell,
> she could tell from Mitchell's behavior that she "had had
> something to drink." A state policeman who earlier in the
> evening had encountered Mitchell and the Lancaster woman
> fighting in the alley behind the bar, and who at that time
> had warned Mitchell to behave herself or he would put her in
> jail, testified in response to a question concerning her sobrie-
> ty at that time, "She was pretty well along, her speech was
> impaired quite a bit." The bartender at the Glen Rio Bar
> testified that she was getting "pretty close" to the point
> where she was too drunk to be sold liquor, and that it was for
> this reason that he closed up the bar.

Besides reshuffling the testimony to build up to a climax, this
revision makes a few other changes. In the sentence summarizing Mrs. Mitchell's testimony, the verb "testified" is changed to
"admitted" and "denied." "Intoxicated" is changed to "drunk."
Although the statement of fact must restrict itself to objective
language and certainly must not indulge in name-calling, it may
properly call a spade a spade; and when it is necessary to inform the court that a man, or even a woman, was drunk, one is
under no obligation to eschew "drunk" and seek a euphemism.
One must, to be sure, sometimes exercise taste and discretion in
deciding whether a given word is a fair, though blunt, descriptive term, or whether it is a biased word, whose use will prejudice the court against oneself more than against one's opponent.
Is "the Lancaster woman" a biased term for referring to plaintiff's companion? And what of calling Mrs. Mitchell "Mitchell"?

The changes made in the paragraph quoted above are merely
in the wording. Reference to the transcript would probably suggest other changes. Why, for example, does the writer reduce
to a subordinate clause the evidence of plaintiff's having been
warned by a state policeman? The transcript would have shown

that this incident could have been enlarged upon, somewhat as follows:

> While the Mitchell party was at the Buddy Bar, Mitchell had been engaged in almost constant argument with her roommate, Frieda Lancaster. At one point the argument developed into a fight, which ended only when the two women were separated by the men present. At about 10.00 p.m. the members of the party were in back of the bar; there they were encountered by a state policeman who told Mitchell and Lancaster to quit fighting and quiet down. Plaintiff Mitchell replied in obscene and abusive language, and the officer found it necessary to order her to behave herself or he would "put her in a place where she would have to."

Appellee's Statement of Facts

Appellee's brief, under the rules of most appellate courts, is not required to include an independent statement of the facts, and in a few states is not permitted to do so.[23] To save time and trouble for the court, appellee should ordinarily confine himself to pointing out any errors in appellant's statement. He should not write a statement of his own except in the rare case in which appellant's statement is so inadequate or confused that it cannot be corrected by pointing out errors.

If appellee has no objection to appellant's statement, he may say simply:

> Appellee has no objections to Appellant's Statement of Facts.

If he has objections, he may introduce them in one of the following ways:

> Appellee objects to the Appellant's Statement of Facts in that it omits certain pertinent facts essential to a full and accurate statement, and without which the statement is strongly biased in Appellant's favor.

---

23. Under a rule providing that "an independent statement of facts by appellee . . . will not be entertained," the court rejected a statement that appellee disagreed with appellant's statement of facts and therefore submitted its own, and said that it therefore would "rely upon the facts submitted by the appellant." Mitchell v. Pettigrew, 65 N.M. 137, 333 P.2d 879 (1958).

The statement of the case made by Appellant in its brief (pp. 5–7) is a fairly accurate and complete statement of the nature and results of this suit in the Courts below. In one important respect, however, Appellee disagrees with the manner in which Appellant has stated the case, and therefore presents this additional statement.

The Plaintiffs-Appellees object to the Statement of Facts in the Brief-in-Chief in the following respects:

1. All of the second and third paragraphs is argumentative in tone and substance and has no place in a statement of facts.

Do not quibble over petty details. Accept appellant's statement except insofar as it presents a distorted, incomplete or unfair picture. When it is unfair, the most effective strategy in offering your correction is not to denounce or fulminate, but rather to bend over backwards to be courteous. This might be called comment by contrast. Never accuse opposing counsel of deliberately falsifying. If you feel you must use an adjective to characterize the omission, let it be "inadvertent." If the facts omitted or misstated are significant, your correction, supported by references to the transcript, will speak as eloquently as any denunciatory words you could use. *Res ipsa loquitur.*

Chapter 12

BRIEFS: ARGUMENT

The argument calls for a style quite different from that of the statement of facts. Objectively is no longer the aim. In the argument, assertions must be put as persuasively and as forcefully as possible. This is especially true for the appellant. He has the burden of demonstrating that the lower court committed error, and error so prejudicial as to call for reversal of the judgment. This is a heavy burden. Statistics show that appeals are successful in only one case out of four or five.[1]

The argument should also be made as interesting as possible. Just as the good trial lawyer tries to present his case before the jury as a gripping drama, so the good appellate lawyer writes that drama into his brief. He should not merely manipulate legal rules as though their application were a mechanical process. The lives and fortunes of living people are at stake, and counsel should not allow the court to forget it.

I. POINT HEADINGS

The points argued on appeal are not the same as the assignments of error made in the trial court. The assignments of error specify the erroneous rulings alleged to have been made by the trial judge. The points in the appellate brief are the separate legal issues raised by these alleged errors. Several errors may all raise the same issue; conversely, one ruling—for example, denial of a motion for a directed verdict—may involve several issues, for the motion may have rested on several legal grounds.

1. Pollack, The Civil Appeal, in Counsel on Appeal 35 (A. Charpentier ed. 1968); Administrative Office of the United States Courts, Annual Report of the Director, 1978, p. 48. Of appeals from civil suits won by the United States, only 10% are successful. Carrington, United States Appeals in Civil Cases: A Field and Statistical Study, 11 Houston L.Rev. 1101 (1974).

Put Your Strongest Point First

The headings for the points asserted tell the judge what the legal issues are and how the argument is organized. This enables him to follow the argument intelligently and to focus on those parts that seem to him crucial or most difficult.

The order in which you put your points is important. If they are logically connected, they should be presented in logical order, so that the second follows naturally from the first. The court will usually find it easier to follow you if you keep the same order in presenting the issues, the propositions of law and the points in your argument. A complex argument may involve several related steps or propositions. Consider whether these should not be developed as sub-points under one major point, instead of as a series of seemingly independent points. When you do this, make use of mechanical aids to clarify for the reader the scheme of your organization. Use Roman numerals for major points, capital letters for sub-points, arabic numerals for sub-sub-points, etc., as you would in organizing an outline.

Your strongest point should normally come first. First impressions are lasting. The human mind does not like to hold judgment in suspense. We begin to lean in one direction or the other almost at once, and having begun to develop a judicial hunch in favor of one side, we do not easily reverse ourselves. Judges from experience if not by temperament are likely to be more open-minded than most of us, but they too are human. If on reading your first point the judge has the impression that your case is weak, the chances that your later points will change his mind are not good.

Let us be clear about what is meant by your strongest point. It is not necessarily the one on which you feel most strongly, nor even the one on which you are most surely on the side of the angels. It is simply the one on which the appellate court is most likely to agree with you. To know what points may appeal to the court, you need to know not only what it has held but also something about the viewpoints and prejudices of its members. Trying to guess what a judge will be thinking as he reads is difficult, but no more so than what the football coach has to do in trying to meet the other team's strategy.

Make Point Headings Assertive and Specific

The headings for your points should not be mere titles, such as "The question of compensation," or "The adequacy of the compensation paid by plaintiff." They should be in the form of declarative sentences. And the propositions asserted should be specific. Avoid what one writer [2] has called "blind headnotes," that is, headings in such general terms that they might fit any of a hundred cases without saying anything specific about any of them:

> The verdict was against the weight of the evidence.
>
> Defendant's motion to dismiss should have been granted.
>
> The complaint failed to state a cause of action.

Almost as futile are headings that lay down a proposition of law without showing its relevance to the instant case:

> It is axiomatic that a court lacking jurisdiction over the person of a defendant is unable to render a personal judgment against him.
>
> The burden of proof of any affirmative defense is on the party who asserts it.
>
> A "marriage" is the civil status of a man and a woman lawfully united in the relation of husband and wife.
>
> When two vehicles approach an intersection at approximately the same time, the one approaching from the right has the right of way.

Do not mistake self-evident generalizations such as those quoted above for strong points, merely because they cannot well be controverted. Just because they are incontrovertible generalizations, the court will know that they cannot go far to decide specific cases. One may have occasion for making such sententious statements in one's brief, and perhaps even making separate points of them. But one should not delude oneself into thinking that because they are sound, they are so strong that they belong at the top of the batting order.

2. Blair, Appellate Briefs and Advocacy, 18 Fordham L.Rev. 30, 38 (1949).

How then can one be more specific? Let us take the last heading quoted above, concerning the intersection collision. It could be worded somewhat as follows:

> When defendant saw plaintiff's vehicle approaching the intersection from his right, at about the same time and speed as his own, it was his duty to yield the right of way to plaintiff; and a judgment for damages caused by his failure to do so should be affirmed.

The following, from the brief for the United States in United States v. Seaboard Airline R. R.,[3] are good examples of headings making very specific assertions:

> I. The statutory requirement that power brakes be in operation on "any train" applied to the respondent's four units, each consisting of an engine and cars completely assembled for an unbroken run of two miles in three instances and of at least one mile in the fourth instance.
>
> . . .
>
> C. The four decisions of this Court on the subject have specifically held so-called "transfer trains" to be subject to the power-brake requirements and have rejected efforts to make exceptions on the basis of absence, in particular operations or places, of one or several of the dangers sought to be averted by the Congress.

The following is from the brief for appellees in International Association of Machinists v. Street:[4]

> II. The union shop contract, by forcing minority employees to accept and pay for political representation by their political foes, violates the First, Fifth, Ninth and Tenth Amendments to the Federal Constitution.

Although point headings should be specific, they should not be too crowded with ideas. Instead of trying to give several reasons to justify the conclusion, it is better to give only the main one. Subordinate ones can be developed in the body of the text; they need not be included in the heading.

---

3. United States v. Seaboard Air Line R. Co., 361 U.S. 78, 80 S.Ct. 12, 4 L.Ed.2d 25 (1959).

4. International Association of Machinists v. Street, 363 U.S. 825, 80 S.Ct. 1604, 4 L.Ed.2d 1521 (1960).

Strive for a Favorable Wording

How you word a point may depend on which side you represent.[5] An unwed mother, shortly after the birth of her child in Iowa, signed a "blanket consent" to its adoption. The child was taken by a couple from New Mexico and moved to Albuquerque. This couple filed a petition in Iowa for adoption. The mother changed her mind and attempted to withdraw her consent. The petition was dismissed by the Iowa courts for want of the mother's consent. The adoptive parents thereupon filed proceedings in New Mexico, under that state's "dependent and neglected children" statute, which provides that a child found destitute, homeless or abandoned and dependent upon the public for support or without proper parental care or guardianship, may be removed from an unfit environment and placed for adoption.

The primary point in the brief for the natural mother read:

A minor child who has at all times since birth lived in the custody of persons of exemplary character and has at all times had care of high order free from any improper or insidious influence is not dependent and neglected within the meaning of section 13–9–2 of the Dependent and Neglected Children Statute; therefore the District Court erred in adjudging Rose Herman to be dependent and neglected.

The brief on behalf of the adopting couple, however, worded its contention this way:

In determining whether a child is dependent and neglected insofar as its natural parent is concerned, the treatment and care received from other persons and the conditions operative upon the child as a result of contact with such persons are irrelevant and do not militate against a finding by the trial court that as to such parent the child is dependent and neglected.

One may easily fall into the practice of starting every point heading with "It was error." At least to avoid monotony, follow

5. See ante, pp. 253–255.

the counsel offered in the chapter on Clarity: start with your subject.

It was error for the trial court to admit testimony of statements given to the police by defendant.	Admitting testimony of statements given by defendant to the police was error.

Appellee's Points

The court is helped in following the argument if the briefs of both parties adopt the same order. Unless good reason exists for doing otherwise, appellee's brief therefore should discuss points in the same order as appellant's. But this should not be done mechanically. If appellee is convinced that the court will consider some other than the appellant's first point to raise the principal issue, appellee should give that issue the place of primary importance. And of course if appellee thinks that the case raises an issue not discussed by appellant at all, he should raise it.

Don't quibble over trivial points. Concentrate on the vital issues. It may be helpful to the court (and so to yourself) to say at the outset of your argument that you are making no issue of certain points. If some of the appellant's points seem insignificant, the appellee may clear away the underbrush by saying by way of introduction to his argument that "to avoid confusion, the appellee will begin by excluding from the discussion certain aspects of the case," naming them.

Point headings should be worded affirmatively. Mere negations are less persuasive and may seem defensive.

II. THE ARGUMENT

Try to gain the court's interest right at the outset by showing that the issue is important. In a case concerning the care and custody of a dependent child, counsel for appellant [6] started his argument as follows:

> This case involves a flat collision of philosophy between the case work approach and the constitutional approach to the

6. Mr. John P. Frank of Phoenix, Arizona. In re Johnson, 86 Ariz. 297, 345 P.2d 423 (1959).

problems of juveniles. It is fitting and proper that these underlying problems, which were fully and fairly recognized as problems of philosophy by the court below (T. 12–13), be brought to this Court in a context which involves a thoroughly respected juvenile judge and two able and experienced case workers. We believe, however, that no judge, no matter how good and fair, nor any case worker, no matter how able and devoted, has been, under our statutes, nor could be, under our Constitution, clothed with the power that judge and the case workers have attempted to wield in this case.

Let us make no bones about what was done here. On a wholly ex parte basis the case workers decided that the boys were no longer dependent children. According to their own candid statement they decided and settled that question even before they had given counsel the informal telephone notice of the coming proceedings. The juvenile court judge received the case worker's report, accepted the recommendations therein, and ruled accordingly without considering any other evidence whatsoever; indeed, he explicitly precluded the presentation of any other evidence.

We believe, first, that the judge did not have the power to do this; and second, that if he had such power, he exercised it mistakenly.

Here as in other writings one must develop a discriminating taste. The following is a commendable student effort to get the interest and sympathy of the court at the outset of his argument. Is it successful?

On rare occasions, the findings of the National Labor Relations Board are so contrary to the weight of the evidence that the record screams a mute appeal for reversal. Such is the case before the Court. The fundamental concepts of fair play have been violated along with a provision of the National Labor Relations Act.

As already said concerning office memoranda, a good way to start is to state the rule or proposition you rely upon, and then show that your case comes within it. Adding the reason for the rule is often helpful, especially when you want to show that your case comes within its intent or spirit.

Use Examples, Figures of Speech, Famous Sayings

You can enliven your style by using examples, metaphors and similes,[7] and by quoting maxims, proverbs and even poetry. Example makes perhaps the most interesting kind of argument, and the one that creates the quickest impression. Since the purpose of an example is to clarify or simplify, it should come from some well-understood incident of daily work or popular sport. If you will keep at hand a good book of quotations, arranged by subjects, and make a practice of consulting it, you will often be delighted to find that the thought you want to express has been marvelously well worded for you by someone else. It does not matter whether it was Plato or Mother Goose, so long as the quotation is apt. In a leading case in which a majority of the United States Supreme Court said there is a high "wall of separation" between church and state, but held that providing bus transportation to parochial school children did not breach that wall, Mr. Justice Jackson, dissenting, was reminded of Byron's Julia, who "whispering, 'I shall ne'er consent,' consented."

Mr. Justice Clark has also resorted to verse, of a sort, to refer indirectly and delicately to a rather common figure of speech. In Order of Railroad Telegraphers v. Chicago & Northwestern R. R.,[8] he said:

> . . . the Court is telling the railroad that it must secure the union's approval before severing the hundreds of surplus employees now carried on its payroll. Everyone knows what the answer of the union will be. It is like the suitor who, when seeking the hand of a young lady, was told by her to "go to father." But, as the parody goes, "She knew that he knew that her father was dead; she knew that he knew what a life he had led; and she knew that he knew what she meant when she said 'go to father.'"

If the relevance of a quotation is not strikingly clear, omit it. But a well-put phrase will be appreciated. Judges have to wade through stacks of briefs that are dull and boring. They are grateful to counsel who brightens his argument with some sparkling jewels of the world's best thought. They may show their

---

7. On the use of figures of speech, see ante, pp. 116–120.

8. 362 U.S. 330, 344, 80 S.Ct. 761, 4 L.Ed.2d 774 (1960).

appreciation by making these gems their own. Remember that
the appellate court must write an opinion, and the material for
that opinion is furnished by the briefs. A crucial passage,
whose wording counsel has taken pains to polish so that it
makes its point in a particularly succinct, epigrammatic way,
may so please the court that it will want to appropriate it for its
opinion. No lawyer, needless to say, objects to this as cribbing;
we are delighted to help write the opinions in our own cases.

Beware of Humor; Avoid Sarcasm

A touch of wit or humor is also a wonderful leavener, but this
is dangerous to attempt. We are all sure that we have a sense
of humor, but the truth is that many of us cannot successfully
be humorous. We may succeed only in being cutting or sarcas-
tic, or our effort may prove to be heavy-handed or in poor taste.
Humor that misses fire is worse than none. Dean Prosser of
California published a collection of specimens of judicial humor;
the general level was not high.[9]

Avoid sarcasm. Irony (saying one thing in a way that shows
the contrary is meant) is sometimes effective, but, like humor,
must be used with discretion and taste. Alexander Hamilton
once said of his opponent in a case, "I have known gentlemen to
split a hair, and I may have tried to do it myself. But I never
before saw anyone decimate a hair and count the pieces before
the court." Lord Hewart answered the argument of a respondent that putting the word "manipulative" before the word "surgeon" showed that he did not hold himself out as a surgeon under the Medical Act by saying, "If the respondent is, as we take
him to be, sincere, there are many ways open to him of telling
the public that he is not a surgeon other than the way of telling
the public that he is a surgeon." [10] And Mr. Justice Jackson,
dissenting in a case involving the validity of an out-of-state divorce, said, "If there is one thing that the people are entitled to
expect from their lawmakers, it is rules of law that will enable

---

9. Prosser, The Judicial Humorist
(1952). Dean Prosser himself had
greater felicity in humorous writing than most of those whom he
quoted. See for example Prosser,
Lighthouse No Good, 1 J.Legal Ed.
257 (1948).

10. Jutson v. Barrow [1936] 1 K.B.
236, 245.

individuals to tell whether they are married, and, if so, to whom." [11]

But do not let these instances tempt you into trying to be a joker. You are presenting your client's side of a serious dispute. Be serious about it.

Propounding Elementary Law

In introducing a legal point it is sometimes necessary to start with a rather elementary proposition, perhaps because it is the foundation upon which counsel means to build his argument. Counsel could perhaps merely refer to it and not state it. But lawyers have an old joke that it is a mistake to assume that the court knows the law. Even an appellate judge cannot be expected to have all the law at his immediate command. Counsel may therefore want to state the rule, to bring it specifically to the court's attention. But propounding it as though he were telling the court something it had never heard before would be tactless. One way to avoid giving the impression of talking down is to introduce the statement with an apologetic phrase, such as "Of course," or "It is elementary law that." This is a shorthand way of saying, "I know that you know this, but for purposes of my argument, it seems necessary to mention it." Another way to do the same thing is to say, "It is unnecessary to point out that"—and then proceed to point it out.

Do Not Shift Your Standpoint

Whether in narrating facts or arguing or explaining law, speak consistently from one viewpoint throughout a passage. Do not speak in one sentence from the viewpoint of one party, and then jump without reason to the other:

> One who is in possession of land, but who has made no discovery of mineral thereon, is protected only so long as he diligently searches for minerals. In order for one to enter even as a bona fide prospector, the original possessor of the land must have either (1) relaxed his occupancy, or (2) maintained his possession for some reason other than a diligent search for minerals.

11. Estin v. Estin, 334 U.S. 541, 553, 68 S.Ct. 1213, 92 L.Ed. 1561 (1948).

Instead of shifting in the second sentence from the standpoint of the one in possession to that of the prospector, the writer should have remained standing where he was:

> One who is in possession of land, but who has made no discovery of mineral thereon, is protected only so long as he diligently searches for minerals. Should he (1) relax his occupancy, or (2) maintain his possession for some reason other than a diligent search for mineral, his possession may legally be disrupted by an entry on the part of a bona fide prospector.

Rhetorical and Other Questions

Attention can be focused on a point by introducing it with a question:

> What then does due process require?
> Does the statute, as applied to the petitioner, abridge freedom of speech?

Writers sometimes become so fond of this device that they overuse it until it becomes tiresome. Or they shoot a rapid-fire series of such questions at the reader. This of course defeats the purpose; the reader cannot concentrate on several issues at once.

The rhetorical question is one that is used as a more striking substitute for an affirmative statement. It assumes that only one answer is possible, and that letting the reader answer it for himself will impress him more than if the writer had given him the answer. The device was much favored in the rich, lush oratory of a century or two ago. Thus Daniel Webster, inveighing against a draft bill in the War of 1812, asked:

> Where is it written, in the Constitution, in what article or section is it contained, that you may take children from their parents and parents from their children and compel them to fight the battles of any war in which the folly or the wickedness of government may engage? Under what concealment has this power lain hidden which now for the first time comes forth, with a tremendous and baleful aspect to trample down and destroy the dearest rights of personal liberty?

This orotund style is rather out of fashion today, but there is still room for a well-worded rhetorical question on occasion:

> Can a republican form of government exist when the majority of citizens are denied the right to participate in affairs of government because they are poor?

> Can we say that men of our time must not even think about the propositions on which our own Revolution was justified?

The Personal Touch

Briefs are written in an impersonal style. Counsel does not write, "I contend," "In my opinion," or "It is our contention." Contentions can be presented impersonally by using the passive: "It is submitted," "It is suggested," "It can be said;" or the subjunctive: "It would seem." But unless the proposition is very dubious, or is purely one's own novel suggestion, it can usually be advanced as a direct assertion.

As already said in discussing letter-writing, however, we can sometimes make use of personal references to get more warmth into our writing—by talking about human beings whenever possible instead of staying always in the realm of impersonal things and abstract ideas. Although the brief-writer cannot usually talk about "you" and "me," he can often make use of "we" or "us."

Every American	All of us in America
It must not be forgotten	We must not forget
It is the duty of every citizen	Our duty is
An example is afforded by	Let us take as an example

Avoid Colloquialisms

Just as counsel would not appear in court to argue his case attired in a sports shirt, so he should not clothe his brief in informal language. The diction should be on a level of dignity commensurate with the dignity of the court to which it is addressed. A jocose tone that might be appropriate and friendly in a letter to a client would be out of place in a brief.

Not only should the general tone be formal, but it should not lapse therefrom. Lapses into colloquialisms or provincialisms give a sudden and jarring drop in tone-level. Such lapses are usually the product of a restricted vocabulary and misjudgment of taste; the writer does not know the word he uses well enough to recognize that it speaks from a different level from the rest of his discourse. Avoid in brief-writing such colloquialisms as:

> He blamed it on her.
> Defendant got off work at twelve noon.
> The incident is over with.
> Federal aid is a must.

One must distinguish between provincialisms and colloquialisms, which are unacceptable, and idiomatic expressions such as "put up with" and "get rid of." Idioms are turns of expression peculiar to the language and usually not following strict rules of grammar, which are nevertheless accepted and dignified. Indeed, they give a racy strength to one's style.

Lapses into colloquial expressions may be intentional, for a homely touch or for satiric or humorous effect. This is pleasing and effective, if done with good taste. If you do it, do so without using apologetic quotation marks:

> The discharge was discriminatory because other employees had been absent or tardy without being "fired."

> Emotional stamina is the quality that enables the trial lawyer to "take it," day after day, when the trial is long and the going rough—enables him—in the pungent language of fistiana—to "roll with the punches," without "taking a nose dive," and without "sniffing the resin."

The quotation marks merely convict the writer of snobbishness. They say, "I really know better; I am stooping to a level beneath myself." If you decide to use an informal expression, have the courage of your conviction and do it without apology.

In informal speech, shortened forms of certain words are now in good standing: ad, auto, phone, photo, taxi. But they should still be avoided in formal writing.

Do Not Overstate

Although argument should be forcefully presented, forcefulness does not mean exaggeration. As an officer of the court, you have a duty to be responsible in your statements. Don't say that the facts of your case are "identical" with those of a precedent. They are never quite that. You may use the quaint legal phrase, "on all fours," or you may say that the facts are similar in all material respects. The novice fails to appreciate the power of understatement. It is a good rule to err on the side of understatement rather than overstatement.

One should also beware of indulging in absolutes. Today more than ever, sophisticated thinking is relative rather than absolute. Ancient philosophers tried to fix every object and every thought in some necessary classification or formula. But since science has revealed all life and all human institutions to be fading into each other by imperceptible degrees, we have come to think of the search for truth as the task of perceiving things relatively and distinguishing shadings of difference. Mr. Justice Frankfurter reflected the modern outlook when he said: "Partly as a flourish of rhetoric and partly because the intellectual fashion of the times indulged a free use of absolutes, Chief Justice Marshall gave currency to the phrase that 'the power to tax involves the power to destroy'." This dictum, Mr. Justice Frankfurter went on, was treated for decades as though it were a constitutional mandate. But it was merely a "seductive cliche," which "was brushed away by one stroke of Mr. Justice Holmes's pen: 'The power to tax is not the power to destroy while this courts sits'." [12]

Do Not Be Intemperate or Insulting

Don't be intemperate. Counsel who has just lost in the court below may be blazing with indignation over his opponent's tactics or the trial court's partiality or obtuseness. Or he may get so fired up by the writing of his own argument that he indulges in exaggerated assertions, overheated argument, personal denunciation, or other lapses in tact and taste. Any such hyperbole should be excised after the fever subsides.

Do not cast aspersions on the intelligence or integrity of opposing counsel. Do not say, "Appellant is confused in his ap-

12. Frankfurter, J., concurring in Graves v. New York, 306 U.S. 466, 489, 59 S.Ct. 595, 83 L.Ed. 927 (1939).

praisal of the case." If you feel compelled to make such a criticism, at least keep it impersonal: "This appraisal of the case confuses. . . ." Never call your opponent a liar. Prove him one, if you have proof, but without personal denunciation. The substance of your criticism may be strong, but it should be *suaviter in modo:*

> The development of the police power in the past two or three decades has been impressive. We have seen People v. Williams, 189 N.Y. 131, 81 N.E. 778 (1907), overruled by People v. Charles Schweinler Press, 214 N.Y. 395, 108 N.E. 639 (1915), and Lochner v. New York, 198 U.S. 45, 25 S.Ct. 539 (1905), criticized with a universality which makes its citation as a precedent today unthinkable. Without meaning to be disrespectful to the able advocacy of our opponent, we may say that his brief is haunted by the ghosts of departed doctrines, and is untenanted by any living principle.[13]

On rare occasions, one may be justified in denouncing an opponent's motives or tactics. A memorandum in support of a motion to strike certain defenses, filed by counsel for the general guardian under a deed of trust, demonstrates that this can be done in strong language without exceeding the bounds of propriety:

> To put it bluntly, those who have set themselves against the children have chosen to make allegations impugning Mrs. X. . . .'s conduct and character, when it is perfectly obvious that those allegations cannot possibly be a subject of legitimate consideration by this Court. These can only be allegations of calculated prejudice, belatedly introduced to confuse, delay and prejudice the determination of the single issue in the case, which could and should have been submitted to the Court before this.

> The Special Guardian has been moved by the offensive nature of the attack made upon Mrs. X. . . and the adoptions to expose the factual sham of the allegations and to seek their dismissal as sham as well as on grounds of legal insufficiency. The General Guardian takes the view, however, that these spurious issues should not be dignified by

13. From respondent's brief in People v. Tilford, 268 N.Y. 557, 198 N. E. 402 (1935), quoted in Blair, Appellate Briefs and Advocacy, 18 Fordham L.Rev. 30, 44 (1949).

any discussion of their factual foundation or total lack of foundation; that they should be taken right out of this case as interjections which are wholly irrelevant and inadmissible for any consideration.

To see how to argue a point forcefully and with feeling, and yet without resorting to sarcasm or ad hominem arguments, one should read important decisions of the United States Supreme Court in which the justices differed strongly. Dissenting opinions are especially likely to be strongly worded. The spokesman for the majority, as the late Mr. Justice Jackson said, "is cautious, timid, fearful of the vivid word, the heightened phrase. . . . Not so, however, the dissenter. . . . For the moment, he is the gladiator making a last stand against the lions." [14] His style is likely to show a strength of feeling and of expression more typical of the advocate than the judge.

Avoid Italics or Underlining to Gain Emphasis

Avoid the use of italics, bold-face type or underlining (in typewritten briefs) as devices for gaining emphasis. The emphasis or forcefulness a lawyer wants in his argument is not gained by these devices.[15] The correct way to stress the desired word or thought is by proper sentence structure and paragraph organization. Only rarely should italics or underlining be used to call attention to a key word that might otherwise be overlooked. They should regularly be used only for three purposes:

(1) Where objection is taken to certain sentences or words in a jury instruction, to call attention to the passages objected to.

(2) Similarly, to show changes in statutory wording, as by an amendment.

(3) To mark unfamiliar foreign words.

14. Jackson, The Supreme Court in the American System of Government 17 (1957). Among the many cases containing strong dissents are: West Virginia State Board of Education v. Barnette, 319 U.S. 624, 63 S.Ct. 1178, 87 L.Ed. 1628 (1943); Wolf v. Colorado, 338 U.S. 25, 69 S.Ct. 1359, 93 L.Ed. 1782 (1949); Bartkus v. Illinois, 359 U. S. 121, 79 S.Ct. 676, 3 L.Ed.2d 684 (1959); Barenblatt v. United States, 360 U.S. 109, 79 S.Ct. 1081, 3 L.Ed.2d 1115 (1959); Kinsella v. Singleton, 361 U.S. 234, 80 S.Ct. 297, 4 L.Ed.2d 268 (1960); Flemming v. Nestor, 363 U.S. 603, 80 S. Ct. 1367, 4 L.Ed.2d 1435 (1960).

15. See ante, p. 105.

Do not italicize foreign words your reader is probably familiar with, or Latin words and abbreviations commonly used by lawyers, such as res gestae, supra, ibid., e. g., i. e., and others listed in Chapter 4.[16] When in doubt whether to italicize or not, don't.

Avoid Footnotes

Footnotes are not normally used in brief-writing. If the thought is important enough to deserve a place in the brief, it can usually be fitted into the text. (A footnote is itself a way of fitting it into the text; the reader will interrupt his reading of the text at that point, to read, or at least glance at, the footnote. If the interruption is undesirable in the reading of the text, it is only slightly less undesirable as a footnote.) There may, however, be historical or other peripheral or incidental matters that deserve mention, but that should not be permitted to interrupt the main line of development. They may be dropped to footnotes.

> Even apart from statute, it is a common law rule of great antiquity [1] that "acceptance of a second office incompatible with one already held works an immediate vacation of the prior office."

The footnote then traces the rule from Dyer's Case, decided in 1557, through the leading case of Millward v. Thatcher, 1876, and other English cases.

Citations to cases may sometimes so seriously interrupt the flow of language that, if rules of court permit, they are better dropped to footnotes. The second sentence of the paragraph quoted on page 288, ante, would be easier to read if the volume and page references were so dropped, leaving the text to read:

> . . . We have seen People v. Williams . . . overruled by People v. Charles Schweinler Press . . . and Lochner v. New York . . . criticized with a universality which makes its citation as a precedent today unthinkable.

The Use of Precedents

Two main lines of argument are usually available, the argument of principle or policy, and the argument on authority. The

16. Ante, p. 67.

strongest brief, of course, is the one that convincingly shows that both these lines lead to the desired conclusion.[17] But sometimes one or the other line is noticeably weak. The precedents may be all too clearly contra. Or while the precedents are favorable, they seem to make for "hard law" in this case. Here counsel will probably want to adopt the strategy often recommended: "When the law is against you, argue the facts; when the facts are against you, argue the law."

When, in a court of last resort, you rest your argument on precedents, remember that you are addressing the court that made the precedents and that it cannot be more bound by them than it wants to be. The weight that precedent will carry will depend on the nature of the issue and the personnel of the court. In certain fields where certainty is of prime importance, a court will be reluctant to overrule itself. In others, it may be more willing to take a fresh look, if counsel can show that the old rule will work injustice in the instant case. But no matter how clearly the precedents seem to support your position, don't try to ram them down the court's throat. Don't say that the cases "require" the court to hold your way. Judges don't like to be ordered about, any more than do the rest of us. A lawyer who thinks he can compel a court to adopt a result that it does not like underestimates the court's ingenuity. It will find a way to distinguish precedents that it does not want to follow. So don't tell the court:

On this record you cannot find

Under the statute, this Court must hold

The Court is bound by these decisions

17. Mr. Justice Rutledge, while a member of the Court of Appeals for the District of Columbia, said concerning briefs in that court:

"Perhaps my major criticism of briefs, apart from that relating to analysis, would deal with the lack of discussion on principle. Some cases are so clearly ruled by authority, directly in point and controlling, that discussion of principle is superfluous. But these are not many. I have been surprised to find how many appealed cases present issues not directly or exactly ruled by precedent." Rutledge, The Appellate Brief, 9 D.C.Bar Ass'n J. 147, 157, and 28 Am.Bar Ass'n J. 251, 253 (1942).

Citing Cases

Do not throw a long list of citations at the court in a solid mass. Almost certainly there will be one or two cases more significant than the others. These may deserve statement of their facts, to show that they are directly in point, and perhaps a one-sentence quotation from the decision, when the court's phrasing is particularly apt. "If the one or two best precedents will not convince," Mr. Justice Jackson once said, "a score of weaker ones will only reveal the weakness of your argument." [18]

The "best" cases may consist of a recent case, an old "leading" case, and perhaps one that contains a particularly full and able discussion of the point, or one whose opinion was written by a particularly eminent judge. But how many cases to cite may depend upon the point at issue, the case and the court. If the point is well established, with a wealth of cases supporting it, a concise way to tell the court so is (after discussing the leading case or cases) to add a sentence such as one of the following:

> This rule has been generally accepted in other jurisdictions. The cases are collected in 6 Wigmore, Evidence, § 1690 (Chadbourne rev. 1972).

> Many cases defining who is an accommodation party under Uniform Commercial Code § 3–415 are collected in 90 A.L.R. 3d 342.

> Beginning with the case of Abbott v. Carney . . . decided more than a century ago, through numerous cases, the most recent of which is Ross v. Starr . . . this court has consistently held. . . .

On federal questions, whether in a federal or state court, a square decision by the United States Supreme Court is decisive, and it would be pointless to add a lot of citations to lower court decisions. If the Supreme Court has not passed on the point, but the Court of Appeals for the local circuit has, that is ordinarily authoritative for the federal district courts in the circuit. On the other hand, if you are in the Court of Appeals, and neither that court nor the Supreme Court has passed on the ques-

---

18. Jackson, Advocacy Before the United States Supreme Court, 37   A.B.A.J. 801, 861; 37 Cornell L.Q. 1; 25 Temple L.Q. 115 (1951).

tion, you will probably want to cite all the cases from other circuits that you can find.

In state courts, similarly, if your court has decided a question, you ordinarily need not bother with cases from other jurisdictions—at least if the court has held with you; if you want to attack or limit the local rule, it may be helpful to show that other states have held the other way.

In a brief addressed to a state court, decisions by the United States Supreme Court do not carry as much weight as the novice might think. On Federal questions, such as the meaning of the United States Constitution or a federal statute, that court's interpretation is, of course, final. But on general questions of law, on which a state court is free to adopt its own law, a decision of the United States Supreme Court carries no more weight than that of the highest court of another state and perhaps less than some. The questions with which the Supreme Court is mainly concerned are broad questions of public policy. It does not have much occasion to deal with such subjects as commercial law.

When for whatever reason it seems useful to make fuller reference to additional cases, this can be more effectively done by working them into the textual discussion than by merely listing them in a long string of citations:

> In the days prior to the Motor Carrier Act, this Court had already upheld the general powers of the states over the insurance of carriers, cf. Sprout v. South Bend, 277 U.S. 163, 172, 48 S.Ct. 502 (1928) and cases following it. The matter is within the general control of the states over their highways; see, e. g., South Carolina State Highway Department v. Barnwell Bros., 303 U.S. 177, 58 S.Ct. 510 (1938) and Maurer v. Hamilton, 309 U.S. 598, 60 S.Ct. 726 (1940). The Commerce Clause is not used to prohibit police regulations, an area in which state control is particularly important, Freeman v. Hewit, 329 U.S. 249, 253, 67 S.Ct. 274 (1946), where the benefit to the state is considerable, there is no discrimination, and the burden is negligible.

> Here the "accumulation of unearned salary" which plaintiff claims is $8,000. This Court has held that delay of even 11 months in bringing suit constitutes laches barring the

claim. Norris v. United States, 257 U.S. 77, 42 S.Ct. 9. The Court of Appeals of the District of Columbia has similarly held that plaintiffs who delayed "over a year" before bringing action were barred by laches. Farley v. Abbetmeier, 114 F.2d 569, 72 App.D.C. 260. Other cases in which delay for a period of 18 months or even less was held fatal are Morse v. United States, 59 C.Cls. 139, app. dis. 270 U.S. 151 (14 months); and Caswell v. Morgenthau, 98 F.2d 296, 69 App. D.C. 15, cert. den. 305 U.S. 596, 59 S.Ct. 81 (18 months).

As the last cases cited in the example immediately above show, the essential facts in a number of cases can be tersely given in parenthetical explanations following the case citation. Other examples of how this device may be used follow:

A finding that a person was incompetent to manage his property, or in need of hospital care and treatment, does not determine that he was so mentally disordered as to come within the legal test of irresponsibility for crime. Southers v. Com., 209 Ky. 70, 272 S.W. 26 (1925) (adjudication of insanity not conclusive of criminal irresponsibility, although defendant was never discharged as cured or restored); Witty v. State, 69 Tex.Cr.R. 125, 153 S.W. 1146 (1913) (adjudication that defendant was insane, and had been so for ten months, during which time the crime charged had been committed, held not conclusive of his irresponsibility at the time of the crime); Apolinar v. State, 92 Tex.Cr.R. 583, 244 S.W. 813 (1922) (fact that defendant had been three times adjudged insane held not conclusive).

The Texas cases do not seem to require diligence on the part of either defendant or counsel. Horhouse v. State, 50 S.W. 361 (Tex.Cr.App.1899) ("the question of diligence is not to be considered by the court"); Walker v. State, 86 Tex.Cr.R. 441, 216 S.W. 1085 (1919) ("a new trial should be granted for proof of facts which show insanity, although no diligence was used to obtain such evidence before the trial").

Another way to handle a large mass of cases which do not seem to deserve discussion in the text is to drop them to a footnote:

The United States Supreme Court,[1] the Court of Claims,[2] and other federal courts [3] have uniformly adhered to the rule

that to constitute an office, the position must have been specifically created by Act of Congress.

The cases are then cited in footnotes.

One of the most common faults of the novice is that of
presenting the precedents by summarizing the facts and the law
of each one in order. The result reads like a page from a digest
system. The cases are strung out one after another with no
connection between them and without any attempt to weld them
into a whole.

Use Quotations with Restraint

Even worse than citing or reviewing a long string of cases is
the practice of quoting from them at length. On rare occasions,
a judge will have put a point in such a pithy or effective way
that you will want to quote his very words. But in most instances you can, for your purpose, say it better in your own
words. If you have two or more good quotations on a point, resist the temptation to give them all. Select the one that is best,
and merely cite the others, "to the same effect."

Many lawyers not only stuff their briefs with too many quotations from cases, but also make the quotations too long. A lawyer will often quote a whole paragraph when more careful reading might convince him that only one sentence is really worth
repeating. Statutory and other legal language is often made up
of long sentences with many qualifying clauses. Some of these
qualifiers may not be relevant for the point you are discussing.
Including them only blurs the focus on the words that are relevant. Omit them, showing the omission with an ellipsis of three
dots. When the omission comes at the end of a sentence, use
four dots. The fourth serves as the period to the sentence. If
the relevant passages in a statute are long, they may be set out
as an appendix instead of in the body of the brief.

Short quotations can be worked into the text, and indicated by
the usual double quotation marks:

> The law does not look with favor on prescriptive rights.
> The Court of Appeals for the Ninth Circuit has stated, per-
> haps more strongly than it is usually put, the law's aversion
> to this way of acquiring rights: "This idea of acquiring title

by larceny does not go in this country." Jasperson v. Sharni-
kow, 150 F. 571, 572.

But quotations that run to more than two or three lines will usually look better "blocked" than enclosed in quotation marks. In typed manuscripts a blocked quotation is indicated by single-spacing and indenting about an inch at both margins. In print-ed matter, smaller type may be used in addition to or instead of the indentation. No quotation marks are used for blocked quo-tations. One advantage of this device is that any quotation marks in the original may be retained without the awkwardness of changing them into inner (single) quotation marks. It also breaks up the solidity of the page and helps the court in follow-ing the argument and picking up the text after the quotation ends.

Do not quote abstract propositions that do not determine the specific issue, and do not quote out of context. Generalizations may sound fine, but they do you no good if opposing counsel can show that in the case quoted the point at issue was materially different. Appellate courts are sensitive to the ever-present danger that some broad proposition they may lay down in one case will return to haunt them in another, in which its applica-tion is more dubious. They have enough trouble with legitimate questions of how far a given rule should be carried; they will resent counsel's creating unnecessary confusion by quoting a rule as though it were applicable to a clearly distinguishable sit-uation. Dicta, of course, should not be quoted as though they were law. A surprisingly large number of lawyers seem to think that any assertion in a judicial opinion is as weighty as any other.

Worse than the habit of quoting at length from prior cases is that of quoting—usually at even greater length—from the rec-ord. In a depressingly large number of briefs, whole pages are filled with quotations. Rarely is any good purpose served by this. Often it only exasperates the judge who has to plow through it.

What To Do About the Cases Against You

Do not ignore authorities that are opposed to your position. You should not only meet contentions and precedents against you cited in your opponent's brief; your responsibility as an officer of the court obliges you also to call the court's attention to a case that appears to be against you, even though your adversary has not cited it.[19]　Since your opponent can usually be counted on to call the court's attention to cases favorable to his side, they are going to be discussed anyway, and it helps rather than hurts your cause for you to discuss them first, doing what you can to minimize their significance.　Thus you steal your opponent's thunder.

Do not be misled, however, into devoting too much attention to your opponent's cases.　"Some attorneys," as Appleman says, "are chronically incapable of resisting argument, when any contention is advanced by an adversary.　Like a disputatious female, they want the last word.　Upon trials, they are handicapped by reason of the fact that a clever opponent continually leads them down by-paths where they waste their energies destroying straw men and losing their lawsuits.　Upon appeals, the same results may follow." [20]

Elaborate analysis and rebuttal of every case cited in an opponent's brief, or too lengthy or too numerous references to his principal cases, may show over-concern about their importance. One should dispose of them as ably and as pungently as one can —and move on.

The best way to dispose of them, of course, is to show that they are irrelevant.　This can sometimes be done in a summary way, as in the following two examples:

> Appellee cheerfully concedes the validity of the decisions cited in the last paragraph of page 10 of appellant's brief; but none of them dealt with the question at issue in this case. The first two concerned only . . . .. The third superficially resembled our case in that the defense of contributory negligence was raised. But the decision in that case rested on
> . . . ..

> Plaintiff's brief contains a lengthy review of cases standing for the proposition that when the Government without condemnation proceedings appropriates private property for

19. Canon 7, EC 7–23, A.B.A. Code of Professional Responsibility, as amended, 1978.

20. Appleman, Approved Appellate Briefs § 3.20 (1958).

public use, it impliedly promises to pay therefor (R. 93–101). This constitutional rule is freely conceded but it has no application in this case. Plaintiff's discussion of these cases assumes the only question in issue, namely, was there a taking? Since the only right that plaintiff had in the buildings was subject to the power reserved by the Government when it granted permission to erect them, to require that they be turned over to it, the Government in exercising that power was not appropriating plaintiff's property but was exercising a property right of its own.

Sometimes the cases contra can be handled tersely by dropping them to footnotes:

Of the few federal cases in which this requirement may seem at first blush to have been disregarded, one or two were decided solely on the question of whether the appointment had been by the "head of the department" ; [1] the others are readily reconcilable with the established rule.[2]

The cases are then cited in footnotes.

Even more summary is a sentence or paragraph saying that certain contentions need not be answered at all:

Appellant's brief, pages 10 to 16, presents a number of contentions dealing with questions of notice. These contentions could be answered, but they were not raised in the court below and not preserved, and so are not properly before this Court. We shall therefore not waste the court's time in replying to them, but shall turn at once to the vital issue in the case, the question whether . . . .

All your writing, whether letters or briefs, should, we have said, be reader-centered. Your reason for summarily dismissing certain contentions should therefore never be to save your own time, but always "not to waste the Court's time," or "to conserve time and exertion for the Court."

Distinguishing a recent decision of the court in which you are arguing is sometimes a difficult task, calling for some skill and tact. The writer of the opinion, if still on the bench, may be presumed to think well of it. Arguing that it is unsound is more likely to stiffen him in his view than it is to convince him, and this is only slightly less true of the judges who concurred. Here, even more than generally, it is unwise to make a direct attack on cases that are against you. Even though a court has power to overrule its own precedents, it will be reluctant to do so. It will, however, usually be less reluctant to decide that the rule laid down in those precedents was not intended to apply to a situation such as this—where you have already shown it would be unjust or unsound—and that the cases are distinguishable and should not be extended to cover the case at issue. The injustice or the bad economic or social effects that will result from such extension, or the embarrassment that the court will be caused in trying to avoid such effects, you will certainly want to point out. But in doing so, don't scold the court; direct your fire at opposing counsel's argument that would bring about this result.

Appellee's Argument

Counsel writing a brief for appellee must not forget that his position has changed from what it was in the trial court—and changed for the better. In the trial court, he was arguing for his position against appellant's; now he is defending the trial court's position. He will therefore want to point out that appellant's contentions have had their day in court, and been rejected; the trial court has weighed the evidence and determined the relevant law, and its decision should not be overturned. "He will, of course, refer to the necessity of the final settlement of issues and an end to litigation, the sanctity of jury trial, the fact that no trial is ever wholly free from trivial error, the fact that it is difficult to believe, under the facts, that any different result would follow upon a second trial, and perhaps make reference to the congestion of court calendars and the expense of protracted litigation. But most of all, the reviewing court must be led to believe that, under the law and the evidence, justice has been substantially served." [21]

Appellee will of course want to demonstrate that appellant's allegations of error are unsound, or that if error occurred it was

21. Appleman, Approved Appellate Briefs § 6.11 (1958). Mr. Justice Thurgood Marshall has observed that lawyers who have a lower court opinion to support them, perhaps even an opinion ably researched and persuasively written, often fail even to mention it in their briefs. Marshall, The Federal Appeal, in Counsel on Appeal (A. Charpentier, ed. 1968) 139–153.

not prejudicial. He will want to distinguish adverse cases either on their facts or on the issue involved. But he should not rest content merely to answer his opponent's contentions. Such a merely negative brief, sniping at appellant's contentions and probing for weak spots, may appear defensive and even apologetic. Appellee's brief should be an affirmative, aggressive presentation of his own position, ardently championing the rightness of the lower court's decision. His answers to appellant's contentions and his arguments to show their weaknesses or fallacies should be woven into the positive argument for his own case.

In a case in which a state court had refused to enjoin a labor union, holding that the subject of the dispute had been preempted by federal law and that the state court therefore had no jurisdiction,[22] the employer moved for a rehearing. Counsel for the union, in its brief opposing the motion, opened its argument as follows:

> Theseus, in Act V of "A Midsummer Night's Dream," says,
>
> > "In the night, imagining some fear,
> > How easy is a bush supposed a bear!"
>
> The instant case presents one of the extremest applications of this bit of the Bard's wisdom. From the tone of the petitions, and from the wave of publicity releases, one would suppose that this Court, following a host of outstanding United States Supreme Court decisions, has somehow shaken the ark of the covenant itself. Tucson counsel, for example, quoting a quote by this Court verbatim from the United States Supreme Court, come to the astonishing conclusion that by the decision of this Court, "Each and every labor dispute in Arizona involving the construction industry is under the sole and exclusive jurisdiction of the National Labor Relations Board."
>
> If this Court had decided that . . ., we would join in general alarm. This Court has made no such decision.

Appellant's Reply Brief

Although rules of court permit filing of a reply brief, this should not be done unless appellee's brief has raised new matter that requires answering, or perhaps has so befuddled an issue

---

22. United Ass'n of Journeymen, etc. v. Marchese, 81 Ariz. 162, 302 P.2d 930 (1956).

that clarifying is called for. The reply brief should be short. It may not reargue matter dealt with in the opening brief, nor itself introduce a new point. But if appellee failed to answer any significant points, the reply brief should point out that such points are thereby impliedly admitted.

Argument in Petitions for Certiorari and Other Discretionary Appeals

When appeal to the upper court is not a matter of right, the appellant has an even heavier burden than in other cases. It is not enough to argue that the decision below is erroneous; the grounds for granting review must be satisfied. The United States Supreme Court will normally take on certiorari only cases of national importance. In a speech before the American Bar Association on September 7, 1949, the late Chief Justice Vinson said:

> Lawyers might be well-advised, in preparing petitions for certiorari, to spend a little less time discussing the merits of their cases and a little more time demonstrating why it is important that the Court should hear them. . . . What the Court is interested in is the actual, practical effect of the disputed decision—its consequences for other litigants and in other situations. A petition for certiorari should explain why it is vital that the question involved be decided finally by the Supreme Court. If it only succeeds in demonstrating that the decision below may be erroneous, it has not fulfilled its purpose.

In one case, the court below had held that a frozen foods processor who freezes vegetables, packs them in bulk containers during the harvesting season, stores them, and after the season repackages them, is exempt from the overtime provisions of the Fair Labor Standards Act. This might seem to be a rather narrow decision in a specialized field, which the Supreme Court might not consider worth bothering with. The Government in its Petition for Certiorari therefore introduced its statement of "Reasons for Granting the Writ" as follows:

> Even limited to its impact upon the frozen foods industry itself, the question presented by this case is of substantial importance in the administration of the overtime provisions of the Fair Labor Standards Act. The frozen foods industry

processes a major, and constantly increasing, share of the national food production.

One ground for granting certiorari is to resolve conflicts between circuits. In a case in which the United States through the ICC charged a railroad with the operation of trains without coupling of air brakes, in violation of the Safety Appliance Act,[23] the court below held the train movements in question to be exempt because the requirement of such brakes on the movements of "any train" did not mean "shifting movements" within yard limits such as were involved here.

The United States in the conclusion of its petition for certiorari said:

> The Safety Appliance Act is now being so differently interpreted in the various circuits that neither the Interstate Commerce Commission nor the railroads have any clear guide as to whether a mass of operations properly fall within the statute. A simple statutory requirement has become a complex economic and sociological problem with the outcome unpredictable even within a single circuit because of the many factors often weighed. We urge this Court to resolve that conflict and reaffirm the clear, simple standard it initially recognized Congress has fixed.

Briefs in opposition to a higher court's taking discretionary jurisdiction will stress the abundance of authority supporting the decision below, the non-recurring nature of the question, or the factual nature of the question (questions of fact are usually beyond the reviewing court's powers of inquiry).

Even where appeal is a matter of right, as under 28 U.S.C.A. § 1257(2), allowing appeal from lower federal courts to the Supreme Court in cases upholding state statutes against the objection of invalidity under the federal Constitution, treaties or laws, it is good strategy to indicate to the court at the outset that the case is important:

> This appeal presents important constitutional questions involving the immunity of the United States and those with whom it deals from discriminatory taxation by the states.

23. United States v. Seaboard Airline R. R., 361 U.S. 78, 80 S.Ct. 12, 4 L.Ed.2d 25 (1959).

Summary and Conclusion

The rules of some courts require a summary of the argument. Even if not required, you may want to give the court a quick summary of your principal points. Most readers like to have the point restated at the end. This helps fix it in mind and gives a tidiness to the development. We like a writer to "wrap it up" for us.

In a brief having only one point, or two or three simple points, no summary may be called for. Sometimes a brief restatement of the thesis will suffice:

> Chapter 37 of the 1950 Session Laws of Texas, as here applied unlawfully discriminates against the United States, its lessees and others with whom it deals. It is therefore repugnant to the Constitution of the United States. The judgment should be reversed.

> Appellant submits that the provision in question does not protect appellee from the results of its own negligence and that the contrary view would create a situation fraught with intolerable consequences.

It is usually better in such a restatement to use words different from those of the original statement, but sometimes, when the original thesis has been worded in a particularly forceful or epigrammatic way, "echoing" it at the end is effective.

For long briefs discussing a number of points, a summary restressing the main arguments is often helpful. It should, of course, be what it purports to be, a summarization of points already made; it must not introduce or suggest new points. The danger of a summary restating the arguments is that it will be too mechanical and bald. High school debaters are likely to end with, "in conclusion, we have proved three points: first . . . second . . . third . . ." This is sound in principle, but it should be done more gracefully.

In Lambert v. California,[24] the issue was the constitutionality of a Los Angeles ordinance requiring any "convicted person" who spent more than five days in the city to register with the police. Brief of amicus curiae for the appellant concluded by

---

24. 355 U.S. 225, 78 S.Ct. 240, 2 L. Ed.2d 228 (1957).

comparing the ordinance with the laws of foreign countries requiring convicted persons to notify the authorities of their addresses and then ended with the following paragraph:

> Consideration of these foreign statutes accentuates the arbitrary features of the Los Angeles ordinance, namely that it (1) fails to restrict its application to multiple or habitual offenders, (2) fails to limit the time following sentence or release during which registration with the Chief of Police is required, (3) fails to provide notice of its requirements, and (4) imposes duties with respect to providing information and being photographed substantially in excess of the "notification of address" required by the foreign laws. Surely an ordinance so indiscriminate in its coverage and so demanding of its subjects is not reasonably restricted to coping with "the evil of professionalism in crime."

The summary should be worded in as vigorous and persuasive language as one can muster. It should aim to impress the court with the soundness and justice of one's cause. Here if anywhere is the place for eloquence and for epigram, if counsel has the gift. Good lines have a powerful impact. At our late date in history, unfortunately, many good lines that may occur to you have already occurred to and been used by others. Don't let that stop you. On the contrary, use them to bolster your statement. Put the idea first in your own words; then quote the authority who said it before. Thus you say in effect, "This is the law. Don't take merely my word for it; John Marshall (Coke, Cardozo, Wigmore) said so too." But give credit. Do not try to pass off someone else's work as your own. Plagiarism is a serious offense.

Certain dealers in musical instruments purchased violins and sold them to other dealers. They were charged with violating federal law, in that they removed from the violins labels marked "Germany/USSR occupied" and substituted labels containing their firm name with a stamp, "Made in Germany." Treasury decisions provided that Western Germany should be treated as one "country" and Eastern Germany as another and that articles made in Western Germany should be marked to indicate Germany as the country of origin, but that goods from Eastern Germany should be marked to indicate Germany (Soviet occu-

pied) as the country of origin.[25]   The brief for the defendant
concluded as follows:

> The Appellees, small business men, not importers or export-
> ers, did not intend to violate any laws. They acted in accord-
> ance with accepted practices in the trade, wholly ignorant of
> the alleged implications of a little known regulation. The
> principle of fair play which is the basis of the rule of strict
> construction of criminal statutes needs no extensive discussion
> nor the support of authorities. The District Court Decision
> was, accordingly, legally sound and just.

The government, however, did not allow this "fair play" argument to go unanswered. Its brief argued that the regulation
must be read together with a statutory provision which permits
punishment only of those who alter or destroy a required marking "with intent to conceal the information given thereby or
contained therein" and cases construing this to mean that only
those who knowingly violate the regulation are punishable. The
government brief concluded:

> The vice of an indefinite statute is that it places the ac-
> cused on trial for an offense which the statute or regulation
> does not define and of which it gives no warning. But where
> the punishment is imposed only for an act which is intention-
> ally done with the purpose of defeating the aim of the stat-
> ute, the defendant does not suffer from lack of warning. Be-
> yond that, we have shown that the regulation in this case has
> a clear meaning which normal persons—and certainly persons
> in the import-export business—would understand and have no
> difficulty in applying.

The summary should emphasize the major issues. A minor
point makes an unemphatic close. How to mention and yet subordinate minor issues is illustrated in the conclusion of Petitioner's Brief in Kremen v. United States.[26]

> Apart from the defects in the indictment, the variance be-
> tween it and the proof made, the inadequacy of the proof of
> petitioners' guilty knowledge, and the errors of the trial

---

25. United States v. Mersky, 361 U.
S. 431, 80 S.Ct. 459, 4 L.Ed.2d 423
(1960).

26. 353 U.S. 346, 77 S.Ct. 820, 1 L.
Ed.2d 876 (1957).

judge's charge, any one of which is enough to require a reversal of the convictions below, there are two major defects in the government's case.

First, . . .

In certain kinds of cases, of which personal injury suits are the best example, the emotional appeal is all on the side of the injured plaintiff. Counsel for the defendant may have to do what he can to counteract this appeal. In a New York case,[27] a child had been injured while using a swing on a public playground. A jury found a verdict for the plaintiff; the Appellate Division affirmed the judgment with one dissent. The brief filed in the Court of Appeals on behalf of the City by Mr. Paxton Blair closed with this paragraph:

> It is impossible to suppress a feeling of sympathy for the infant plaintiff. But the Trial Justice and the jury seem to have yielded too much to sentiment, and to have sought negligence where none in fact or in law existed. To allow the judgment to stand would be to impose upon the city, in carrying on activities unattended by profit, a burden too severe to be borne. To fulfill the requirements of due care as interpreted by the Courts below would involve here a substantial increase in playground supervisors for each park (which would involve closing some playgrounds to counteract the extra expense), or the removal of all devices capable, in any conceivable circumstances, of causing harm to children rendered dizzy while at play. The requirements are a "counsel of perfection," beyond reasonable attainments, and attended by public disadvantages which would nullify any gain capable of flowing from their adoption.

How well adapted to its purpose the language of this passage is may not be immediately apparent. Great art in writing is often self-effacing. What is notable about the passage is the skillfulness with which it counters emotion not with emotion but with factual statements which create a pattern of emotion—in T. S. Eliot's words, "a situation, a chain of events . . . such that when the external facts, which must terminate in sensory experience are given, the emotion is immediately evoked."

27. Peterson v. City of New York,
267 N.Y. 204, 196 N.E. 27 (1935).

A brief amici curiae filed by a Committee of Law Teachers Against Segregation in Legal Education, in the case of Sweatt v. Painter,[28] concluded as follows:

> Every branch of the government, in its own way, has the duty of meeting a challenge of our times that Democracy is unreal, a promise without fulfillment. This requires more than words. It requires that we bring our practices up to our pretensions. The account by General Bedell Smith of his experiences as Ambassador to Russia, as reprinted in the *New York Times*, dealt at some length with the publication *Amerika*, which our country distributes in Russia. In the *Times* General Smith reprinted two pictures from *Amerika* as samples of our message to Moscow. One of those pictures was of an unsegregated school room. Is this *really* our message to the world, or must we send a postscript that there is a special exception for young men studying the Constitution of the United States in the State of Texas? The Texas legislature has no authority to answer that question for the rest of America. The equal protection clause has answered it.

Finally, here are the closing words not of a brief but of an application for executive clemency filed by Gladstein, Andersen, Leonard & Sibbett, of San Francisco, addressed to the Governor of California:

> One final word: the Governor has the obligation to do justice, but he also has the right and power to grant mercy. After all is said and done, the taking of this life will not restore a single one of the victims to life. It will only bring anguish and heartache to a wife and two young infants. It will deprive petitioner of a chance to make of himself the kind of useful human being he was before the terrible events of that fatal night of April 4, 1957. Even if petitioner is required to spend the rest of his years in the penitentiary he may nonetheless make some small contribution to society and may in some small measure make amends for his participation in the events of that night. To take his life, we submit, would be an act of blind vengeance, it would be meaningless, and it would be brutal. It would not serve any socially useful purpose, deterrent or otherwise.

28. 339 U.S. 629, 70 S.Ct. 848, 94 L.
Ed. 1114 (1950).

> We call upon the Governor to exercise his executive clemen-
> cy in this case and to spare the life of Manuel Joe Chavez.

In encouraging attempts at eloquence, one runs the risk of in-
stigating some outrageous crimes against the English language.
Some people have so little ear for language, so little sensitivity
to the distinction between sentiment and sentimentality, or even
between the sublime and the ridiculous, that their efforts to be
eloquent produce only beery bathos, or unadulterated corn.[29]
Unless you do it well, better not do it at all. Chapter 13, entitled A Touch of Eloquence, will offer some suggestions that may
help you do it well.

Formal Conclusion

Whether there is a summary of the argument or not, the last
line or paragraph should be a formal conclusion saying what you
want the court to do:

> The judgment below should be affirmed.

> The judgment of the court below should be reversed and
> the cause remanded with instructions to dismiss the com-
> plaint against appellant.

> The judgment appealed from should be reversed and the
> complaint dismissed, with costs in all courts.

> For the above reasons, we respectfully submit that the
> judgment of the court below should be reversed.

When necessary, be sure to specify the relief asked in addition
to reversal, such as dismissal of the indictment or reinstatement
of the judgment of the trial court.

Proofread!

One final word of advice: proofread your work before you let
it go out. This applies not only to briefs but to anything you
write, from letters to wills. The best of typists make mistakes,
and so do printers. Typographical errors will appear most often
as misspellings. Misspelling is one of the most obvious marks of
illiteracy, so the reader who finds you apparently misspelling

---

29. See example from an actual
brief quoted on p. 142.

words may mark you down for an ignoramus. If he is kind, he may prefer to assume that you knew better but were merely careless about proofreading. A careless lawyer, however, is not the sort that even the most charitable person cares to entrust with important interests.

Misspellings and other typographical errors in the text can usually be caught by careful reading, but misspellings in names and errors in numerals, as in case citations, can be found only by checking against the original. Your cause is harmed if counsel for the other party can casually correct one of your citations by referring to "Fisser v. Int. Bank, 282 F.2d 231 (cited by plaintiff as Fisher v. Int. Bank, 282 F.2d 281)." This sort of thing will prompt the court to conclude that you are guilty of citing authorities at second hand.

> In conclusion, Appellant contends that he has brought to the attention of this Court and earlier decision which was previously overlooked and deems it controlling on the issues involved herein.

One need read only this one sentence to understand why the decision was overlooked. Counsel is obviously careless—in research as in proofreading. He is also not a very effective writer. Why does he "contend" that he has brought a case to the Court's attention? If he has done so, why not say "he has," instead of contending that he has? And why does he merely "deem" it controlling? The answer to this we can guess: he doesn't know what the word means.

After all the work of research and writing, one may be tempted to hand the manuscript over to a typist with a feeling of relief that the job is done. But it is not done. The most meticulous care in checking citations and quotations, and in polishing the wording for maximum effect, can all be ruined if the final draft contains some howler that makes a shambles of your statement. Careful proofreading is a relatively minor chore. It is worth doing carefully.

Chapter 13

A TOUCH OF ELOQUENCE

The qualities of precision, conciseness, simplicity, clarity and forcefulness, discussed in previous chapters, are the essentials of style—for a lawyer even more than for most writers. In much of his writing, such as drafting pleadings, contracts or statutes, the lawyer not only does not need, but must actually avoid, the more literary qualities of eloquence or ornamentation. But occasions will arise when he will want more than cold clarity or logic. He should be able, when necessary, to express himself with some grace and elegance.

As an illustration of lawyer's language that has both simplicity and emotional warmth, Sir Norman Birkett has quoted the opening by counsel for the defense, John Inglis, in the famous murder trial of Madeleine Smith:

> Gentlemen, the charge against the prisoner is murder, and the punishment for murder is death, and that simple statement is sufficient to suggest to you the awful nature of the case which brings you and me face to face.[1]

You may want to appeal to emotions not only in addressing a jury, but even in writing a brief for an appellate court. During World War II, certain promoters obtained an interest in a dormant corporation which once had manufactured brake-shoes and which still owned an idle old plant. They went to Washington to get a government contract. The time was shortly after Pearl Harbor; war materials of all kinds were desperately needed; and so they found no difficulty in obtaining from the Navy, a "letter of intent," stating that it was anticipated that the Navy would place an order with the company for 150 gun mounts. But the company failed to furnish a satisfactory performance bond, and a Navy inspector who visited the plant two months

1. Birkett, Law and Literature, in
The Lawyer's Treasury 127, 136–37
(1956).

310

after the letter was issued found the building locked; when he finally got a caretaker to open it, the only signs of life were pigeons nesting in the rusty machinery. Nothing apparently had been done to get into production. The Navy therefore cancelled the letter of intent. Unfortunately, just as it was being decided to cancel, an award of contract was mailed out by the Navy's award section. A telegram correcting the error was sent the next day. But the company sued for breach of contract, and the Court of Claims held that the mailing of the notice of award constituted the execution of a contract, which was not vitiated by the mistake, and gave the company judgment for $80,000 profits it might have made if allowed to perform.

Counsel for the government felt this was unjust. But appeal from the Court of Claims lies only to the United States Supreme Court, and that court is too busy to be willing ordinarily to grant certiorari in cases that do not involve legal questions of general national importance. It seemed unlikely that it would take this case, involving only the question of whether the facts spelled out a breach of contract. Counsel felt called upon in the government's petition for certiorari to try to arouse the judges' sense of injustice, and to this end tried especially to conclude on a strong note. The closing paragraph read:

> The demoralizing effect of this judgment, if allowed to stand, upon the Government's capacity to procure materials in war times cannot be exaggerated. By this judgment, a dormant corporation which never lifted a finger or spent a cent to carry out its undertaking to manufacture desperately needed armaments and whose contract was finally cancelled because of such failure to act, is handed a judgment of $80,000, being 4% profit on the total price under the contract which it did nothing to perform. Other contractors, more zealous in answering their country's need, were sweating blood to meet the seemingly impossible production goals that had to be met, and not all of them made money, especially on their first contracts. By this judgment, contractors are advised that even in the most desperate hour of their country's history, it was shrewder and safer to do nothing than it was to assume the risks of production.

The court did grant certiorari, and ultimately reversed the judgment.[2]

The qualities that make for grace, polish and effectiveness of expression are not easily identified. Why do certain combinations of words move us more strongly than others?

> She walks in beauty, like the night.

Everyone would agree that this conjunction of simple words, simply arranged, makes an effective sentence, but we do not know why. There is, as C. E. Montague once said, "a kind of dazzling unreason" about the effect that certain combinations of words has upon us. Good writing is an art. As is true of other arts, it is not acquired by mechanical application of rules. Wide reading and much practice, as already said, are the best recipe. Some persons develop it (they surely are not born with it) as some develop an ear for music. Others seem to remain tone deaf.

But this is of no help and little consolation to the law student who must write, and who wants to learn to write as well as may be possible. He wants suggestions that will help him to choose the right word or phrase, the right arrangement of words and phrases within the sentence and the right arrangement of sentences, to get a smooth flow of ideas and to evoke the emotion or impression desired.

"The man who writes professionally," said Professor Isaac Goldberg, "and who considers his job to be something more than word-slinging—who likes now and then to get a lilt into his line —to add in rhythm and cadence a subtle something that makes of the phrase a whole that is greater than the mere sum of its parts—will naturally experiment with words, with synonyms, with paraphrases." [3] The good writer, like the good practitioner of any craft, has done enough experimenting to have learned a number of ways to do the job well. The rest of this chapter points out what some of these are.

2. United States v. Penn Foundry & Mfg. Co., 337 U.S. 198, 69 S.Ct. 1009, 93 L.Ed. 1308 (1949).

3. Goldberg, The Wonder of Words 373 (1938).

Alliteration

Alliteration is defined by Webster as "repetition of the same sound at the beginning of two or more consecutive words or words near one another."

The Fowlers (The King's English, p. 292) say, "Alliteration is not much affected by modern prose writers of any experience; it is a novice's toy." It is true that it is a rhetorical and oratorical device, and rhetoric and oratory are no longer as much esteemed as they once were. But a device that Winston Churchill did not scorn to use need not be scorned by the rest of us:

> We cannot fail or falter.
>
> We shall not flag or fail.
>
> Let us to the task, to the battle and the toil.
>
> I have nothing to offer but blood, toil, tears and sweat.

Repetition of similar sounds in a sentence gives harmony and swing. It catches our attention. That is why political and advertising slogan writers love it:

> Fifty-four forty or fight
>
> Rum, Romanism and rebellion
>
> Tippecanoe and Tyler too
>
> Better Buy Buick

In nominating Richard M. Nixon for the presidency of the United States, Governor Mark Hatfield called him "a man to match the momentous need" of the times, a man who had "demonstrated courage in crisis from Caracas to the Kremlin . . . a fighter for freedom, a pilgrim for peace." Does this strike you as effective?

Alliteration may be used not only as a mnemonic device but also stylistically to get emphasis and euphony. Poets use it much:

> In a somer seson when soft was the sonne.—Piers Plowman.
>
> Even the weariest river winds somewhere safe to sea.—Swinburne.
>
> The moan of doves in immemorial elms and the murmur of innumerable bees.—Tennyson.

It has also been used effectively in prose:

> The mind and the mood of the masses is the soil of the policy.—Glenn Frank.

> A nation's army is only the clenched fist of its factories and farms.—Glenn Frank.

> The American people have always loved a man who could talk like a pirate and act like a Presbyterian, and Jackson could do both to perfection.—From a speech on Andrew Jackson.

As is true of any artistic device, alliteration can be overdone. If the reader senses not merely that the words flow smoothly, but that they are alliterative, the emphasis is too heavy. You don't want sentences that sound like, "Peter Piper picked a peck of pickled peppers."

Here are the opening words of a book on psychiatry and law:

> There was a time when the medicine man and the lawgiver had much in common. Both were men of mystery and magic, members of a sacerdotal class in close communion with the gods.

Notice that the second sentence has a series of four m sounds, followed by three hard c sounds. Is the effect good? Is it overdone? Are the four m sounds too much? Are the c sounds? Are the two together one following the other, too much?

Alliteration usually refers to the recurrence of consonant sounds. Recurrence of vowel sounds is called assonance: his escape from the jail, the home chosen by his host.

Rhythm: Metre

Aristotle described prose as neither possessing meter nor destitute of rhythm. Isocrates said, "Let not prose be altogether prose, for it would be dry; nor metered, for that would attract too much attention."

The warning of the ancient Greeks against metrical prose has been repeated by others. Robert Louis Stevenson said, "Prose may be rhythmical but it must not be metrical." The Fowlers were withering in their scorn of metrical prose: "The novice who is conscious of a weakness for the high-flown and the inflated should watch narrowly for metrical snatches in his prose; they are a sure sign that the fit is on him." [4]

But rhythm, most experts agree, is desirable. The impact of a sentence depends not only on the words used to convey the thought but also on the total effect created by their arrangement. Rhythm of some kind is present in any well-written prose, even the most matter-of-fact. Writing is rhythmical if the words fall naturally into groupings whose length and arrangement is such that the sounds roll smoothly off the tongue. Writing that has no rhythm is lifeless.

Rudolf Flesch is opposed even to rhythm. "Do not use rhythm," he says. "(Maybe your reader won't catch on)." [5]

The reader may not "catch on" to the fact that a sentence has rhythm, but because it rolls smoothly he may get the strong impression that it is a good sentence. After a date with a young lady, you may not remember any details about her dress or how she did her hair, but you may nevertheless have a distinct impression that the effect was stunning. So the person looking at a painting, or listening to music, or reading good writing, feels that it is pleasing, although he may not know and may not even care to know the devices by which the effect was obtained.

There are no rules for prose rhythm. Unlike that of poetry, it is irregular. You must develop an ear for it. The rhythm of a sentence may call for a word of one syllable and be spoiled by one of three syllables. Or it may call for a word accented on the first syllable rather than on the second.

Here is another sentence taken from the book on law and psychiatry already mentioned. In this sentence, there is one superfluous word that spoils the rhythm:

> The seeds of most mental disorders, of vice and crime, of alcoholism and perversion, of brutality, hatred, miserliness, and innumerable other highly unlovely traits are sown in the first years of childhood.

In the confusion caused by numerous revisions, the manuscript that was sent to the printer contained this one word

4. H. W. and F. G. Fowler, The King's English 295 (1908).　　　5. Flesch, The Art of Plain Talk 105 (1946).

which was not intended to be included. It is, as you probably sensed from reading it, the twenty-second word in the sentence. "Innumerable other unlovely traits" would have sounded much better.

Would it have been still better also to *add* a word—the word "all," between "are" and "sown"? The best way to answer this is to read the sentence aloud both ways and decide whether "are sown" or "are all sown" sounds more euphonious.

Here is the pledge of allegiance, in its original form and as since revised. Which version has the better rhythm?

I pledge allegiance to the flag, and to the republic for which it stands, one nation, indivisible, with liberty and justice for all.

I pledge allegiance to the flag of the United States of America and to the republic for which it stands, one nation, under God, indivisible, with liberty and justice for all.

One device for getting rhythm into one's writing is rise and fall. Consider this famous sentence written by Mr. Justice Holmes:

But when men have realized that time has upset many fighting faiths, they may come to believe even more than they believe the foundations of their own conduct that the ultimate goal desired is better reached by free trade in ideas— that the best test of truth is the power of the thought to get itself accepted in the competition of the market, and that truth is the only ground upon which their wishes safely may be carried out.

The sentence moves in a curve, like the flight of an airplane. It rises in a gradual ascent, reaching its highest altitude with the word "ideas," maintains that height for a time (through "market,"), then begins to lose altitude, and glides gracefully down ("upon which their wishes safely may be carried out"). The gentle downward curve at the end is called a cadence.

Rhymes—Something to Avoid

While a certain amount of rhythm in one's prose is desirable, rhyming is not. Economy of the reader's attention requires that we minimize friction in the process of communication between writer and reader. We want no distracting stimuli that will interfere with smooth transmission. The unexpected appearance of rhyme in prose—like grammatical error, misspelling, and wrong choice of words—is a distraction. One should therefore try to avoid having too many words in the same sentence that rhyme or contain the same sound. Several such words in close proximity to each other offend the inner ear, even when absorbed only through the eye. Lawyers use many abstract words, which often end in "ation," "otion," "ty," or "ship." Two or three such words in a sentence gives a jingling effect.

Your communication to the Administration bears the connotation

The interest of society in the security of property

The actual contractual work

It is presumed that he assumed

Jingling rhymes are especially noticeable when formed by the first and last words of a short sentence.

Our nation must be saved from foreign domination.

Words that *almost* rhyme are just as noticeable as those that actually do.

Washington set the precedent of a two-term limit for President.

Even where there is no rhyming effect, it is well to avoid repeating the same word so often in a sentence that the repetition becomes noticeable. Words that give trouble are "in," "of," and "that."

The essence of many of the opinions of the Court of Appeals on the subject of

That that was the incident that led to that result is utterly untrue.

Reiteration

The chapter on Conciseness warned against pointless repetition—the use of two or three words with the same meaning, or two or three phrases or clauses that repeat one thought. But as there mentioned, repeating words and phrases is not always pointless. It may be done deliberately, to gain emphasis (as pointed out in the chapter on Forcefulness) or cohesion or clarity. It may also be done to gain emotional effect.

Winston Churchill used reiteration of words very effectively:

> Do not let us speak of darker days; let us speak rather of sterner days. These are not dark days: these are great days —the greatest days our country has ever lived; and we must all thank God that we have been allowed, each of us according to our stations, to play a part in making these days memorable in the history of our race.

> We shall not flag or fail. We shall fight in France, we shall fight on the seas and oceans, we shall fight with growing confidence and growing strength in the air, we shall defend our island, whatever the cost may be, we shall fight on the beaches, we shall fight on the landing grounds, we shall fight in the fields and in the streets, we shall fight in the hills; we shall never surrender.

Others have also used it:

> What do we mean when we say that first of all we seek liberty? I often wonder whether we do not rest our hopes too much upon constitutions, upon laws and upon courts. These are false hopes; believe me, these are false hopes. Liberty lies in the hearts of men and women; when it dies there, no constitution, no law, no court can save it; no constitution, no law, no court can even do much to help it. While it lies there it needs no constitution, no law, no court to save it.—Judge Learned Hand.

> When I hear any man talk of an inalterable law, the only effect it produces upon me is to convince me that he is an inalterable fool.—Sydney Smith.

> When ideas compete in the market for acceptance, full and free discussion exposes the false and they gain few adherents. Full and free discussion even of ideas we hate encourages the testing of our own prejudices and preconceptions. Full and free discussion keeps a society from becoming stagnant and unprepared for the stresses and strains that work to tear all civilizations apart.

> Full and free discussion has indeed been the first article of our faith.—Mr. Justice Douglas.[6]

Repetition cannot be used in quite the same way in writing as in speaking. In speaking, as said in the chapter on Simplicity, one can repeat essentially the same words and get variety in expression by stressing a different word or phrase the second time, or varying the inflection or the tempo. The printed page does not have these devices. Variety in expression must therefore be obtained by rearranging or substituting words.

While intentional reiteration may be pleasing and effective, merely accidental repetition of sound is a blemish. Especially should one avoid the use of the same word in two different senses.

> He wept—something he had never done before before a jury.

Parallel Construction

Arranging words, phrases and sentences in groups of two or three often aids in building up emotional effect. Lincoln could have said "government of, by and for the people," or even more concisely, "a people's government," and said just as much as "government of the people, by the people and for the people." But he was not trying merely to be concise. He used three parallel phrases unnecessary for the sense but very conducive to deepening emotional reactions with each repetition.

Parallel construction, or balance, helps give emphasis, coherence and rhythm. The ear likes to hear the pattern of one sentence or clause echoed in a second. As with other devices, it is necessary to guard against over-use, but for a climax, or a conclusion, this can be very effectual. Here again, Churchill is masterly:

> Death and sorrow will be the companions of our journey; hardship our garment; constancy and valor our only shield. We must be united, we must be undaunted, we must be inflexible.

6. Dissenting in Dennis v. United States, 341 U.S. 494, 584, 71 S.Ct. 857, 95 L.Ed. 1137 (1951).

The only guide to a man is his conscience; the only shield to his memory is the rectitude and sincerity of his actions.

"Not in vain" may be the pride of those who survived and the epitaph of those who fell.

Balanced sentences are also found in judicial opinions.

We are not final because we are infallible, but we are infallible only because we are final.—Mr. Justice Jackson.[7]

Jurisdiction exists that rights may be maintained. Rights are not maintained that jurisdiction may exist.—Judge Cardozo.[8]

The constitutional protection of religious freedom terminated disabilities, it did not create new privileges. It gave religious equality, not civil immunity. Its essence is freedom from conformity to religious dogma, not freedom from conformity to law because of religious dogma.—Mr. Justice Frankfurter.[9]

Freedom to publish means freedom for all and not for some. Freedom to publish is guaranteed by the Constitution, but freedom to combine to keep others from publishing is not.—Mr. Justice Black.[10]

Dissenting in the case upholding a New York law allowing "dismissed time" for religious instruction of school children,[11] Mr. Justice Black said:

State help to religion injects political and party prejudices into a holy field. It too often substitutes force for prayer, hate for love, and persecution for persuasion.

In the same case, Mr. Justice Jackson, also dissenting, said:

My evangelistic brethren confuse an objection to compulsion with an objection to religion. It is possible to hold a faith with enough confidence to believe that what should be

---

7. Brown v. Allen, 344 U.S. 443, 540, 73 S.Ct. 397, 97 L.Ed. 469 (1953).

8. Berkovitz v. Arbib, 230 N.Y. 261, 272, 130 N.E. 288, 291 (1921).

9. Dissenting in West Virginia State Board of Education v. Barnette, 319 U.S. 624, 653, 63 S.Ct. 1178, 1192, 87 L.Ed. 1628 (1943).

10. Associated Press v. United States, 326 U.S. 1, 20, 65 S.Ct. 1416, 1424, 87 L.Ed. 2013 (1945).

11. Zorach v. Clauson, 343 U.S. 306, 72 S.Ct. 679, 96 L.Ed. 954 (1952).

rendered to God does not need to be decided and collected by Caesar.

The day that this country ceases to be free for irreligion it will cease to be free for religion—except for the sect that can win political power. The same epithetical jurisprudence used by the Court today to beat down those who oppose pressuring children into some religion can devise as good epithets tomorrow against those who object to pressuring them into a favored religion.

The number three has always had a special attraction for the human race. We make trinities of our most important concepts. So in our speech, we like the sound of words, phrases and clauses that come in three's. Many of Francis Bacon's best-remembered aphorisms are in this form.

Reading maketh a full man, conference a ready man, and writing an exact man.

Some books are to be tasted, others to be swallowed, and some few to be chewed and digested.

Wives are young men's mistresses, companions for middle age, and old men's nurses.

If the first two of the three clauses are short and parallel in movement and the third longer and more elaborate, we can get not only rhythm but climax. In the great case of Ex parte Milligan, 71 U.S. 2, 120 (1866), Mr. Justice Davis said:

The Constitution of the United States is a law for rulers and people, equally in war and in peace, and covers with the shield of its protection all classes of men, at all times, and under all circumstances.

Mrs. Franklin D. Roosevelt ended a foreword to a series of lectures by Chester Bowles with the following paragraph:

Hearing these lectures, he [my husband] would have understood, as I can understand, the real significance of what Mr. Bowles is telling us: that there is much to do, that the hour is late, and that we must find a President this year who has the will to work, the heart to inspire us, and the wisdom to show us the way.

Notice that both Mr. Justice Davis and Mrs. Roosevelt used three clauses, or phrases, the third of which in turn used three more.

Antithesis

When the ideas expressed in parallel statements are opposed or in contrast, the device is called antithesis, the setting of one thing over against another. Bringing opposing ideas together in this way makes them stand out with bold distinctness, and so has more impact on the reader. A sentence in this form can be pithy and forceful.

> To err is human; to forgive, divine.—Pope.
>
> It hath been an opinion that the French are wiser than they seem, and the Spaniards seem wiser than they are.—Bacon.
>
> Religion has not civilized man—man has civilized religion. God improves as man advances.—Robert Ingersoll.
>
> A cynic is a man who knows the price of everything and the value of nothing.—Wilde.
>
> It is difficult to make our material condition better by the best of laws, but it is easy enough to ruin it by bad laws.—T. Roosevelt.
>
> Let us never negotiate out of fear. But let us never fear to negotiate.—John F. Kennedy.

In antithetical statements as in writing generally, the more concise wording is apt to be the more vigorous; separating the contrasting ideas by punctuation alone (comma, semi-colon or colon) is usually stronger than using a word, such as "but" or "whereas." Too many lawyers, if they wrote Pope's line in their usual style, would write, "To err is human, whereas to forgive is divine."

In Lincoln's writing, as one critic has said, "a delicate balancing of contrasted thought is conveyed in an equally delicate balancing of phrase, that pleases and attracts the mind, no less than the ear, of him who hears it. A tendency toward veiled antithesis, indeed, may be set down as a definite feature of Lincoln's oratory. It enters into nearly all of his most finished utterances; and it is the more effective in that it does not spring from conscious artifice, but is entirely natural; for it arose from the supremely logical workings of an intellect that had been trained to see the other side of every question, to set one fact against another, to weigh and to compare, and then to render judgment with a perfect impartiality. This it was that gave to Lincoln's controversial oratory its great persuasive power; for it struck the note of absolute sincerity and of intense conviction." [12]

No Time for Style?

The student may feel that this talk of rhythm and cadence is overrefined, that a busy lawyer has no time for such concern with sensitivity. Too often this is true; the lawyer working under pressure cannot give the time he would like to give, not only to his writing, but also to the investigation of facts and legal research. But this means he is not performing at his highest level of competence, and it hurts his case. Able lawyers know the importance of expressing their thoughts in the most effective way possible, and they devote time and effort to putting them into the best form they can.

When Abraham Lincoln took office in 1861, he was certainly under at least as much pressure as any practicing lawyer is likely to be. Seven states had seceded from the Union and formed a provisional government. Fort Sumter had been under siege for several months. If ever a situation demanded action and did not permit wasting time in word-polishing, this was it. Yet Lincoln in preparing his inaugural address took time to seek the best advice he could get. And the men whose advice he sought agreed on the importance of what that address should say. They all made thoughtful suggestions. W. H. Seward suggested adding a paragraph at the end, and submitted a proposed draft. Lincoln adopted the suggestion, but made some revisions. Below is Seward's original and Lincoln's revision. Seward had made some revisions of his own; his draft contains words he had first written and then stricken out. Notice the changes he made and the further changes that Lincoln made. Evaluate each one in your own mind and try to imagine the reasons for making it. Was it

12.   Harry Thurston Peck, quoted in Rickard, Technical Writing 320 (3d ed. 1931).

made to give precision, simplicity, clarity, forcefulness, balance, rhythm, cadence?

Seward's original manuscript (with changes): [13]

> I close. We are not, we must not be aliens or enemies but fellow-countrymen and brethren. Although passion has strained our bonds of affection too hardly they must not, ~~be broken, they will not,~~ I am sure they will not be broken. The mystic chords which proceeding from ~~every ba~~ so many battle fields and ~~patrio~~ so many patroit graves pass through all the hearts and ~~hearths~~ all the hearths in this broad continent of ours will yet ~~harmo~~ again harmonize in their ancient music when ~~touched as they surely~~ breathed upon ~~again~~ by the ~~better angel~~ guardian angel of the nation.

Lincoln's revision:

> I am loth to close. We are not enemies, but friends. We must not be enemies. Though passion may have strained, it must not break our bonds of affection. The mystic chords of memory, stretching from every battlefield, and patriot grave, to every living heart and hearthstone, all over this broad land, will yet swell the chorus of the Union, when again touched, as surely they will be, by the better angels of our nature.

Literary taste, as said in our introductory chapter, takes time to develop. One learns to appreciate good writing much as one comes to appreciate good music, by hearing much of it. Even without conscious effort, one tends to adopt in one's own writing the characteristics of writing one reads. With conscious effort, one can do even more to emulate good style.

POSTSCRIPT

From what is said in this book, it is not to be assumed that the writing of lawyers is worse than that of most people. Others also are tempted at times to indulge in pompous or pretentious words. Others also fail to think through exactly what

---

13. The incident is related in Nicolay and Hay, *Abraham, Lincoln: A History*. Vol. III, 336–344. Quoted in Robbins, An Approach to Composition Through Psychology, pp. 321–322 (1929).

they want to say before they try to say it, and neglect to read critically and to revise what they have written.

What Sir Ernest Gowers has said in defense of government officials can also be said of lawyers. Most lawyers, like most officials, "write grammatically correct English. Their style is untainted by the silly jargon of commercialese, the catchpenny tricks of the worse sort of journalism, the more nebulous nebulosities of politicians, or the recondite abstractions of Greek or Latin origin in which men of science, philosophers and economists often wrap their thoughts. Sometimes it is very good, but then no one notices it. Occasionally it reaches a level of rare excellence." [14]

The manifold faults and bad practices we have pilloried in this book are not all characteristic of the writing of most lawyers or most law students. (Any student who habitually commits every error in the book would be a poor prospect for the profession!) The student should concentrate on correcting those errors he does commit. Some he can learn to avoid before he puts them down. When about to begin a sentence with "It is" or "There is," he can remember that this is a weak start, and can look for a stronger opening word; when "very" comes to mind, he can recall that this word is almost never a help. But no one should expect to attain perfection in his first draft. The key to good writing is rewriting.

If you will reread your early drafts for style, you will find intensifying adverbs that you put there to add force but which you now see merely sound like bluffing or exaggeration. You will find nouns qualified by one or more adjectives; if you think, or consult a thesaurus, you will be able to find a single noun that will do the job by itself, and do it more pungently. You will find loose, unharnessed sentences that you can rearrange and tighten.

When you think you have a passable draft, read it aloud. Or have a friend, perhaps your spouse, read it to you. As you listen, you will hear passages that sound flat or awkward. If the reader's voice falters, if he stresses the wrong word, if the

14. Gowers, Plain Words, Their
ABC 291-2 (1957).

rhythm breaks, the passage needs reworking.   Perhaps it needs to be thrown away, in favor of a fresh start.

Finally, with much labor and perhaps a little luck, you succeed in wiping out all evidence of the sweat and toil that went into it.   You have a paragraph that sounds easy and natural. For that is the aim of all the labor—to make it sound unlabored. "A picture is finished," said the painter Whistler, "when all trace of the means used to bring about the end has disappeared."

If you succeed, you will have the gratifying feeling as you re-read your work that the words you have used and your arrangement of them hit just the right note to produce the effect you want.   Phrases, sentences, whole paragraphs, ring pleasingly in your mind and your ear.   "This is good!" you will say, a little surprised and more than a little pleased.   That is your reward, the sense of satisfaction with a job well done that is the ultimate reward of any craftsman.

INDEX

†